Aspects of Jewish Power

in the

United States

Volume IV
of
The International Jew
The World's Foremost Problem

Being a Reprint of a Fourth Selection
of Articles from
THE DEARBORN INDEPENDENT

Reprinted 2004 by
Liberty Bell Publications
PO Box 890
York, SC 29745
www.libertybellpublications.com
803.684.4408

ISBN: 1-59364-007-2

Printed in the United States of America

FOREWARD
To the Bi-Centennial Edition

In the year 1920 Henry Sr. published *The International Jew*, a comprehensive survey of Jewish Power in the United States and throughout the world. This four-volume work was originally serialized in the *Dearborn Independent,* the house organ of the Ford Motor Company.

These books have been best-sellers in many parts of the world, and have been translated into the languages of most civilized countries. Sadly, there are many countries today where possession of these books has been made punishable by confiscation or worse. In Germany, for example, a person who wants to borrow *The International Jew* from a library must first prove that he needs it for historical research. In other words, an ordinary tax-paying member of the public who supports the public library with his hard-earned money is unable to further his knowledge or satisfy his curiosity in this regard.

It is therefore in the interest of spreading truth that we republish these books in full so that new generations shall see for themselves how our problems of today are the same problems which have "mysteriously" occurred since the turn of the century. The fact that even the wealthy Henry Ford, Sr. could be forced to withdraw these books, starkly illuminates the power of the Jews, even in the 1920's. To reprint *The International Jew* now, when the Jews are so much more powerful, is some indication of the tremendous courage of the publisher.

Every American who loves his country should make it his duty to buy sufficient copies for donation to libraries, universities, business associations, etc. Most important, every American parent should have at least one set at home to pass on to his children.

In further support of the findings and conclusions of *The International Jew,* an excellent companion book, *The Dispossessed Majority,* by Wilmot Robertson, exposes the rapid increase of Jewish power since the first publication of Henry Ford's great work. No conscientious, thinking American should be without these amazing, fact-filled books.

Preface

THIS is the fourth volume of reprinted studies in the Jewish Question as they appeared in THE DEARBORN INDEPENDENT. The articles follow the same general line as the previous volume in showing the various angles of Jewish influence and achievement in the affairs of the people of the United States, but they do not by any means exhaust either the number of the angles nor the depth of the significance in the angles traced.

Deliberate public opinion has shown many signs of a new alertness to the movement which was proceeding deftly and unnoticed in the midst of America, and many checks have been put in operation. The work of THE DEARBORN INDEPENDENT was undertaken at a disadvantage because of the tremendous emphasis of the American mind on racial peace and because of the ease with which racial propagandists can make a purely economic and political matter assume the aspects of a religious controversy. THE DEARBORN INDEPENDENT opened the Question to public gaze, and was therefore assumed to be the attacker. In this country our sense of fairness always leaves the advantage with the attacked, and false accusations quickly fall. The country has seen, however, the truth of the statements and has observed the mild and unprejudiced manner in which they were made, so that it may now be said that truth has made its way.

Most gratifying are the signs which Jews themselves have given that certain abuses must be quickly stopped. A Jewish leader has appealed for the removal of the exemption which nullifies the Constitution of the United States in favor of the Jew with reference to the use of liquor. Other Jewish leaders have sought to compel Jewish theatrical controllers to observe elementary decency in their productions.

These articles have always held that the cleansing must come from within Judah itself. It is recognized that racial pride might prevent many improvements being attempted under fire, but American Jews cannot afford to be ruled by a false pride in this respect. These are days of judgment for all the corruptive forces of society and the Jews cannot expect to escape responsibility for their part in these things.

May, 1922

Contents

		Page
LXII.	How Jews Gained American Liquor Control	7
LXIII.	Gigantic Jewish Liquor Trust and Its Career	19
LXIV.	The Jewish Element in Bootlegging Evil	31
LXV.	Angles of Jewish Influence in American Life	41
LXVI.	The Jews' Complaint Against "Americanism"	53
LXVII.	The Jewish Associates of Benedict Arnold	67
LXVIII.	Benedict Arnold and Jewish Aid in Shady Deal	81
LXIX.	Arnold and His Jewish Aids at West Point	95
LXX.	The Gentle Art of Changing Jewish Names	109
LXXI.	Jewish "Kol Nidre" and "Eli, Eli" Explained	121
LXXII.	Jews as New York Magistrates See Them	133
LXXIII.	Jews are Silent, the National Voice is Heard	143
LXXIV.	What Jews Attempted Where They Had Power	155
LXXV.	The Jewish Question in Current Testimony	167
LXXVI.	America's Jewish Enigma—Louis Marshall	179
LXXVII.	The Economic Plans of International Jews	193
LXXVIII.	A Jew Sees His People As Others See Them	207
LXXIX.	Candid Address to Jews on the Jewish Problem	223
LXXX.	An address to "Gentiles" on the Jewish Problem	235

United, then, by the strongest feelings of solidarity the Jews can easily hold their own in this disjointed and anarchic society of ours. If the million of Christians by whom they are surrounded were to substitute the same principle of co-operation for that of individual competition, the importance of the Jew would immediately be destroyed. The Christian, however, will not adopt such a course, and the Jew must, inevitably, I will not say dominate (the favorite expression of the anti-Semites) but certainly possess the advantage over others, and exercise the supremacy against which the anti-Semites inveigh without being able to destroy it."
——*Lazare.*

LXII.

How Jews Gained American Liquor Control

TO those who have been surprised and confounded by the widespread evidence, which even the newspapers have been unable to suppress, that the bulk of the organized bootlegging which is being carried on in this country is in the hands of Jews, it would have been less of a surprise had they known the liquor history of this country.

The claim made for the Jews, that they are a sober people, is undoubtedly true, but that has not prevented two facts concerning them, namely, that they usually constitute the liquor dealers of the countries where they live in numbers, and that in the United States they are the only people exempted from the operations of the Prohibition law.

Here as elsewhere the principle holds true that "the Jew is the key." The demoralization which struck the liquor business, causing its downfall, and the demoralization which has struck Prohibition enforcement for a time, cannot be understood without a study of the racial elements which contributed to both phenomena. If in what follows the Jews find objectionable elements, they should remember that their own people put them there. It is impossible to doubt that if the organized Jews of the United States were to make one-thousandth of the protest against the illegal liquor activities of their own people that they make against the perfectly legal and morally justifiable exposures being made in THE DEARBORN INDEPENDENT, the result would be not only favorable but immediate.

There was a time when the term "whisky" had a much more respectable connotation than it has today. There was a time when to use whisky and even to make it, were customs sanctioned by the better class of public opinion.

It is a common explanation of the difference between *then* and *now*, that people of the latter period became more sensitive morally than their forbears, that whereas the previous generations guzzled its whisky, innocently oblivious of the evil in it, the latter generation developed a stronger moral discrimination and banned the custom.

The truth is this: the people did not become better; *the whisky became worse.* When the entire story of the people's justifiable indignation is written, the competent historian will trace along with the people's rising disgust, the whisky's decreasing quality.

Attention to this matter will materially assist an understanding of the fact that Jews and bootlegging are so continuously and prominently connected in the public prints these days.

Readers of the old romances know how proud the master was of his wines. Vintages ripened under certain skies, on certain hills, where certain waters flowed, with cellarage in certain soils, had a faculty of aging gracefully, mellowing to a smoothness and purity and desirableness that made for cheer and health without the alloy of sordid inebriety. The bouquet of wine, the perfected essence of the grape subjected to the further courses of nature, has been a theme of praise for centuries. If it were uttered today the source of the utterance would be suspected, and very probably with good reason, of being in pay of the "wets." For the vile stuff which civilization threw out is not at all the wine of popular custom and century-long esteem.

Nevertheless, it is not difficult for even a modern to grasp the fact that there was an art in making wine and strong drink, in which art men took pride. That art required time, experience, a love of good quality.

It is a little difficult to speak of this art in connection with whisky—wine being a more poetic word—yet it is a matter of knowledge that three places in the world have devoted to the production of whisky the same spirit which France and Portugal devoted to their wines. These three districts are Glenlivet in Scotland, the region of Dublin in Ireland, and the Blue-Grass region of Kentucky. Why in these three regions? First, because there were men—non-Jews, of course—who were willing to wait ten years to produce a good article. Second, the waters of these regions are of a quality which is beautifully adapted to the making of pure goods. Pure whisky, it should be remembered, is a vegetable product matured by natural forces and no other. Grain, water and time—not even artificial heat added, nor any other thing—completes the best whisky product.

In older times in America there were men who were as choice of their whiskies as of their horses or books. There was then such a thing as quality. But there was not such thing as delirium tremens. That came later, with the disappearance of pure whisky. A distiller seldom grew rich—he was too engrossed in maintaining the quality of his product; and it consumed much time.

There were certain brands known nationally because of their mildness and purity—purest wine of the choicest grapes, aged in the best adapted cellars, was not more mild or pure. There are names that remain until this day—Pepper, Crow, Taylor, and others—the names of men who took time and pains, whose names became "brands" which guaranteed quality and purity. These men were distillers in the true sense, not manufacturers nor compounders, but *distillers* in a time when distilling was both a science and an art, and not a mere name to conceal a gigantic fraud on the public.

In time to come, when the people's justifiable moral indignation will permit a study of the steps by which the reputation of whisky came to its present low degree, they will see how much better it would have been, how much more efficacious and clarifying, if the attack on whisky had included an exposure of the men who had driven whisky out of the country and were selling rank poison as a substitute. The saloon, the brewer, the man who used strong drink were all of them made the target for attack; the Jews who demoralized the whole business went on collecting their enormous and illegitimate profits without so much as their identity being revealed.

Whisky ceased to be whisky and beer grew less like beer; the results upon humanity became apparent and deplorable. So society raised the license fee and increased the restrictions. To meet this, the Jewish compounders turned out still cheaper stuff, and still more vicious mixtures. Licenses went up, and quality went down; the Jewish compounders always getting a larger margin of profit. And through the long, long fight no one, with one or two notable exceptions, had the sense and the courage to point a finger at the solid racial phalanx lined up behind the whole rotten combination.

Distilling is one of the long list of businesses which has been ruined by Jewish monopoly. Those who favor Prohibition will probably thank the Jew for his work in that direction. It may be that the Jew is destiny's agent to demoralize the business that must pass away. But set against that the fact that it is Jewish influence that demoralizes Prohibition, too, and both "wets and "drys" have an interesting situation to consider.

In general, the Jews are on the side of liquor and always have been. They are the steadiest drinkers of all. That is why they were able to secure exemption from the Prohibition laws; their religious ceremonies require them to drink an amount which the law has considered to equal ten gallons a year. And so the Prohibition law of the United States—a part of the Constitution of the United States—is made legally ineffective to the extent of ten gallons a year a Jew. The amount, of course, is very much more; it is always easy to get 100 gallons through a 10 gallon loophole. In fact, thousands of gallons have come through that 10-gallon loophole.

It will come to many people as new knowledge that the

liquor business of the world has been in the hands of Jews. In the United States the liquor business was almost exclusively in the hands of Jews for 25 years previous to Prohibition, during the period, in fact, when the liquor trade was giving point and confirmation to Prohibition arguments. This knowledge has an important bearing on the interpretation of our times.

In the volume, "The Conquering Jew," published by Funk & Wagnalls Company in 1916, John Foster Fraser writes:

"The Jews are masters of the whisky trade in the United States. Eighty per cent of the members of the National Liquor Dealers' Association are Jews. It has been shown that 60 per cent of the business of distilling and wholesale trade in whisky is in the hands of the Jews. As middlemen they control the wine product of California. Jews visit the tobacco-growing States and buy up nearly all the leaf tobacco, so that the great tobacco companies have to buy the raw product from them. The Jews have a grip on the cigar trade. The American Tobacco Company manufactures about 15 per cent of the cigars smoked in the United States. The Jews provide the rest."

It was also true in Russia, Poland, Rumania. The Jewish Encyclopedia states that "The establishment of the government liquor monopoly (in Russia in 1896) deprived thousands of Jewish families of a livelihood." They controlled the liquor traffic, the vodka business which undermined Russia. The government made the liquor business a national monopoly in order to abolish it, which was done. Liquor in Russia was Jewish, as the Encyclopedia testifies. Anyone reading carefully the article on Russia, especially pages 527 and 559 in the Jewish Encyclopedia, will be in no doubt as to the fact. In Rumania the whole "Jewish Question" was the liquor question. The land of the peasants came into control of the liquor sellers, and the business of handling liquors was a strict Jewish monopoly for years. In Poland the same was true. It is not surprising, therefore, that in the United States whisky also became Jewish.

For convenience in detailing this story, most of the observations made will center in the state of Kentucky. Almost every one of age knows the phrase "fine old Kentucky whiskies." It was once a phrase that meant something. Kentucky produced, in her limestone regions, the kind of water that served best with the grain ingredients of whisky. The word "Bourbon," known mostly as a kind of whisky, is really the name of a county in Kentucky where "Bourbon whisky" was first made. How profoundly the region in which whisky is manufactured affects the product may be gathered from the fact that a primitive Kentucky distiller named Shields, who became famous for a brand of Bourbon made from the waters of Glen's Creek, conceived the idea of lowering his costs by transferring his distillery to Illinois, where he would be nearer the rich cornfields. He was disappointed. Illinois water would not make Bourbon. "The rule of the region" is supreme. Jamaica rum owes its characteristic to the waters of Jamaica. Port Wine is best produced in the region of Duro in Portugal, champagne in the region of Rheims in France, and beer in Bavaria. And so, in Kentucky there was the right combination of elements which made the whisky product of that state world famous.

An alcoholic spirit from grain may be made in *any* climate and by many methods. Neutral spirits, high wines and alcohol, are not indigenous anywhere. They can be made in any back room or cellar, in very little time. Little care is required. A concoction of drugs and spirits, properly colored and flavored, fraudulently labeled "whisky" and passed out over the bar, is a crime against the art of distilling, against the human nervous system, and against society.

Readers may recall that in 1904, Dr. Wiley, then chief of the United States Bureau of Chemistry, had a great deal to say about this. But because he did not point out that the evil he was attacking was fostered by a single class of men bent on gain at the cost of ruin to an American industry and to countless thousands of American citizens, few paid any attention to him. The public supposed that Dr. Wiley was discussing a technical question which interested American distillers only. It vastly more interested the American citizen, if he had but known it, if anyone had but had the clear vision and the courage to expose the great Jewish whisky conspiracy.

The difference between the non-Jewish and the Jewish method, as illustrated in the history of American whisky, is thus described by Dr. Wiley:

"The aging of whisky takes years of time. It is expensive. The whisky leaks out. It is allowed to stand for four years at least. The object of this is to permit the oxidation of the alcohols . . . .There is a loss of interest on the value of the whisky while it is aging; hence it is an expensive process.

"But the manufacture of compounded, or artificial whisky has for its purpose the avoiding of this long and expensive process. The makers begin with the pure article of spirits which can be made in a few hours . . . . To this is added enough water to dilute it to the strength of whisky. The next step is to color it. . . . this is done by adding burnt sugar and caramel. The next thing is to supply the flavors . . . . By the way I have described, in two or three hours the compounder can make a material which looks like, smells like, tastes like, and analyzes like genuine whisky, but it has a different effect on the system. The people who drink this whisky are much more liable to receive injury from it than those who drink the genuine article."

All sorts of practices were resorted to. Drugs and raw "crops" of whisky were bought up and the business of "rectifying," as it was called, began the ruin of the natural and wholesome process of distilling. Quick money, regardless of what happened to the customer: that was the motive of the rectifying business.

This rectifying business was mostly Jewish. Here and there a non-Jew was associated with Jewish partners, but rarely. The way had been found to trade on the reputation of the term "whisky" by compounding a liquid which looked and tasted like whisky but the effect of which was harmful. That was the capital fraud—the capture of the name "whisky" for a synthetic poison. There was a concealment of the meaning of "rectified spirits," a deceptive use of the word "blend," and even a most fraudulent misrepresentation concerning aging. If chemical deception could be used to make a whisky taste as if it were nine years old, then it was advertised as "Nine Years in the Wood." Here is a bit of Jewish court testimony:

Q. Is your make of whisky nine years old?

A. Nine years old, but I want to explain in that respect that the whisky may not have existed nine years before it was put into that bottle. . . .That brand of whisky which we brand as nine years old blended, means that it is equal to nine-year-old whisky in smoothness and quality.

Q. How did you arrive at the fact which you put upon this bottle that the whisky was nine years old?

A. Because it is comparatively nine years old.

Q. How do you arrive at that result?

A. By sampling. You take the whisky that is allowed to remain in the original package for nine years and compare it with our nine-year old blend and you will find them in smoothness the same. Therefore, we class it as nine-year old whiskey.

Let the reader form his own judgment on that type of mind. The whiskey bore a name resembling a time-honored brand of pure goods, and it flaunted the name Kentucky, when it was not whisky at all, was *not* a Kentucky product, but was compounded of neutral spirits from Indiana, prune juice from California, rock candy from anywhere, and raw Illinois whisky from Peoria to give it flavor.

Although Louisville, Kentucky, became head-quarters of whisky men, it was Cincinnati, Ohio, a thoroughly Judaized city, which became a greater headquarters for the pseudo-whisky men, the compounders, mixers and rectifiers. The list of Cincinnati liquor dealers reads like a directory of the

Warsaw ghetto. In Louisville the Judaic complexion of the city, as well as society, is very noticeable; indeed, most of the leading Jews in the whisky business are now Kentucky "Colonels."

The Jewish character of the whisky business since the Civil War may be visualized, by the simple expedient of noting how many of the better known brands have been at various dates under Jewish control:

There is "Old 66," owned by Straus, Pritz & Co.

"Highland Rye," owned by Freiberg & Workum.

"T. W. Samuel Old Style Sour Mash," owned by Max Hirsch, the Star Distilling company.

"Bridgewater Sour Mash and Rye Whiskies," "Rosewood and Westbrook Bourbon Whiskies," distilled by J. & A. Freiberg.

"T. J. Monarch" and "Davies County Sour Mash Whiskies," controlled by J. & A. Freiberg.

"Louis Hunter 1870," "Crystal Wedding," and "Old Jug," blended by J. & A. Freiberg.

"Gannymede '76," put out by Sigmund and Sol H. Freiberg.

"Jig-Saw Kentucky Corn Whisky," "Lynndale Whisky," Brunswick Rye and Bourbon," by Hoffheimer Brothers Company.

"Red Top Rye" and "White House Club," by Ferdinand Westheimer & Sons.

"Green River" came into the control of E. La Montague.

"Sunnybrook," a widely advertised brand, on whose advertising matter a man in a United States Inspectors uniform stood behind as if endorsing it, was at the time owned by Rosenfield Brothers & Co.

"Mount Vernon," as from the Hannis Distilling Company, was at the time owned by Angelo Meyer.

"Belle of Nelson" came into control of the Jewish trust, which was brought to legal birth by Levy Mayer and Alfred Austrian, the latter being the Chicago attorney whose name will be recalled in connection with the baseball articles in this series.

"James E. Pepper" was owned by James Wolf. "Cedar

Brook" was owned by Julius Kessler & Co. It was formerly the old "W. H. McBrayer" brand, but the real W. H. McBrayer, knowing the new methods that were arising in liquor-making, requested in his will that his name should not be used as a brand after he had ceased to see that the product was worthy of his name.

In the Pittsburgh and Peoria districts, the same story held true; the alleged whisky made in those districts was controlled, with one exception, by Jews.

The Great Western Distillery, in Peoria, owned by a corporation of Jews. Two of its brands were "Ravenswood Rye" and "Ravenswood Bourbon."

The Woolner Distillery made "Old Grove Whisky" and "Old Ryan Whisky," and "Bucha Gin."

In the city of Peoria alone there are fifteen great fortunes, all held by Jews, and for the most part made in what passed in Peoria for Whisky.

Take the city of Cincinnati alone and note what even an incomplete list reveals as to the names of the men classified as "distillers":

Bernheim, Rexinger & Company; Elias Bloch & Sons; J. & A. Freiberg; Freiberg & Workum; Helfferich & Sons; Hoffheimer Brothers Company; Elias Hyman & Sons; Kaufman, Bare & Company; Klein Brothers; A. Loeb & Co.; H. Rosenthal & Sons; Seligman Distilling Company; Straus, Pritz & Company; S. N. Weil & Company, and F. Westheimer & Sons; with many other Jews concealed under fancy trade names and corporation designations. It is the same throughout Ohio, which state, incidentally, is one of the most Jew-ridden states in the Union.

The lists here given do not by any means begin to indicate the numbers of the Jews who were engaged in the liquor business, they only indicate the complexion which the business takes on when a search is made behind the "brands" and the trade names. Any citizen in any city of size will have no trouble in confirming the statement that most of the rectifiers and wholesalers and brokers in the whisky trade of his city also were Jews.

But it is not only the fact that the liquor business was controlled by Jews that assumes importance. That is a fact which no one will deny—not even the Jewish defenders. But it is the additional fact that there was spread over this country the machinery of a vicious system which while it was destined to ruin the liquor business—as perhaps it deserved to be ruined —also ruined hundreds of thousands of citizens who trusted that "pure and unadulterated" meant what the words were intended to convey. It would be a separate story to tell of all the manipulation of labels, the piracy of brand names, the conscienceless play upon the words "pure and unadulterated" of which the un-American "compounded liquor" combine was guilty. Of course, the stuff was "pure and unadulterated"—so is carbolic acid—but it was not whisky! There were law violations galore, and it was well enough recognized in the rectifying business as a regular practice to appropriate annually a certain sum to pay the fines that were bound to be assessed against it. A riot of adulteration and chicanery ensued, with whisky being made in many saloon cellars and the dangerous secrets of synthetic booze-making being peddled abroad among the customers of the trust.

Presently the saloon men became aware of the fact that they were the goats of the game. Seldom was the Jew engaged in dishing out five-cent beers or ten-cent whiskies; it remained for the "boob Gentile" to do that; the Jew was at the wholesale end where the real profits were made. But it was the saloon man who took the brunt of the blame. The Jewish "distillers," as the compounders and blenders of the Louisville and Peoria districts were called, wore silk hats and their respectability was unquestioned. The saloon men made an eleventh hour effort to save their business, but the stuff they were pouring out had not improved, and Prohibition came, sweeping the saloon away, but, as the sequel will show, not depriving the Jewish compounder of his profits.

How much of the liquor business of the United States was

in whisky and how much in rectified spirits?

The Twelfth Census of the United States, 1900, said: *"Most of the distilled liquors consumed as a beverage by the American people pass through rectifying houses.* The different classes of rectified spirits range from the cheapest concoctions of neutral spirits and drugs to the simple blending of young and old whisky."

Twenty years ago statistics showed that 80 per cent of the so-called whisky put up in the United States was imitation whisky. Chief Chemist Wiley, whose concern was not with the quantity but with the quality, gave it as his information "that over half the whisky in this country was compounded whisky. Less than half was genuine; and while they usually mix a little old whisky with it, they often sell it purely and simply as it is, whisky which has no claim to be called whisky under the real meaning of that term."

But all that was only a beginning. The time came when the vision of a great liquor combination rose in certain minds in this country. It was planned to sweep the good brands and the bad brands alike into one common management—whose control the reader will by this time suspect—and thus not only capitalize the reputation which the old-time American distillers had made through years of honest distilling, but use the trade names of pure goods as a mask for a deluge of the dishonest kind of liquor which left a trail of suicide, insanity, crime and social wreckage in its path.

This, with independent testimony as to the Jewish direction of it all, will form the subject matter of a separate story.

Issue of December 17, 1921.

LXIII.

Gigantic Jewish Liquor Trust and Its Career

IT has been shown how the American whisky business became Jewish. The *distillers* of pure whisky which required years to make, were driven out by the *manufacturers* of drugged and chemicalized liquors which could be made in three or four hours. The latter, being cheaper and more intoxicating, so completely usurped the market that the public never knew that it was not whisky. It had stolen the name of whisky, and under that name the righteous indignation of the people prohibited it; and under that name still it is being sold by bootleggers at an advance of 1,000 per cent. The use of the fraudulent label is not new, it is not a product of Prohibition days; it began with the advent of Jewish capital into the liquor business. Whisky, carefully and scientifically made, purified by long years of repose in the warehouse, was an American product; "red eye," "forty rod stuff," "knock 'em dead" and "squirrel whisky" mixed and sold the same day, were Jewish products.

The Pure Food Law came into the fight to protect the American industry, but it was flouted at every turn. Bad liquor was in such a deep state of public disgrace that the people paid little attention to Chief Chemist Wiley's efforts. They thought when he said "whisky" he meant the stuff that they knew as "whisky," and they disregarded him. The degeneration of the liquor business became deeper and deeper, to the amazement of both its friends and its foes, and no one had the key to the situation because no one saw, or seeing, had courage to expose, the Jewish program behind the scenes.

To resume the story: Even after the cheap compounded liquors which masqueraded as "whisky" had won a commanding place in the market, to the serious detriment of the business in pure brands, the Jewish compounders were far from satisfied. There remained a few American brands whose names, by reason of their dependability, topped the list. Their very quality, though of limited quantity, was a constant challenge to the vicious mixtures of which the rectifiers produced millions of gallons a year.

How to remove those standard American brands, with their honest labels, from the market?—that was the problem which the leaders of the Jewish compounding business tackled. The first report was, characteristically, to trickery. Shipments of pure goods would be sidetracked somewhere en route, while the rectifiers drew off half the whisky and refilled the barrels with mixed compounds. People who have been amazed at the stunts of the bootleggers,—the sidetracking of whisky shipments, the "robbery" of loaded trucks, and so on—would not be so surprised if they knew that every trick was used by the compounders of bad liquor twenty years ago! It was Jewish then, as it is Jewish now, but no one dared say so. Merely to list the tricks would require too much space. It was a nasty business from any point of view.

But still the standard brands held their place in public confidence. The Jew who claims to be the superior of the American in skill did not think of making a better whisky and thus winning the market; he thought to get rid of the leaders of the better whisky that the vicious, adulterated product might own the field.

It was the day of Trusts. Big Business was amalgamating. It occurred to the leaders of the compounding business that if they could sweep all the honest distilleries into a combine with all the back-room rectifying places, put them all under one management and run down the quality of famous brands to the standard of cheap ones—cashing in on the names of the brands, and doubly profiting by decreasing the cost which quality requires—they could thus accomplish in a financial way what had been formerly tried by less respectable methods.

The inception of the idea of a "whisky combine" was legitimate. The Kentucky distillers (who must at all times be distinguished from compounders and rectifiers) endeavored in 1898 to establish a combination that would unite all the legitimate distilleries in the fight against the flood of counterfeit whisky. It is, however, significant that there was not enough capital in the legitimate whisky business to finance the plan. But when the idea was picked up by the makers of spurious liquor, there were millions of dollars at their command—just as today, with industry suffering, there are millions of Jewish capital at the disposal of the motion picture business!

In the Louisville *Courier-Journal*, February, 1899, the story of the first operations toward a combine is told, the language being inflated, of course, that hesitant distilleries might be stampeded. "Absorbed Kentucky Distilleries in a Mammoth Combine. Capital Stock $32,000,000. Some of the Biggest Plants in the State Involved. Sixteen in Louisville. Controls 90 per cent of the Product and Nearly All Standard Brands."

"Levy Mayer, of Chicago, has acted as counsel in the drawing up of the papers. He becomes the general counsel of the new company."

This article contained a list of Kentucky distilleries, all of them American—that is, non-Jewish. It was the well-established brands, the names of quality, that were sought. These names were all non-Jewish.

"Levy Mayer, the general counsel of the new company, said tonight: 'The Kentucky Distilleries and Warehouse Company is a reality and will bring prosperity to the state of Kentucky where depression has prevailed for some years on account of the discord which has existed among the distillers of Bourbon whisky, who for a generation prior enjoyed a great prosperity.'"

A most ingenuous statement. But Mr. Mayer is a most ingenuous man. However, there is some truth in his statement: It was true that the legitimate distillers had suffered from depression, not because the American people were not consuming liquor, however, but because the American people had been turned from pure whisky to "red eye"; and Mr. Mayer's smooth statement that this depression was "on account of the discord which has existed among the distillers of Bourbon whisky" needs revision to "the fight between the non-Jewish makers of real whisky and the Jewish makers of compounded liquor."

In the story of the combine a great deal is heard of Mr. Mayer and Alfred Austrian. Mayer is a Chicago Jew who is worth a story by himself. He is one of those Jews with whom candidates for the American presidency—mostly those candidates who are in debt—feel it necessary to stay, when he invites them. Mr. Austrian is sufficiently well known by his connection with the baseball scandal. He was attorney for Rothstein, the gambler, whose name figured so prominently in that scandal, and who is credited with doing things to the grand jury testimony in a way that makes a pretty tale. Austrian also appeared for two St. Louis Jew gamblers, implicated in the baseball scandal, who were afterward indicted. Austrian is also credited with being the author of the so-called "Lasker Plan" of baseball reorganization. The services of Mayer and Austrian to the liquor interests of Chicago and Cook County, were and are important.

There were Jewish names previously appearing. About 1889 Nathan Hoffheimer had tried to bring all the Kentucky whisky business under one head, and later Morris Greenbaum tried it. It will probably be conceded that both these men are Jews, and it is provable by the records that they were endeavoring to consolidate the whisky business. But the big stunt was really pulled off under the guidance of the two Chicago Jews, Mayer and Austrian.

"The various companies forming the Trust are:

"*American Spirits Manufacturing Company, $35,000,000*; Kentucky Distilling and Warehouse Association, $32,000,000; the Rye Whisky Distillers Association, $30,000,000; the

Standard Distilling Company, $28,000,000; and the Spirits Distributing Company, $7,500,000.

"*The forerunner of the gigantic combination of the whisky interests of the country was the organization of the American Spirits Manufacturing Company* upon the ruins of the old whisky trust which was controlled and directed by Joseph Greenhut. . . . .

"*Attorney Levi Mayer, of Chicago, who has been legal adviser of the whisky people from the inception of the American Spirits Manufacturing Association*, was called to New York Saturday last to confer over the legal form of the charter and the closing of the negotiations."

The italicized portions indicate the connection, and it was a connection maintained to the end, and may indeed be continued yet.

Then, in the current accounts of this merger of the liquor business under Jewish control, another name appears. On March 15, 1899:

"Angelo Meyer, a big whisky buyer of New York, is in Louisville trying to buy a big lot of whiskies." It appears that Mr. Meyers put on a poor mouth and told how hard it was to buy whisky in big lots.

And then on March 17, two days later, this appeared: "Mr. Angelo Meyer, the wealthy Philadelphia whisky man, has been appointed one of the general managers of the business of the Kentucky Distilleries Company, and is engaged in appointing men to take charge of the various departments of the combine's affairs."

The discrepancy in the above two paragraphs need not be charged to the untruthfulness of the newspaper reporter. Reporters as a rule faithfully report what they are told; but sometimes what they are told is not true.

"Mr. Meyer has commonly been called the Napoleon of the whisky trade. He is largely interested in the recently formed combine.

" 'We intend to make plenty of whisky. No brand will be

killed,' said Mr. Meyer."

Henceforth the names of Levy Mayer, Alfred Austrian and Angelo Meyer appear most frequently in the reports.

"Alfred Austrian, who is Levy Mayer's legal representative, says that all the distilleries now negotiated for will be absorbed in three weeks more."

"In an interview today Mr. Angelo Meyer said, 'I believe confidently that in the next five years a business calling for 10,000,000 gallons of whisky a year will be built up.' "

In April, 1899, another Jewish movement appeared: "Joseph Wolf, the Chicago whisky dealer, who is said to own more Kentucky whisky, independent of the Kentucky Distilleries and Warehouse Company, than any other individual corporation, is behind the new whisky combine formed in Chicago with a capital stock of $3,00,000. The purpose of the new trust, which it is said will be given the title of the Illinois Distilleries and Warehouse Company, is to fight the Kentucky Distilleries and Warehouse Company."

The few remaining Kentucky distillers were wary; they regarded Wolf, probably with reason, as simulating enmity to the other part of the Jew-made whisky trust, in order to sweep into his net the remaining independents.

"Alfred Austrian and C. H. Stoll, attorneys for the Kentucky Distilleries and Warehouse Company, will leave Louisville today for Chicago to confer with Levy D. Mayer, chief counsel for the trust; and in fact, counsel for three big whisky and spirits combines."

"Alfred Austrian, of Chicago, left last night for Cincinnati to close the deal for the celebrated Sam Clay distillery of Bourbon County."

Under an exciting headline detailing the departure of the Jew Lawyer Austrian to Chicago to see the Jew lawyer Mayer, there is the story of a still greater whisky combine:

"The projected combination of all the whisky interests of the country will probably be completed in Chicago today. A rye whisky trust is now being formed, and will soon be ready for incorporation and presentation to men with capital . . . . It is said that the capitalization of the rye whisky trust will be $60,000,000, and the combined capitalization of the five companies will amount to about $175,000,000 . . . . Levy Mayer, of Chicago, Alfred Austrian, of Chicago, and C. H. Stoll, of New York, are the attorneys for the three trusts, Mr. Mayer being the chief counsel.."

And still later, a statement by Levy Mayer:

"The new rye distillery combination will be the largest individual whisky amalgamation in the world. It is controlled and is being financed by the same people and the same trust companies of New York and Philadelphia now controlling and financing the Kentucky Distilleries and Warehouse Company, whose capital is $32,000,000; the Standard Distilling and Distributing Company, with a capital of $28,000,000; the American Spirits Manufacturing Company, with a capital of $35,000,000; and the Spirits Distributing Company, with a capitalization of $15,000,000.

"Rumor has it," and Mr. Mayer smiled as he patted a big bundle of legal documents, "that after the rye consolidation has been perfected all the separate companies will be merged into one central company, which will have an aggregate capital close to $200,000,000. A whisky combination of that size will certainly hold foremost place among the world's liquor trusts and organizations."

Another dispatch: "Alfred Austrian today returned to Louisville from New York, where he assisted in forming the combine of the American Spirits Manufacturing Company (and the three other companies).

"Mr. Austrian leaves tonight for Chicago, where he expects to close the deal with Elias Bloch & Sons to purchase the Darling distillery in Carroll County, and with Freiberg and Workum to secure their two plants in Boone County.

Here it is possible to see the Jewish agents of Jewish capital hurrying to and fro with every assurance of success, working along well-defined lines, known to themselves but concealed from the public, building up a colossal structure which public opinion was to hurl down in two decades. But two decades were enough for enormous revenues to be derived from the criminal debasement of all kinds of liquor, which became more apparent from the time of the giant consolidation.

Whisky became so rotten that in Kentucky, the pioneer whisky state, there were only four whole "wet" counties by 1908. The first decade of absolute Jewish control put even the first whisky state in the "dry" column.

The Jewish compounders did not care how they marketed their goods, so long as they could sell them in quantities. The cheap "barrel house" appeared with its windows full of gleaming bottles and gaudy labels and "cut rate" whisky prices. The compounders became saloon owners toward the end of the saloon era, and many Jews went into the "barrel house" business for a quick clean-up. The proportion of vicious dives increased everywhere, and the moral guardians of society were amazed at "the wave of vice" that was "sweeping over the country"; but they did not have the key that explained it. The whisky business was riding to a wild finish, but the men at the helm knew exactly what they were doing, every moment of the time. To look back upon that period, with all the facts at hand, makes it more and more apparent how fitting is the term, "boob Gentile."

Why, even Norman Hapgood knew how bad it was, and *Collier's Weekly*, under his editorship, was the first journal in the land to print the names of Jews in connection with the liquor debauchery of the country. But those were the good old days, when Hapgood could tell the truth even about Hearst, the man for whom he now writes his graceless palaver of pro-Jewish propaganda.

In *Collier's Weekly*, during the year 1908, solid truths appeared, which are in point today as proofs of what was transpiring. There was a specially scathing attack on what was called "nigger gin," a peculiarly vile beverage which was compounded to act upon the Negro in a most vicious manner Will Irwin spoke of this gin as "the king iniquity in the degenerated liquor traffic of these United States." This author and *Collier's* started a new fashion in giving publicity not only to the names of certain brands of liquors, but also the names of the men who made them. It turned out that the maker of a brand of "nigger gin" which had spurred certain Negroes on to the nameless crime, was one Lee Levy. Mr. Irwin wrote:

"Because the South is not through with Lee Levy, and because its citizens may at last drive him out of business—if they cannot get him behind the bars—one declaration of the *Commercial Appeal* is worthy of reply. That paper raises a question of fact—it charges that Levy's gin, Dreyfuss, Weil & Company's gin, Bluthenthal & Blickert's gin, the Old Spring Distilling Company's gin, do not exist; or that, if they exist, their sales are insignificant. Let me present my own evidence on that point."

Mr. Irwin then details some of his experiences. The gin which he was discussing was provocative of peculiar lawlessness, its labels bore lascivious suggestions and were decorated with highly indecent portraiture of white women. "I bought, for evidence, many other brands, some emanating from the big liquor cities and some put up by local people; but I could always get Levy's. I never saw it in any saloon which bars the Negro.

"In Galveston, which prides itself on its clean government, some brand or other was for sale in nearly all the corner grocery 'drums.'

"In a Negro street of New Orleans I saw five saloon shop windows in one block which displayed either Lee Levy's or Dreyfuss, Weil & Company's. This latter firm is more clever in its work than the others, much more delicate and subtle in its labeling policy. It takes one who understands the Negro and his slang to appreciate the enigma of their wording; it all comes in a 'caution label' on the obverse of the bottles.

".... Such gins were sold everywhere in Birmingham ...."

a bottle of the stuff, half empty, had been taken from a Pickens County Negro just after his arrest for the nameless crime.

"Levy—so the gossip of the liquor trade has it—grew rich through this department of his business. Dreyfuss, Weil & Company advertise everywhere that theirs is 'the most widely sold brand in the South.' And more and more one hears of tragedies that lie at the end of this course. "That is a sample— an expurgated sample—of what went on in every part of the country. Newspaper reporters will remember how the police used to wonder about the change that came over certain foreign communities. "They come here nice people," the experienced police captain would say, "but in a short time they are giving us all sorts of trouble. They don't do that in their own country."

"It's the drink," someone would suggest.

"No, they drink in their own country, they drink all the time here. It's the *kind* of drink they get here that does it—the 'rot gut,' that drives them wild." That was the captain's diagnosis, made a thousand times, but no one was the wiser. No one saw the key, which was the Jew.

In the South a terrible lynching period came and divided the country into pro-lynching and pro-Negro parties, but still no one saw the reason for it all. The race question rose to threatening proportions, the Americans of North and South looked at each other askance, there was a cooling of sympathy between the regions. Northerners were inclined to look at Southerners as unjust and inhuman in their treatment of the Negro, and Southerners were inclined to look upon Northerners as temperamentally unsympathetic and stupidly ignorant of what the conditions were.

Behind it all were the products of men like Lee Levy and Dreyfuss, Weil & Company, to use only the names quoted from *Collier's*.

The ancient Jewish policy of Divide-Conquer-Destroy was in operation. Jewish policy favors disunion as a preparation to the kind of union which Jewish leaders want. Jewish influence was strong for disunion in the Civil War. Jewish influence is directly behind the present attitude of the Negro toward the white man—look at the so-called "Negro welfare societies" with their hordes of Jewish officials and patrons! Jewish influence in the South is today active in keeping up the memory of the old divisions. And, with reference to the Negro question, "nigger gin," the product of Jewish poisoned liquor factories, was its most provocative element.

Trace the appearance of this gin as to date, and you find the period when Negro outbursts and lynching became serious. Trace the localities where this gin was most widely sold and you will find the places where these disorders prevailed.

It is extremely simple, so simple that it has been overlooked. The public is being constantly deceived by an appearance of complexity, where there is none. When you find the fever-bearing mosquito, yellow fever is no longer a mystery.

The same policy of "Divide-Conquer-Destroy" tells the story of the liquor traffic. Jewish influence divided between distilling and compounding, drove out distilling, and in the end destroyed the traffic as a legalized entity.

It needs to be said, however, that the destruction is not part of the Jewish intention. "Divide and Conquer" is the formula as the Jewish leaders conceive it, as, indeed, it is stated in the Protocols. The "destroy" comes as Nemesis upon Jewish achievements. Russia was divided and conquered, but just as the Jews had conquered it, the canker worm of fate began to consume their conquest. The story is repeated wherever Jewish intrigue has succeeded. Whatever the Jews can succeed in making Jewish, falls!

It may be fate. It may be Destiny's way to the survival of the fittest. That which succumbs to complete Judaization, as Jewish leaders conceive it, may deserve to fall. The justification of its destruction may appear in the possibility of its Judaization. Anything that can be Judaized is to that extent sentenced to oblivion.

The story of Jewish control of liquor has now been carried

through two stages, the "Divide and Conquer" stages. The third stage follows with swift and relentless steps. Blind though the country was to the Jewish character of the liquor business, it was not blind to the ravages of that business upon society.

There came a sentiment that moved ceaselessly through the country, and mounted to stormy power; people could only speak of it as a "wave." The term became hackneyed by overuse, but it was accurately descriptive. The indignation of the people, the arousal of their just moral resentment was as a flood which rose to cleanse the land. The attack was on liquor, and the attack was just. The attack was on liquor and it came none too soon. The country was drenched in vile concoctions which rapidly undermined large sections of the population.

Crime increased and domestic misery was everywhere. The people attacked the only thing they could see—they attacked the stuff and the places that distributed it. They did not see the $200,000,000 Jewish whisky combination, they did not see the sinister devices by which strong drink was made vile and viler with the growth of Jewish control.

The people rose and swept away the saloon. They did not sweep away the stocks of liquor. They did not sweep away Jewish interest in liquor. They left the source untouched. And that source is still existent.

There remains another chapter of the narrative: the coming of Prohibition and of the illicit traffic in liquor. It remains to be seen whether the same thread carries through the latter phases.

Issue of December 24, 1921.

XIV.

The Jewish Element in Bootlegging Evil

A STUDENT of the liquor history of the United States is left wondering, not that Prohibition came, but that the authorities ever allowed matters to go so far as to compel the people to take the issue into their own hands. That is the point where those who believe in "personal liberty" and those who believe in "public safety" ought to meet each other. It cannot be contended that every believer in Prohibition is a crank, nor can it be contended that every believer in "personal liberty" is a drunkard or a liquor guzzler; each of them stands for a principle that is a principle of right. But the Prohibitionist has been able to command victory over the "personal liberty" advocate because the stuff that the Prohibitionist is against ought not to be sold nor used under any circumstances, whereas the stuff the "personal liberty" advocate thinks he favors is not the stuff he thinks it is at all.

If the element in question were poisoned tooth paste, or opium, or any other concededly dangerous substance, both the Prohibitionist and the "personal liberty" advocate would agree. What the honest "personal liberty" advocate needs to learn is that the liquor which caused the adoption of Prohibition was the most dangerous to the individual and society.

It is scarcely to be hoped that all the "personal liberty" groups will come to agree with this, because most of them are formed of the very men who made and profited by the drugged and chemicalized substances which were sold over the bar and in bottles.

Liquor men themselves must agree with the facts. Even Bonfort's Wine and Spirits Circular admitted years ago that "the bulk of spirits sold today in glass under well-known brands is not what it is represented to be." "The truth of the matter is (we dislike to say it) the wine and spirit trade of this country is honeycombed with fraud, and the most radical measure should be applied and applied vigorously."

"Many a dealer prominent socially, morally, religiously and in philanthropic circles will take a lot of neutral spirits, only a few days old, flavor them with a little heavy-bodied whisky, and brand them on the label or glass with the name of any state or county desired, and with any age, and this he will do with all smiles and glee and inward delight that is said to characterize the bold buccaneer when he cuts a throat and scuttles a ship."

These excerpts show how near the official publications of the liquor trade could come to describing the practice and indicating the Jew. The last quotation was a direct hit at Louisville liquor Jews, one of which compounders furnished a room at the Y. M. C. A. of that city, another of whom adorned the town with public gifts, all of whom are Kentucky "Colonels"; though their ancestry is not exactly Kentuckian, nor even American.

The wine companies of Ohio, whose vineyard on Kelleys Island and elsewhere had built up a standard business, joined in the protest. They pointed out that counterfeit wines were flowing out of factories in Cleveland and Cincinnati, while the legitimate wine districts of Sandusky and Put-in-Bay were being saddled with the stigma of poisoned goods. As all the counterfeit business was in the hands of Jews, the statement is unavoidable that the whole movement of the degradation of liquor was Jewish.

Then came Prohibition. The Constitution of the United States was amended, the amendment being ratified by 45 states. The issue had been actively before the nation longer than any other issue except the slavery question, so that the people's action on it must be regarded as deliberate. And the liquor business was legally ended. BUT—

What was the Jewish attitude toward Prohibition while it

was being argued before the nation? What has been the Jewish attitude toward Prohibition since it has been adopted?

Both questions can be answered the same way. There are, of course, Kentuckians and others who have convinced themselves that the Jewish compounders foresaw Prohibition and welcomed it, because they saw that it would increase their profits 1,000 per cent. But whatever the truth of that may be, there are no available records to support it. The Jews destroyed the business—that is true; but whether intentionally, for greater illegitimate profits, we cannot say. There are, however, records of Jewish activity during the reform agitation. The Jews were against Prohibition. Their press and pulpit were against it. Their whole influence in politics and finance were against it. They were the backbone of the entire "wet" propaganda, and are today. The great temperance organizations will tell you that Jews did not contribute to their work. One national Prohibition organization admits a gift of $5 in many years. Will Irwin, investigating the early Prohibition movement in the South for *Collier's* in 1909, found that *The Modern Voice*, a Jewish religious weekly which is still published, was engaged in carrying the "wet" propaganda into the southern states. *The Modern Voice* lost more votes than it made for its lack of taste in printing a halftone picture of Christ endorsing the liquor traffic. J. K. Baer, one of the editors of this Jewish paper, explained his activity in this direction by saying, "We are a Jewish weekly, and the Jews are opposed on moral grounds to prohibition." A Mr. Rosenthal was associated in the work. This was typical of the Jewish press everywhere. The Jewish stage was enlisted, every man and girl, just as it is now, to deride those who protested against the destruction of the American people by counterfeit whisky and wine. Jazz music, the movies, fake medical "experts"—every agency under Jewish control was mobilized to assist the fight for a continuance of the privilege of drugging the people's drink.

This will scarcely be denied, at least by Jews. Some

"Gentile fronts" may feel obliged to rush to the defense of the Jews by denying it, but their work is unnecessary. Jews themselves make no bones about it. They did not favor Prohibition, but they did not fear it; they knew that they would be exempt, they knew that it would bring certain illegitimate commercial advantages; they would be winners either way. Jewish luck!

It is not surprising, therefore, that violation and evasion of the Prohibition law has had a deep Jewish complexion from the very beginning. THE DEARBORN INDEPENDENT would be glad to be excused from making the raw statement that bootlegging is a 95 per cent controlled Jewish industry in which a certain class of rabbis have been active; we, therefore, avail ourselves of the report of an address of Rabbi Leo M. Franklin, of Detroit, president of the Central Conference of American Rabbis, as given before that body at Washington in April, 1921, confirming the general fact:

"In making the recommendation I gave you in my message in regard to this matter, and in going to the extreme in suggesting that we appeal to the government to rescind that part of the Prohibition law which gives rabbis permission to issue permits for the purchase and distribution of wine for ritual purposes, I did so after very mature consideration. I am sure that after (his successor) shall have been in the chair of the conference for any length of time, he will come to exactly the same conclusions as I did.

"You gentlemen, members of the conference, who have dealt with this situation as a local question have had, here and there, some small question to solve; but when you become president of the conference and have letters from every part of the country, almost day by day, asking you as president of the conference to give the necessary authority to all sorts of men in all sorts of conditions, to purchase and distribute wine for ritual purposes, then you will take a different angle on this whole situation.

"I pointed out to one of my colleagues, next to whom I was

just now sitting, that within the past month I have received requests from three different men calling themselves rabbis in their communities, for authorization to purchase and distribute wine. I know that I am not exaggerating when I say that during this last year I received requests from not less than 150 men in all parts of the country for permits to distribute wine. . . . I had the applicants investigated, and I may say to you that in nine cases out of ten we found those who were attempting to use this conference, through its executive officers, for the obtaining of this authority, were men who had not the slightest right to stand before their communities as rabbis.

"What were they for the most part? They were men without the slightest pretense at rabbinical training or position who, for the purpose of getting into the wholesale liquor business, if you will, organized congregations. Nothing on God's earth could prevent them from doing so. They simply gathered around them little companies of men; they called them congregations; and then, under the law as it now exists, they were privileged to purchase and distribute wine to these people. And I call your attention to the fact that many of the so-called members of these congregations were not members of one congregation only! (Laughter.) This is not a laughing matter. They were not only members of one congregation, but members of two, three, four and upward. Why, you don't know what good Jews many have become since this law has gone into effect!

"What is more, gentlemen, perhaps some of you don't realize what popularity has come to the—sermon, and how many Jews have suddenly come to realize the beauty and the duty of the Kiddush on Friday night. I tell you it is a mighty serious problem, and say what you will, our conference, under present conditions, is being used as a medium by unscrupulous men, by the dozens and by the hundreds, to carry on a bootlegging business in the name of religion . . . .

"Now you say there have been just small scandals here and there. A wine company in New York was raided last week and a quarter of a million dollars' worth of wine was taken away by the authorities, supposed to be for ritual purposes. Don't forget that rabbi after rabbi last week in New York, a few of whom I happen to know, and in Rochester, Buffalo, Flint, Michigan, and Port Huron, Michigan—in any number of small towns throughout the country, if you have read your papers carefully, you will find that Rabbi So-and-So has been arrested as a bootlegger."

The discussion of this subject by the other rabbis present was very interesting. There was a request that "personal experiences be debarred," but some crept in. Rabbi Cohen, for example, was quite explicit. "Being one of those who opposed the whole Prohibition law, I am not in sympathy with the whole Prohibition law .... It seems to me that we rabbis ought not to stand in the way of our own members in their legitimate ways of getting wine for their homes... If a member wants the wine, I would like to be in a position that he may have the wine, even though he may not absolutely have to have it."

Rabbi Cohen pronounced the typical Jewish view. If the fool Gentiles want to prohibit themselves from having liquor, let them do it, but if there is a loophole for the Jews such as the rabbinical permit offers, it should be used generously for any "member," "even though he may not absolutely have to have it."

The pre-Prohibition Jewish liquor business is also the post-Prohibition Jewish liquor business. That fact is established by mountainous evidence. This does not mean, of course, that every bootlegger you meet is a Jew, nor that you will ever meet a Jew serving as an itinerant bootlegger. Unless you live in Chicago, New York or other large cities, an actual meeting with the Jew in this minor capacity will not be frequent. The Jew is the possessor of the wholesale stocks; he is the director of the underground railways that convey the stuff surreptitiously to the public; seldom does he risk his own safety in being the last man to hand the goods to the consumer and to take the money.

But notwithstanding all this carefulness, the bulk of the arrests made in the United States have been among Jews. The bulk of the liquor permits—a guess of 95 per cent would not be too high—are in the hands of Jews. More and more the Jews are being appointed as Prohibition enforcement officers at the central points of distribution. It is a fact, as Rabbi Franklin showed, that part of the trouble arises over the abuse of what has been called "rabbinical wine," but big as it seems by itself, it is really a small part in comparison with the whole. Numbers of lesser rabbis have profited from the sale of liquor, no doubt of that. And not only among their own people, but from any people making the demand. "If you sign a Jewish name you can get it" is the watchword. Newspaper offices have been kept "wet" in some cases by "rabbinical wine," which accounts for the dribble of "wet" propaganda in the so-called humorous and other columns of the evening journals.

It happens that "rabbinical wine" is a euphemism for whisky, gin, Scotch, champagne, vermuth, absinthe, or any other kind of hard liquor. The stocks that existed when Prohibition went into force have not only *not* decreased, but have actually increased, because of the increase in the "doctoring" of the stuff. It has been cheapened, its bulk has been increased and it has been made, if anything, more deadly than before. "As fatal as bootleg whisky" is a saying founded on thousands of deaths.

The wholesale stocks of compounded liquor remained in the hands of the men who owned them, while the retail stocks in stores and saloons had to be disposed of. That was one of the first big mistakes—that the little fellow was compelled to get rid of his stock, while the big fellow was permitted to keep his. The so-called rabbis, who had advance information of the special privileges which the Jews were to enjoy under the Prohibition law, were very active in buying up the smaller stocks and storing them away. Of course, no one could prevent them. Was it not "ritual wine"?—even though it was any kind of liquor, it went under the "cover name" of "ritual wine," and of course, as everybody knows, great scandal resulted. Protests like that of Rabbi Franklin indicate that a part of Jewish public opinion resents the policy of exempting Jews from the Prohibition law, but this is minority opinion. What the Central Conference of American Rabbis may think is of little consequence to the mass of Jews in America. The people to scrutinize with regard to this are not the Rabbi Franklins, who are amenable to the significance of American opinion, but those Jews who do not consult with Americanized rabbis, but run the political end of Jewry as they choose.

There *is* no reason why the Jews should be exempt from the operation of the Constitution of the Untied States at all, yet the Constitution is suspended in their favor when the Ten-Gallon Permit is given.

But it would be a great mistake to suppose that there is or could be any objection to the Jews' ritualistic use of wine, or that the present scandal with regard to law violation rises from that. It is not a religious question at all. It is purely a commercial question. The people who are breaking the Prohibition law are the same people who broke the Pure Food law with regard to the ingredients of whisky. They are essentially a lawbreaking class.

The "Gentile boobs" who patronize bootleggers today are being sold a liquor which is never what it is represented to be, in spite of names blown in the bottles, in spite of seals and in spite of labels. The most conscienceless fraud is being perpetrated on gullible people at an increase in profit of from 400 to 1,000 per cent. The stuff brought from Havana is Jew whisky shipped there, "doctored" still more and shipped back at increased prices—the "Gentile boobs" fancying they are getting something extra special "Just brought in from Havana."

Twenty years ago Jewish liquor dealers of Chicago were using genuine James E. Pepper bottles refilled with vile ingredients compounded in back rooms. Twenty years ago there were counterfeit whiskies sold in the United States bearing forged Canadian Government stamps. The forgers of the labels were Jewish liquor houses. Twenty years ago there was unlimited faking of liquor labels, a Chicago printing house furnishing Jewish liquor houses with clever imitations of any reputable label in use, to be placed on bottles containing doped goods. Foreign, American and Canadian labels were unscrupulously adopted and brazenly advertised everywhere.

These abuses did not wait for Prohibition; they were daily Jewish practices twenty years ago.

The only difference now is that the stuff which is sold is still worse.

The enforcement of the Prohibition law ought to be rigidly complete, for the same reason that the enforcement of the Pure Food law should have been complete years ago—it is necessary to prevent the wholesale harming of an ignorant public.

The maintenance of *the idea of drink* in the minds of the people is due to Jewish propaganda. There is not a dialog on the stage today that does not drip with whisky patter. As all the plays making much noise this year are not only Jew-written, Jew-produced and Jew controlled, but also Jew-played (the stage swarms with Jewish countenances this year), the drip of whisky patter is constant. If theatergoers were at all observant they would see that most of their money goes to support pro-Jewish propaganda in one form or another, which is, of course, a tribute to Jewish business genius—what other people could embark on a pro-racial propaganda and make the opposite race pay for it?

This *idea of drink* will be maintained by means of the Jewish stage, Jewish jazz and the Jewish comics until somebody comes down hard upon it as being incentive of treason to the Constitution. When a Jewish comedian can indulge in a 15-minute monologue "panning" the United States, defaming Liberty, heaping contempt upon the Pilgrims, and. openly praising a violation of a portion of the Constitution of the United States—and when choruses sing this sort of thing, and slap-stick artists take it up, and it becomes evident that the country is being ringed around every week by repeated attacks upon what the people have established—it is certain not to be very long before a heavy hand will be laid on the whole business.

The Department of Justice should pay some attention to the treason nightly spouted on the legitimate stage before Americans who pay as high as $5 each in support of the propaganda.

First and last, the illicit liquor business in all its phases, both before and after Prohibition, has always been Jewish. Before Prohibition it was morally illicit, after Prohibition it became both morally and legally illicit.

And it is not a cause for shame among the majority of the Jews, sad to say; it is rather a cause for boast. The Yiddish newspapers are fruitful of jocular references to the fact, and they even carry large wine company advertisements week after week.

As before Prohibition the key to the steady degeneration of the liquor business was the fact of Jewish domination, so now the key to the organized and lawless rebellion against a recently enacted article of the Constitution is also Jewish. Prohibition enforcement officers will find a shortcut to successful enforcement along this line. And if law-abiding Jews would help with what they know, the work could be soon accomplished.

Issue of December 31, 1921.

LXV.

Angles of Jewish Influence in American Life

THE Jewish Question exists wherever Jews appear, says Theodor Herzl, because they bring it with them. It is not their numbers that create the Question, for there is in almost every country a larger number of other aliens than of Jews. It is not their much-boasted ability, for it is now coming to be understood that, give the Jew an equal start and hold him to the rules of the game, and he is not smarter than anyone else; indeed, in one great class of Jews the zeal is quenched when opportunity for intrigue is removed.

The Jewish Question is not in the number of Jews who here reside, not in the American's jealousy of the Jew's success, certainly not in any objection to the Jew's entirely unobjectionable Mosaic religion; it is in something else, and that something else is the fact of Jewish influence on the life of the country where Jews dwell; in the United States it is *the Jewish influence on American life*.

That the Jews exert an influence, they themselves loudly proclaim. One is permitted to think that they really claim a stronger influence than they possess, especially in those higher regions where excellent and determinative influences have been at work. The Jews claim, indeed, that the fundamentals of the United States are Jewish and not Christian, and that the entire history of this country should be rewritten to make proper acknowledgment of the prior glory due to Judah. If the question of influence rested entirely on the Jewish claim, there would be no occasion for doubt; they claim it all. But it is kindness to hold them to the facts; it is also more clearly explanatory of conditions in our country. If they insist that they "gave us our Bible" and "gave us our God" and "gave us our religion," as they do over and over again with nauseating superciliousness throughout all their polemic publications—*not a single one of these claims being true*—they must not grow impatient and profane while we complete the list of the real influences they have set at work in American life.

It is not the Jewish people but *the Jewish idea,* and the people only as vehicles of the idea, that is the point at issue. As it was Prussianism and not the German people that was the objective in the recent war, so in this investigation of the Jewish Question, it is Jewish influence and the Jewish Idea that are being discovered and defined.

The Jews are propagandists. This was originally their mission. But they were to propagate the central tenet of their religion. This they failed to do. By failing in this they, according to their own Scriptures, failed everywhere. They are now without a mission of blessing. Few of their leaders even claim a spiritual mission. But the mission idea is still with them in a degenerate form; it represents the grossest materialism of the day; it has become a means of sordid acquisition instead of a channel of service.

The essence of the Jewish *Idea in its influence on the labor world* is the same as in all other departments—the destruction of real values in favor of fictitious values. The Jewish philosophy of money is not to "make money," but to "get money." The distinction between these two is fundamental. That explains Jews being "financiers" instead of "captains of industry." It is the difference between "getting" and "making."

The creative, constructive type of mind has an affection for the thing it is doing. The non-Jewish worker formerly chose the work he liked best. He did not change employment easily, because there was a bond between him and the kind of work he had chosen. Nothing else was so attractive to him. He would rather draw a little less money and do what he liked to do, than a little more and do what irked him. The "maker" is always thus influenced by his liking.

Not so the "getter." It doesn't matter what he does, so long as the income is satisfactory. He has no illusions, sentiments or affections on the side of work. It is the "geld" that counts. He has no attachment for the things he makes, for he doesn't make any; he deals in the things which other men make and regards them solely on the side of their money-drawing value. "The joy of creative labor" is nothing to him, not even an intelligible saying.

Now, previous to the advent of Jewish socialistic and subversive ideas, the predominant thought in the labor world was to "make" things and thus "make" money. There was a pride among mechanics. Men who made things were a sturdy, honest race because they dealt with ideas of skill and quality, and their very characters were formed by the satisfaction of having performed useful functions in society. They were the Makers. And society was solid as long as they were solid. Men made shoes as exhibitions of their skill. Farmers raised crops for the inherent love of crops, not with reference to far-off money markets. Everywhere The Job was the main thing and the rest was incidental.

The only way to break down this strong safeguard of society—a laboring class of sturdy character—was to sow other ideas among it; and the most dangerous of all the ideas sown was that which substituted "get" for "make." With the required manipulation of the money and food markets, enough pressure could be brought to bear on the ultimate consumers to give point to the idea of "get," and it was not long before the internal relations of American business were totally upset, with Jews at the head of the banking system, and Jews at the head of both the conservative and radical elements of the Labor Movement, AND, most potent of all, the Jewish Idea sowed through the minds of workingmen. What Idea? The old idea of "get" instead of "make."

The idea of "get" is a vicious, anti-social and destructive idea *when held alone*; but when held in company with "make" and as second in importance, it is legitimate and constructive. As soon as a man or a class is inoculated with the strictly Jewish Idea of "getting"—("getting mine;" "getting while the getting is good;" "honestly if you can, dishonestly if you must—but *get* it"—all of which are notes of this treasonable philosophy), the very cement of society loses its adhesiveness and begins to crumble. The great myth and fiction of Money has been forced into the place of real things, and the second step of the drama can thus be opened up.

Jewish influence on the thought of the working-men of the United States, as well as on the thought of business and professional men, has been bad, thoroughly bad. This is not manifested in a division between "capital" and "labor," for there are no such separate elements; there is only the executive and operating departments of American business. The real division is between the Jewish idea of "get" and the Anglo-Saxon idea of "make," and at the present time the Jewish idea has been successful enough to have caused an upset.

All over the United States, in many branches of trade, Communist colleges are maintained, officered and taught by Jews. These so-called colleges exist in Chicago, Detroit, Cleveland, Rochester, Pittsburgh, New York, Philadelphia and other cities, the whole intent being to put all American labor on a "get" basis, which must prove the economic damnation of the country. And that, apparently, is the end sought, as in Russia.

Until Jews can show that the infiltration of foreign Jews and the Jewish Idea into the American labor movement has made for the betterment in character and estate, in citizenship and economic statesmanship, of the American workingman, the charge of being an alien, destructive and treasonable influence will have to stand.

The last place the uninstructed observer would look for traces of Jewish influence is in the Christian church, yet if he fail to look there he will miss much. If the libraries of our theological seminaries were equipped with complete files of Jewish literary effort in the United States during the past 15 years, and if theological students were required to read these Jewish utterances, there would be less silly talk and fewer "easy marks" for Jewish propaganda in the American pulpit.

For the next 25 years every theological seminary should support a chair for the study of Modern Jewish Influence and the Protocols. The fiction, that the Jews are an Old Testament people faithful to the Mosaic Law, would then be exploded, and timid Christians would no longer superstitiously hesitate to speak the truth about them because of that sadly misinterpreted text: "I will bless them that bless thee, and curse him that curseth thee."

There is a mission for the pulpit to liberate the Church from what the New Testament Scriptures call "the fear of the Jews."

The pulpit has also the mission of liberating the Church from the error that Judah and Israel are synonymous. The reading of the Scriptures which confuse the tribe of Judah with Israel, and which interpret every mention of Israel as signifying the Jews, is at the root of more than one-half the confusion and division traceable in Christian doctrinal statements.

The Jews are *not* "The Chosen People," though practically the entire Church has succumbed to the propaganda which declares them to be so.

The Jewish tinge of thought has of late years overspread many Christian statements, and the uninstructed clergy have proved more and more amenable to Jewish suggestion.

The flaccid condition of the Church, so much deplored by spokesmen who had regard for her inner life, was brought about not by "science," not by "scholarship," not by the "increase of light and learning"—for none of these things are antagonistic even to incomplete statements of truth—but by *Jewish-German higher criticism.*

The defenders of the faith have fought long and valiantly against the inroads made by the so-called Higher Criticism, but were sadly incapacitated in their defense, because they did not see that its origin and purpose were Jewish. It was not Christian; it was not German; it was Jewish. It is almost wholly discounted today in the practical life of the church, but it still adheres to the darker corners of the colleges, along with the Red Bolshevism which is taking root there under Jewish influences.

Let the Christian minister who wishes to know the source of Jewish influence in the church look over the names of the more notorious "German" Higher Critics of the Bible, and consider their race. Add to them one Frenchman, an atheist and a Jew, and you have modern "liberal" sources very complete:

      Wellhausen   Kuehne
      Strauss   Hitzig
      Ewald   Renan

It is perfectly in keeping with the Jewish World Program that this destructive influence should be sent out under Jewish auspices, and it is perfectly in keeping with non-Jewish trustfulness to accept the thing without looking at its source. A great many so-called "liberals" played the Jewish game for a time; they are now coming back to the old citadel which stood in its own strength and without their patronage while the fever of the Higher Criticism raged.

The church is now victim of a second attack against her, in the rampant Socialism and Sovietism that have been thrust upon her in the name of flabby and unmoral theories of "brotherhood' and in an appeal to her "fairness." The church has been made to believe that she is a forum for discussion and not a high place for annunciation. She has been turned from a Voice into an echo of jangling cries. Jews have actually invaded, in person and in program, hundreds of American churches, with their subversive and impossible social ideals, and at last became so cocksure of their domination of the situation that they were met with the inevitable check.

Clergymen ought to know that seven-eighths of the economic mush they speak from the pulpit is prepared by Jewish professors of political economy and revolutionary leaders. They should be informed that economic thought has been so completely Judaized by means of a deliberate and masterly plan of camouflaged propaganda, that the mass-thought of the crowd (which is the thought mostly echoed in "popular" pulpits and editorials) is more Jewish than Jewry itself holds.

The Jew has got hold of the church in doctrine, in

liberalism, so-called, and in the feverish and feeble sociological diversions of many pulpits and adult classes.

If there is any place where a straight study of the Jewish Question should be made, with the Bible always in hand as the authoritative textbook, it is in the modern church which is unconsciously giving allegiance to a mass of Jewish propaganda.

It is not a reaction that is counseled here; it is progress along constructive paths, the paths of our forefathers, the Anglo-Saxons, who have to this day been the World-Builders, the Makers of cities and commerce and continents; and not the Jews who have never been builders or pioneers, who have never peopled the wilderness, but who move in upon the labors of other men. They are not to be blamed for not being Builders and Pioneers, perhaps; they are to be blamed for claiming all the rights of pioneers; but even then, perhaps, their blame ought not to be so great as the blame that rests upon the sons of the Anglo-Saxons for rejecting the straightforward Building of their fathers, and taking up with the doubtful ideas of Judah.

Colleges are being constantly invaded by the Jewish Idea. The sons of the Anglo-Saxon are being attacked in their very heredity. The sons of the Builders, the Makers, are being subverted to the philosophy of the destroyers. Young men in the first exhilarating months of intellectual freedom are being seized with promissory doctrines, the source and consequences of which they do not see. There is a natural rebelliousness of youth, which promises progress; there is a natural venturesomeness to play free with ancient faiths; both of which are ebullitions of the spirit and significant of dawning mental virility. It is during the periods when these adolescent expansions are in process that the youth is captured by influences which deliberately lie in wait for him in the colleges. True, in after years a large proportion come to their senses sufficiently to be able "to sit on the fence and see themselves go by," and they come back to sanity. They find that "free love" doctrines make exhilarating club topics, but that the Family—the old-fashioned loyalty of one man and one woman to each other and their children—is the basis, not only of society, but of all personal character and progress. They find that Revolution, while a delightful subject for fiery debates and an excellent stimulant to the feeling of supermanlikeness, is nevertheless not the process of progress.

And, too, they come at length to see that the Stars and Stripes and the Free Republic are better far than the Red Star and Soviet sordidness.

When a Supreme Court Justice addressed one of the greater American universities, a student came to him after a lecture and said: "It gave me so much pleasure to hear your lectures, for they were *the first kindly words I have heard said about our government since the commencement of my university career.*"

For years the secular magazines have been carrying articles on the question, "*What is Wrong With the Colleges?*" The answer is perfectly clear to those who can discern Jewish influence in American life.

The trouble with the colleges has progressed along precisely the same lines that have been described above in connection with the churches. First, Jewish higher criticism in the destruction of young men's sense of respect for the ancient foundations; second, Jewish revolutionary social doctrines. The two always go together. They cannot live apart. They are the fulfillment of the Protocol's program to split non-Jewish society by means of ideas.

It is idle to attack the "unbelief" of college students, idle to attack their "radicalism"—these are always the qualities of immaturity. But it is not idle to show that social radicalism ("radicalism" being a very good word very sadly misused) and antagonism to the religious sanctions of the moral law, both come from the same source. Over the fountain of Revolutionism and Anti-Christian belief place the descriptive and definitive term "Jewish," and let the sons of the Anglo-Saxons learn from what waters they are drinking. That source is not Mosaic, but Jewish—there is a world of difference between them.

The central group of Red philosophers in every university is a Jewish group, with often enough a "Gentile front" in the shape of a deluded professor. *Some of these professors are in the pay of outside Red organizations.* There are Intercollegiate Socialist Societies, swarming with Jews and Jewish influences, and toting Jewish professors around the country, addressing medics and lits and even the Divinity schools, under the patronage of the best civic and university auspices. Student lecture courses are fine pasture for this propaganda. Intercollegiate Liberal Leagues are established everywhere, the purpose evidently being to give students the thrill of believing that they are taking part in the beginning of a great new movement, comparable to the winning of Independence or the Abolition of slavery. As stein parties gradually cease as a college diversion, Red conferences will come in; it is part of the effervescence of youth.

The revolutionary forces which head up in Jewry rely very heavily on the respectability which is given their movement by the adhesion of students and a few professors. It was so in Russia—everyone knows what the name "student" eventually came to signify in that country. And as a result, while Sovietists are glorifying the "success" of the Revolution, men like Maxim Gorky are sending out appeals for food to prevent the intelligentsia from starving to death.

The Jewish Chautauqua, which works almost exclusively in colleges and universities, together with Bolshevism in art, science, religion, economics and sociology, are driving straight through the Anglo-Saxon traditions and landmarks of our race of students. And these are ably assisted by professors and clergymen whose thinking has been dislocated and poisoned by Jewish subversive influences in theology and sociology.

What to do about it? Simply identify the source and nature of the influence which has overrun our colleges. Let the students know that their choice is between the Anglo-Saxons and the Tribe of Judah. Let the students decide, in making up their allegiance, whether they will follow the Builders or those who seek to tear down.

It is not a case for argument. Radicalism and religious indifference are states of mind. Normal men usually grow out of them in good time. Others are caught and held to the end. But the treatment is not argument.

The only absolute antidote to the Jewish influence is to call college students back to a pride of race. We often speak of the Fathers as if they were the few who happened to affix their signatures to a great document which marked a new era of liberty. The Fathers were the men of the Anglo-Saxon -Celtic race. The men who came across Europe with civilization in their blood and in their destiny; the men who crossed the Atlantic and set up civilization on a bleak and rock-bound coast; the men who drove west to California and north to Alaska; the men who peopled Australia and seized the gates of the world at Suez, Gibraltar and Panama; the men who opened the tropics and subdued the arctics—Anglo-Saxon men, who have given form to every government and a livelihood to every people and an ideal to every century. They got neither their God nor their religion from Judah, nor yet their speech nor their creative genius—they are the Ruling People, Chosen throughout the centuries to Master the world, by Building it ever better and better and not by breaking it down.

Into the camp of this race, among the sons of the rulers, comes a people that has no civilization to point to, no aspiring religion, no universal speech, no great achievement in any realm but the realm of "get," cast out of every land that gave them hospitality, and these people endeavor to tell the sons of the Saxons what is needed to make the world what it ought to be.

If our sons in college follow this counsel of dark rebellion and destruction, it is because they do not know whose sons they are, of what race they are the scions.

Let there be free speech to the limit in our universities and free intercourse of ideas, but let Jewish thought be labeled Jewish, and let our sons know the racial secret.

The warning has already gone out through the colleges. The system of procedure is already fully known. And how simple it is:

First, you secularize the public schools—"secularize" is the precise word the Jews use for the process. You prepare the mind of the public school child by enforcing the rule that no mention shall ever be made to indicate that culture or patriotism is in any way connected with the deeper principles of the Anglo-Saxon religion. Keep it out, every sight and sound of it! Keep out also every word that will aid any child to identify the Jewish race.

Then, when you have thus prepared the soil, you can go into the universities and colleges and enter upon the double program of pouring contempt on all the Christian landmarks, at the same time filling the void with Jewish revolutionary ideas.

The influence of the common people is driven out of the public schools, where common people's influence can go; but Jewish influence is allowed to run rampant in the higher institutions where the common people's influence cannot go.

Secularize the public schools, and you can then Judaize the universities.

This is the "liberalism" which Jewish spokesmen so much applaud. In labor unions, in church, in university, it has tinctured the principles of work, faith and society. This will not be denied, because the proof of it is too thickly written over Jewish activities and utterances. Indeed, it is in exerting these very influences that Jewry convinces itself it is fulfilling its "mission" to the world. The capitalism attacked is non-Jewish capitalism; the orthodoxy attacked is Christian orthodoxy; the society attacked is the Anglo-Saxon form of society, all of which by their destruction would redound to the glory of Judaism.

The list could be extended—the influence of the Jewish idea on Anglo-Saxon sports and pleasure, on the Anglo-Saxon-Celtic idea of patriotism, on the Anglo-Saxon-Celtic conception of the learned professions; the influence of the Jewish idea runs down through every department of life.

"Well," one very badly deluded Anglo-Saxon editor, wrapped up in Jewish advertising contracts, was heard to say, "if the Jews can get away with it, then they have a right to." It is a variant of the "answer" of Jewish origin, which runs thus: "How can a paltry 3,000,000 run the 100,000,000 of the rest of us? Nonsense!"

Yes, let it be agreed; if the Jewish idea is the stronger, if the Jewish ability is the greater, let them conquer; let Anglo-Saxon principles and Anglo-Saxon power go down in ruins before the Tribe of Judah. *But first let the two ideas struggle under their own banners; let it be a fair struggle.* It is not a fair fight when in the movies, in the public schools, in the Judaized churches, in the universities, the Anglo-Saxon idea is kept away from Anglo-Saxons on the plea that it is "sectarian" or "clannish" or "obsolete" or something else. It is not a fair fight when Jewish ideas are offered as Anglo-Saxon ideas, because offered under Anglo-Saxon auspices. Let the heritage of our Anglo-Saxon-Celtic fathers have free course among their Anglo-Saxon-Celtic sons, and the Jewish idea can never triumph over it, in university forum or in the marts of trade. The Jewish idea never triumphs until first the people over whom it triumphs are denied the nurture of their native culture.

Judah has begun the struggle. Judah has made the invasion. Let it come. Let no man fear it. But let every man insist that the fight be fair. Let college students and leaders of thought know that the objective is the regnancy of the ideas and the race that have built all the civilization we see and that promise all the civilization of the future; let them also know that the attacking force is Jewish.

That is all that will be necessary. And it is against this that the Jews protest. "You must not use the term 'Jew.' " Why? Because unless the Jewish idea can creep in under the assumption of other than Jewish origin, it is doomed. Anglo-Saxon ideas dare proclaim themselves and their origin. A proper proclamation is all that is necessary today. Compel every invading idea to run up its flag!

Issue of May 21, 1921.

LXVI.

The Jews' Complaint Against "Americanism"

FROM the earliest record of the Jews' contact with other nations, no long period of years has ever passed without the charge arising that the Jews constitute "a people within a people, a nation within a nation." When this charge is made today it is vehemently denied by men who pose as the defenders of their people, and the denial is more or less countenanced by all the Jews of every class.

And yet there is nothing more clearly stated in Jewish teaching, nor more clearly indicated in Jewish life, than that the charge is true. *But whether the truth should be used against the Jews* is quite another question. If the Jews are a nation, their nationality founded upon the double ground of race and religion, it is certainly outside the bounds of reason that they should be asked or expected to de-racialize, de-nationalize and de-religionize themselves; but neither is it to be expected that they should bitterly denounce those who state the facts. It is only upon a basis of facts that a solution of any problem can come. Where blame attaches is here: that the evident facts are denied, as if no one but the Jews themselves knew that there are such facts.

If the Jews are to be continuously a nation, as they teach, and if the condition of "a nation within a nation" becomes more and more intolerable, then the solution must come through one of two things: a separation of the "nation" from the rest of the nations, or an exaltation of the "nation" above the rest of the nations. There is a mass of evidence in Jewish writings that the leaders expect both of these conditions to come—a *separate* nation and a *super-nation*; indeed the heart of Jewish teaching is, as quite fully illustrated in the last article, that Jewry is *a separate nation now,* and on the way to becoming a *super-*

nation. It is only those appointed to address the Gentiles who deny this: the real rabbinate of Israel does not deny.

Now, in any investigation of the Jewish Question, the student is struck over and over again by the fact that what the Jews most complain of, they themselves began. They complain of what they call anti-Semitism; but it must be apparent to the dullest mind that there could never have been such a thing as anti-Semitism were there not first such a thing as Semitism.

And then take the complaint about the Jews having to live in ghettos. The ghetto is a Jewish invention. In the beginning of the invasion of European and American cities the Jews always lived by themselves because they wanted to, because they believed the presence of Gentiles contaminated them. Jewish writers, writing for Jews, freely admit this; but in writing for Gentiles, they refer to the ghetto as a surviving illustration of Gentile cruelty. The idea of contamination originated with the Jews; it spread by suggestion to the Gentiles.

And so with this fact of the separate "nation"; it was the Jews who first recognized it, first insisted upon it and have always sought to realize that separateness both in thought and action.

Nay, more, the true and normal type of Jew today believes that the influence of Americanism, or of any civilized Gentile state, is harmful to Judaism.

That is a serious statement and no amount of Gentile assertion will be sufficient to confirm it. Indeed, it is such a statement as the Gentile mind could not have evolved, because the trend of Gentile feeling is all in the opposite direction, namely, that Americanization is a good thing for the Jew. It is from authoritative Jewish sources that we learn this fact, that what we call civilizing influences are looked upon as being at enmity with Judaism.

It is not the Gentile who says that Jewish ideals, as ideals, are incompatible with life in our country; it is the Jew who says so. It is he who inveighs against Americanism, not the American who inveighs against Judaism.

The Jews' Complaint Against "Americanism"

As this article is one with the last, the same method of impassive presentation of the testimony will be followed. Readers of this study of the Jewish Question should know that neither rhetoric nor emotion will contribute a single element to the solution of the Question. We prefer to leave rhetoric and emotion to the anti-Semites who call names and to the pro-Semites who are apparently reduced to the same necessitous level.

Now, the first thing to know is this; that though Americanism is yet unfinished, Judaism has been complete for centuries; and while no American would think of pointing to any part of the country or to any group as representing the true and final type of Americanism, the Jews quite unhesitatingly point to parts of the world and to certain groups as representing the true type of Judaism.

Where is the type to be found which Jewish writers recognize as the true one?

The Jew of the ghetto is held up in Jewish treatises as the norm of Judaism.

The visitor in New York has perhaps seen on Central Park west the massive synagogue of the Spanish and Portuguese Jews. Its famous rabbi was the Rev. Dr. D. de Sola Pool. He is the author of the following words:

"In the ghetto the observance of Judaism was natural and almost inevitable. The regimen of Jewish life was the atmosphere that was breathed * * * Not only did public opinion make it possible for men to go bearded, to keep the head covered at all times, to carry the palm branch in the public street, or to walk the street in stockinged feet on fast days, but public opinion made it almost impossible for a Jew to profane the Sabbath or the Passóver regulations, or openly to transgress any of the main observances"— and, as we shall later see, the learned rabbi considers these conditions more preservative of Judaism than are American conditions.

Rev. Dr. M. H. Segal expresses the view that Jewry in the more modern portions of Europe and America was really kept alive by the infusions of immigrants from Poland and Lithuania. Asserting, in agreement with other Jewish leaders, that the Jewish center of the world has been, until now, in Russia and Poland, Dr. Segal says:

"The war has destroyed the last traces of the declining Jewish society which had dragged out its feeble existence in the semi-medieval ghettos of Poland and Lithuania. With all their growing feebleness, these communities were yet the last refuge of Judaism in the Dispersion. In them there had still survived something of the old Jewish life, some of the old Jewish institutions, practices and traditions. *These communities also supplied such vitality as they could afford to the attenuated and atrophied Judaism in the communities of the more modern states of Europe and America.*"

The idea is not at all uncommon—that large infusions of "real Jews" from the Old World ghettos are desirable and necessary in order to keep Judaism alive in countries like the United States.

Israel Friedlaender, whose name just at present is held in peculiar honor by the Jews, and justly so, was a man of most enlightened intellect, and he too recognized the service of the ghetto stream to Judaism. In his lecture, "The Problem of Judaism in America," he speaks about the de-Judaizing tendency of absolute freedom, such as the Jew has always enjoyed in the United States. This tendency, he says, is corrected in two ways—by anti-Semitic influences and "by the large stream of Jewish emigration, on the other hand, which, proceeding from the land of oppression to the lands of freedom, *carries with it, on or under the surface, the preserving and reviving influences of the ghetto.*"

The same authority, in an article entitled "The Americanization of the Jewish Immigrant," frankly prefers the Jew fresh from the ghetto to the Jew who has been influenced by American life.

He says that he "prefers the kaftan-clad, old-fashioned Jew, with his unattractive appearance and ungainly manners, whose whole life is dominated by the ideals and mandates of an ancient religion and civilization * * * to that modernized, amphibious creature, the gaudily attired, slang-using, gum-chewing, movie-visiting, dollar-hunting, vulgar and uncultured, quasi-Americanized 'dzentleman.' "

The "kaftan-clad, old-fashioned Jew" of whom Mr. Friedlaender writes, is the Polish Jew, 250,000 of whom are coming to the United States as "a preserving and reviving influence" upon Judaism in the United States.

Not to use more space, however, on the identity of the normal type of Jew as precisely stated by those who have expressed themselves on this subject, it is possible to preserve the idea and add its logical complement, by quoting some testimony on the Jewish view of Americanization.

What now follows is of special interest because it is so generally stated and received throughout Jewish circles, that the center of Jewry has shifted to America. That is the form in which Jewish spokesmen make the statement: they say "America," not the United States.

A little story—a true one—may be worth while here. It may throw a sidelight on the use of the word "American" as used in the testimony. A certain editor of an American newspaper gave a trifling bit of publicity to this series of articles. Jewish advertising was withdrawn from his columns by the chairman of the Anti-Defamation Committee of the local Lodge of B'nai B'rith, which chairman was also an advertising agent who handled all the Jewish advertising in that city. The editor, not being a wise man, yielded to the bulldozing methods used upon him, and in a half-hearted bit of editorial praise for the Jews used the word "Americanism." The advertising agent toyed with the word in the manner of one who, having a weak Gentile in his power, would make the best of it.

"Why did you say 'Americanism'? Why did you not say 'civilization'?" he asked.

The editor to this day thinks it was a bit of captiousness. It was not. There is meaning in it.

To "Americanize" means, in our ordinary speech, to bring

into sympathy with the traditions and institutions of the United States, but the Jews do not mean only the United States when they say "America." They mean also South and Central America —where so many revolutions have occurred. There are large numbers of Jews in Argentina, and many are found in other countries. The next place to be extensively colonized will be Mexico. If the people of the United States see a Jewish ambassador sent to represent them in Mexico, they must know that the invasion of that country is about to begin. If the ambassador is not himself a Jew, it will be well to scrutinize his connections; there may be reasons which will make it necessary to employ a "Gentile front" for a time.

Now, it would probably give a wrong twist to the fact to say that the Jewish leaders are anti-American, but it is true that they are against the "Americanization" of the Jewish immigrant stream. That is, the trend of "Americanization" is so different from the trend of "Judaism" that the two are in conflict. This does not indicate treason toward American nationalism, perhaps, so much as it indicates loyalty toward Jewish nationalism.

But the reader must himself be the judge as to how far the difference goes. The testimony which will now be given divided itself into two parts: first, that relating to the American state in particular; second, that relating to any Gentile state.

After he had spoken in praise of the old type of Jew; as seen in the foreign ghettos, Dr. D. de Sola Pool added:

"To a large extent the adult Jewish population of the United States has been reared in Jewish communities of this type of Jewish inevitableness. To a large extent the young generation is being reared in an atmosphere in which this type of Jewishness is unknown, or at least strange and impossible. *Jewish religious observance in the United States is becoming increasingly difficult and increasingly rare.*"

Describing the antagonism between the American and the Jewish tendencies, he continues with this reference to the effect of "Americanism" on Jewish modes of worship:

"On the platform officiate a cantor and a preacher, who turn their backs to the ark and address themselves to their congregation. The tallith and similar externals are un-American, and have consequently been sacrificed. The 'American' worships with bare head; therefore the American of Jewish persuasion must also doff his headgear when at worship. Hebrew, and Oriental language, is not an American tongue. The American prays in English, which all understand, and accordingly the American of Jewish faith has Anglicized his ritual. Such a ritual is not susceptible of being chanted with traditional Jewish Chazzunath, and the music of the temple has therefore been brought up to date by the introduction of an organ, sacred music borrowed from non-Jewish neighbors, and mixed choirs in which non-Jewish singers are almost the rule * * * The Jewish Sabbath is out of keeping with the environment, and the only way in which it seemed to be possible to save it was by celebrating it with a Friday evening temple service after supper, and resting, and sometimes also attending temple on Sunday."

It is not difficult to detect underneath these words the tone of criticism for such "Americanization." It is a criticism which is fully justified by conditions. And it must be remembered that it was not uttered by a "kaftan-clad, old fashioned Jew," but by a learned rabbi with a magnificent temple on Central Park west, a man whom our government has seen fit to honor.

But that is not all that Dr. de Sola Pool objects to. Nor does he mince words in making his objection known: "If so far, Reform has avoided the logical end of the process and has stopped short of identifying itself with Christianity, it has Americanized Judaism by dropping the elements that are characteristically Jewish and un-American, and has thereby created an almost non-sectarian Judaism housed in an almost non-sectarian Temple."

It will be noticed that the learned doctor used the word "American" as one accustomed to quite another atmosphere. A further illustration is found in this:

"Neglect of the un-American dietary laws is usually the first step that the Americanizing Jew takes in asserting his

Americanism."

"The "un-American dietary laws" are, of course, the Jewish dietary laws. But if any Gentile writer had so referred to them, he would have been abused as a hostile witness.

It is very curious indeed to read the long list of complaints against modern conditions in their power to bring about the "decay of Judaism." The ghetto, which makes for separateness, is frequently heralded as the true safeguard of Judaism. Intercourse with the world is dangerous. "Americanizing" influences are distrusted.

No doubt many and many a Gentile parent in New York, Boston, Louisville, Dallas and other American cities has witnessed the spectacle of Jewish teachers and "welfare workers" instructing Gentile children in the principles of Americanism, but did anyone ever see a Gentile teacher instructing Jewish children in Americanism?

Recently when the American Legion asked permission of the government to establish Americanization classes at Ellis Island, where tens of thousands of Polish Jews gain entry into the United States, the reply was a refusal, and the reason was that all the space for charitable institutions was already taken. What charitable institutions? How many of them were Jewish?

"The beginning of this decay," says Israel Friedlaender, referring to the effect of modern life on Judaism, "is obviously coincident with the beginning of Jewish emancipation, that is to say, with *the moment when the Jews left the ghetto to join the life and culture of the nations around them.*"

Mr. Friedlaender even went so far as to say that pogroms against the Jews were "fortunate" in that they drove the Jews back to their Judaism—"*Fortunately*, however, Russian Jewry was halted on its downward rush toward national self-annihilation. The process of assimilation was cut short by the pogroms, and ever since then the Jews of Russia have stood firmly their ground. * * * "

That may be the reason why some Jewish spokesmen of the Jews in America are trying to make this series of articles appear as a "pogrom." There is plenty of evidence to indicate that Jewish leaders have regarded "pogroms," in modern times at least, as very useful in preserving the solidarity of Jewry. However, those who are responsible for the present series of articles, much as they hope to benefit the general situation of the humbler Jews by showing the use which the leading Jews are making of them, must decline to be counted among those who justify "pogroms" on any ground whatsoever.

Justice Brandeis, of the United States Supreme Court, is also an exponent of the idea that, released from ghetto influences, the Jew becomes less of a Jew. He says:

"We must protect America and ourselves from *demoralization*, which has to some extent *already set in among American Jews. The cause of this demoralization is clear*. It results, in large part, from the fact *that in our land of liberty all the restraints by which the Jews were protected in their ghettos were removed* and a new generation left without necessary moral and spiritual support."

Justice Brandeis is a Zionist on these very grounds. He wants the land of Palestine because there the Jews, as he says, "may live together and *lead a Jewish life.*"

Not the United States, but Palestine, is Justice Brandeis' hope for the Jews; he says of Palestine that "*there only can Jewish life be fully protected from the forces of disintegration.*"

Arguing the same question, the Rev. Mr. S. Levy says: "I shall probably be told that the reestablishment of Jews as a nation would mean the recreation of the ghetto. I am frankly prepared to admit the force of the criticism, but with an important qualification dependent on the interpretation of the word 'ghetto.'

"In so far as the national center will insure the existence of this Jewish environment, Jewish atmosphere, and Jewish culture, there *will* be a recreation of the ghetto. (The italics are Mr. Levy's.)

"The continuance of Judaism, then, is dependent on the existence of an area with an aggregation of Jews living in a Jewish environment, breathing a Jewish atmosphere and fostering a Jewish culture, and these factors must predominate over all other influences."

It is therefore plain that, however startling and improbable the statement may seem when made by a Gentile, the Jews themselves regard the influences of modern lands as inimical to Judaism.

But there is still a further consideration, which is distinctly set forth in Jewish writings, namely, that the trend of the modern State is harmful to all that Judaism holds to be essential to its moral and spiritual welfare.

The modern State is changing, and Jewish observers sense the fact more readily than do the rest of the people, because Jews see in the change both an opportunity and a menace. If the State continues to change according to the trend of the general mind of the world, Jewish ideas of supremacy will find less and less opportunity to be realized—that is the menace. If the change, or the spirit of change, can be seized and twisted to Jewish purposes, as was done in Russia, and a Jewish type of State erected on the ruins of the old—that is the opportunity. Readers of these articles know that stimulation of "the spirit of change" is one of the clearest planks in the World Program.

As Cyril M. Picciotto points out in his "Conceptions of the State and the Jewish Question," there is a tendency to "increase the control of the State over the individual." This, of course, has nowhere been done so thoroughly as in Russia under the Jewish-Bolshevik regime, but it is not of this that Mr. Picciotto speaks, it is of the tendency observed in the Gentile states; and he asks: "In the face of such a tendency in political development (which it is not rash to assume will be more pronounced in the future than in the past) *how does the Jew stand?*"

He adds: "The time is not far distant when the development of the State will continue on organic and collectivist lines. The central authority will embrace an ever wider area, and will make such a penetration into the recesses of individual freedom as would have been thought inconceivable thirty of forty years ago. Compulsory military service, compulsory education, compulsory insurance are but milestones on the road which logically leads to the adoption of a State morality, a State creed, and of a common way of life. To say this is merely to indicate the probable trend, not to approve it."

"How, then, is the State of the future going to deal with a people in its midst which largely preserves its separateness of blood, which in its fasts, its festivals, its day of rest, its dietary laws, its marriage ceremony, suggests a distinct historic entity?"

The question is a disturbing one to Jews, as is shown by Rabbi Segal's words in "The Future of Judaism." He even says that "the medieval State, with all its tyranny and obscurantism" was more favorable to the Jews than the modern type of State. "Its defective organization permitted both individuals and whole classes to live their life in their own way. Hence the medieval State enabled the Jews to organize themselves on semi-national lines, and, as far as circumstances permitted, to create afresh in their dispersion the national institutions and practices of their ancient commonwealth."

They did this, of course, by establishing the ghetto.

"But this has *become an absolute impossibility in the modern State*," continues the rabbi. "The rise of democracy and the transference of the ultimate power of government from the oligarchy to the majority involves the practical suppression of weak minorities. The identification of the State with the culture and aspiration of a particular nationality leads inevitably to the crippling of and gradual extinction of those *classes who do not share that particular culture and those aspirations.* The State, moreover, enforces a system of education which is purposely designed to fashion and to mold all the inhabitants * * * It also maintains a thorough-going organization which embraces all the departments of the public and private life of all its inhabitants, irrespective of class, race or tradition. *There is thus no room in the modern State for Jewish* culture, for Jewish national life, or for a specifically Jewish society, with its own specific institutions, customs and practices. * * *

"Therefore, Judaism can live and work only with a

specifically Jewish society and within a Jewish national organization. The medieval ghetto, with all its narrowness, with all the unhealthy and abnormal conditions of its existence, yet contained such a semi-national society; therefore, *Judaism flourished in the medieval ghetto. The modern State, on the other hand, has broken up that specifically Jewish society* * * * "

Now, there are the reactions of leading Jewish minds to conditions in America particularly, and to conditions in the modern Gentile State generally. The statement of the antagonism which exists between the two is clear and complete. The Gentiles do not notice that antagonism, but the Jews are always and everywhere keenly aware of it. This throws a light, a very strong light, on all the revolutionary programs to break up the present control of society, by sowing dissensions between capital and labor so-called, by cheapening the dignity of government through corrupt politics, by trivializing the mind of the people through theaters and movies and similar agencies, and by weakening the appeal of distinctively Christian religion. A breakdown of Gentile seriousness is the opportunity of the Jew. A colossal war is also his opportunity, as witness his seizure of the United States Government during the recent war. Judaism says that Americanism and Gentile nationalism generally, are harmful to it. Judaism has therefore the alternative of changing and controlling Gentile nationalism, or of constructing a nationalism of its own in Palestine. It is trying both.

This all harks back to what Lord Eustace Percy is quoted in the Jewish press as saying: that the Jew participates in revolutions "not because the Jew cares for the positive side of radical philosophy, not because he desires to be a partaker in Gentile nationalism or Gentile democracy, but *because no existing Gentile system of government is ever anything but distasteful to him.*"

And the same author—"In a world of completely organized territorial sovereignties, he (the Jew) has only two possible cities of refuge: *he must either pull down the pillars of the whole national state system or he must create a territorial sovereignty of his own.* In this perhaps *lies the explanation both of Jewish Bolshevism and of Zionism,* for at this moment Eastern Jewry seems to hover uncertainly between the two."

Issue of October 23, 1920

LXVII.

The Jewish Associates of Benedict Arnold

AS the Jewish propagandists in the United States cannot be trusted to give the people all the facts— even though these propagandists have the facts in their possession—it devolves upon some impartial agency to do so. The Jewish propagandists are accorded the utmost freedom of the newspapers of the United States —by reason of Jewish advertising being more than 75 per cent of all the advertising done in this country—and thus a wide web of false impressions is constantly being woven around the Jewish Question. The most recent is the widespread publication of a new "exposure" of the origin of the Protocols. This makes the sixth "final" and "complete" exposure that the Jews have put forth for public consumption. The Jews have still time to repent and tell the truth. Suppose they make the seventh the whole truth with a true repudiation of the Protocols.

It is THE DEARBORN INDEPENDENT'S purpose to open up from time to time new angles of the Jewish Question, so that the candid reader who would be informed of the extensive character of Jewish influence may obtain a general view of it.

The part taken by Jews in the wars of the United States has been a subject of considerable boasting by Jewish publicists. It is a most interesting subject. It deserves the fullest possible treatment. It is not THE DEARBORN INDEPENDENT'S present purpose to challenge the Jewish boast; it is, however, our purpose to fill in the omitted parts of the story, and supply the missing links in several of the most interesting episodes in American history. This will be done on the basis of unquestioned historical authority, mostly of a

Jewish character, and solely in the interests of a complete understanding of a matter which Jewish leaders have brought to the front.

The first subject which will be treated in this series is *the part of Jews in the treason of Benedict Arnold.*

Benedict Arnold, the most conspicuous traitor in American history, has been the subject of considerable comment of late. Among the commentators have been American Jews who have failed to make known to the American public the information which may be found in Jewish archives concerning Benedict Arnold and his associates.

To begin with, the propensity of the Jews to engage in the business of supplying the needs of armies and to avail themselves as far as possible of war contracts, is of long standing and notice.

An authority on this matter, Werner Sombart, says in his "Jews and Modern Capitalism" (pp. 50-53):

"The Jews throughout the sixteenth, seventeenth and eighteenth centuries were most influential as army-purveyors and as the moneyed men to whom the princes looked for financial backing . . . . we cannot attempt to mention every possible example. We can only point the way; it will be for subsequent research to follow.

"Although there are numerous cases on record of Jews acting in the capacity of army-contractors in Spain previous to 1492, I shall not refer to this period, because it lies outside the scope of our present considerations. We shall confine ourselves to the centuries that followed, and begin with England.

"In the seventeenth and eighteenth centuries the Jews had already achieved renown as army-purveyors. Under the Commonwealth the most famous army contractor was Antonio Fernandez Carvajal, 'the great Jew,' who came to London some time between 1630 and 1635, and was very soon accounted among the most prominent traders in the land. In 1649 he was one of the five London merchants intrusted by the council of state with the army contract for corn. It is said that he annually imported into England silver to the value of £100,000. In the period that ensued, especially in the wars of William III, Sir Solomon Medina ('the Jew Medina') was 'the great contractor,' and for his services he was knighted, being the first professing Jew to receive that honor.

"It was the same in the wars of the Spanish Succession; here, too, Jews were the principal army-contractors. In 1716 the Jews of Strassburg recall the services they rendered the armies of Louis XIV by furnishing information and supplying provisions. Indeed, Louis XIV's army-contractor-in-chief was a Jew, Jacob Worms by name; and in the eighteenth century Jews gradually took a more and more prominent part in this work. In 1727 the Jews of Metz brought into the city in the space of six weeks, 2,000 horses for food and more than 5,000 for remounts. Field Marshal Maurice, of Saxony, the victor of Fontenoy, expressed the opinion that his armies were never better served with supplies than when the Jews were the contractors. One of the best-known of the army contractors in the time of the last two Louises was Cerf Beer, in whose patent of naturalization it is recorded that ' . . . . in the wars which raged in Alsace in 1770 and 1771 he found the opportunity of proving his zeal in our service and in that of the state.'

"Similarly the house of Gradis, of Bordeaux, was an establishment of international repute in the eighteenth century. Abraham Gradis set up large storehouses in Quebec to supply the needs of the French troops there. Under the Revolutionary Government, under the Directory, in the Napoleonic wars it was always the Jews who acted as purveyors. In this connection a public notice displayed in the streets of Paris is significant. There was a famine in the city and the Jews were called upon to show their gratitude for the rights bestowed upon them by the Revolution by bringing in corn. 'They alone,' says the author of the notice, 'can successfully accomplish this enterprise, thanks to their business relations, of which their fellow citizens ought to have full benefit.' A parallel story comes from Dresden. In 1720 the

Court Jew, Jonas Meyer, saved the town from starvation by supplying it with large quantities of corn. (The Chronicler mentions 40,000 bushels.)

"All over Germany, the Jews from an early date were found in the ranks of the army-contractors. Let us enumerate a few of them. There was Isaac Meyer in the sixteenth century, who, when admitted by Cardinal Albrecht as a resident of Halberstadt in 1537, was enjoined by him, in view of the dangerous times, 'to supply our monastery with good weapons and armor.' There was Joselman von Rosheim, who in 1548 received an imperial letter of protection because he had supplied both money and provisions for the army. In 1546 there is a record of Bohemian Jews who provided greatcoats and blankets for the army. In the next century another Bohemian Jew, Lazarus by name, received an official declaration that he 'obtained either in person or at his own expense, valuable information for the imperial troops, and that he made it his business to see that the army had a good supply of ammunition and clothing.' The Great Elector also had recourse to Jews for his military needs. Leimann Gompertz and Solomon Elias were his contractors for cannon, powder and so forth. There were numerous others: Samuel Julius, remount contractor under the Elector Frederick Augustus of Saxony; the Model Family, court-purveyors and army-contractors in the Duchy of Aensbach in the seventeenth and eighteenth centuries are well known in history. In short, as one writer of the time pithily expresses it, 'all the contractors are Jews and all the Jews are contractors.'

"Austria does not differ in this respect from Germany, France and England. The wealthy Jews, who in the reign of the Emperor Leopold received permission to resettle in Vienna (1670)—the Oppenheimers, Wertheimers, Mayer Herschel and the rest—were all army-contractors. And we find the same thing in all the countries under the Austrian Crown.

"Lastly, we must mention the Jewish army-contractors who provisioned the American troops in the Revolutionary and

Civil wars."

Sombart's record ceases there. He does not go on to mention "the Jewish contractors who provisioned the American troops in the Revolutionary and Civil wars." That task shall be THE DEARBORN INDEPENDENT'S from time to time in the future.

It is in the study of Jewish money-making out of war that the clues are found to most of the great abuses of which Jews have been guilty. In the present instance, it was in the matter of profiteering in war goods, that the Jewish connections of Benedict Arnold were discovered.

"Wars are the Jews' harvests" is an ancient saying. Their predilection for the quartermaster's department has been observed anciently and modernly. Their interest being mostly in profits and not in national issues; their traditional loyalty being to the Jewish nation, rather than to any other nation; it is only natural that they should be found to be the merchants of goods and information in times of war—that is, the war profiteers and the spies. As the unbroken program is traced through the Revolutionary War, through the American Civil War, and through the Great War of recent occurrence, the only change observable is the increasing power and profit of the Jews.

Although the number of Jews resident in the American colonies was very small, there were enough to make a mark on the Revolutionary War; and while there was no wholesale legislation against Jews as there was in the Civil War, there were actions against individuals for the same causes which in 1861-5 obtained more extensively.

The Journals of the Continental Congress contain numerous entries of payments made to Jews, as well as the records of various dealings with them on other scores. For drums, for blankets, for rifles, for provisions, for clothing—these are the usual entries. Most of the Jewish commissars were Indian traders (the extent to which the Jews dealt with the American Indians has not as yet been made a subject of research it deserves). The Gratz family of Pennsylvania carried on a very extensive Indian trade and amassed a vast fortune out of it. A most curious lot of information concerning the dealings of the Colonies with the Jews is obtainable by a search through the old records.

The Jews of Colonial New York were both loyalists and rebels, as the tide turned. They profited under loyalism by the contracts which they secured, and by buying in the confiscated property of those who were loyal to the American cause. It is interesting to note that some of the purchasers of the extensive Delancey properties were Jews. Delancey was a patriot whom New York afterward honored by giving his name to an important thoroughfare. That same New York has recently by official action separated the name of Delancey from that thoroughfare, and substituted the name of Jacob H. Schiff, a Jew, native of Frankfort-on-Main.

We enter immediately into the limits of the Benedict Arnold narrative by making mention of the Franks family of Philadelphia, of which family several members will claim our attention.

The Franks were Jews from England who settled in America, retaining their English connections. They were in the business of public contracts, principally army contracts. They were holders of the British army contracts for the French and Indian wars, and for the succeeding Revolutionary War.

To get the picture, conceive it thus, as it is taken from Jewish sources:

Moses Franks lived in England, doing business with the British Government direct. He had the contract for supplying all the British forces in America before military trouble between the Colonies and the Home Government was thought of. He was the principal purveyor of the British Army in Quebec, Montreal, Massachusetts, New York and in the country of the Illinois Indians. It was all British territory then.

Jacob Franks lived in New York. He was American representative of Moses Franks of England. He was the

American agent of the Franks Army Purveyors Syndicate—for that is what it was.

In Philadelphia was *David Franks*, son of Jacob, of New York. David was the Franks' agent for the state or colony of Pennsylvania. He was at the seat of the colonial government, the center of American politics. He was hand in glove with many of the fathers of the American Government. He was an immensely rich man (although but an agent) and carried a high hand at Philadelphia.

At Montreal was another *Franks—David Solesbury Franks*— also in the business of army contractor. He was a gay young man, described as "a blooded buck," who knew all the arts of turning an honest penny out of the needs of armies and the distress of nations. This young man was a grandson or grand nephew of the Moses Franks of England, as he was a nephew of the David Franks of Philadelphia.

Here and there were other Franks, all intent on business with the non-Jewish government, but the four here mentioned carry along the main parts of the tale.

A moment's digression will give us at once a view of the looseness of the liberalism of some of the Fathers of the Country, and a view of the equanimity with which David Franks, of Philadelphia, could pass from one role to another—a facility which cost him dearly when war came on.

John Trumbull, an artist of considerable note at the time, whose paintings still adorn the National Capitol, was invited to dine at Thomas Jefferson's home, among the guests being Senator Giles, from Virginia. Trumbull tells the story:

"I was scarcely seated when Giles began to rally me on the Puritanical ancestry and character of New England. I saw there was no other person from New England present, and, therefore, although conscious that I was in no degree qualified to manage a religious discussion, I felt myself bound to defend my country on this delicate point as well as I could. Whether it had been prearranged that a debate on the Christian religion, in which it should be powerfully ridiculed on the one side and weakly defended on the other, was to be brought forward as promising amusement to a rather free-thinking dinner party, I will not presume to say, but it had that appearance, and Mr. Giles pushed his raillery, to my no small annoyance, if not to my discomfiture, until dinner was announced.

"That I hoped would relieve me by giving a new turn to the conversation, but the company was hardly seated at table when he renewed the assault with increased asperity, and proceeded so far at last as to ridicule the character, conduct and doctrines of the Divine Founder of our religion; Mr. Jefferson in the meantime smiling and nodding approval on Mr. Giles, while the rest of the company silently left me and my defense to our fate, until at length my friend David Franks took up the argument on my side. Thinking this a fair opportunity for avoiding further conversation on the subject, I turned to Mr. Jefferson and said, 'Sir, this is a strange situation in which I find myself; in a country professing Christianity and at a table with Christians, as I supposed, I find my religion and myself attacked with severe and almost irresistible wit and raillery, and not a person to aid in my defense but my friend Mr. Franks, who is himself a Jew.'"

This episode throws a curious light on the character of Thomas Jefferson's "philosophical unbelief," the unlovely fashion of that day; it also illustrates a certain facility in David Franks.

Relations between the Colonies and the Mother Country became strained. Political feelings ran high. The lines of division between "American" and "British" began to appear for the first time. At first there was a degree of agreement among all the population, except the government officials, that a protest against governmental abuses was justified and that strong representations should be made in behalf of the Colonists. Even loyalists and imperialists agreed with that. It was a question of domestic politics. But when presently the idea of protest began to develop into the idea of rebellion and independence, a cleavage came. It was one thing to correct the Empire, another thing to desert it. Here is where the people of the Colonies split.

Mr. Jacob Franks in royalist and loyalist New York, was, of course, royalist and loyalist. As army-contractor for the British Government, he had no choice.

Mr. David Franks, down in Philadelphia, was a little nearer the heart of the new American sentiment, and could not be so royal and loyal as was his kinsman north. In fact, David Franks tried to do what is modernly called "the straddle," attempting to side with the Empire and with the Colonies, too.

It was natural. His business was in Philadelphia. He may also have wished to remain as long as possible in the position of a spy, and send information of the state of public feeling to the royalists. Moreover, he was received in good society and his reputation for wealth and shrewdness won him attentions he could not otherwise have commanded.

So, in 1765 we find him joining the merchants of Philadelphia in the pact not to import articles from England while the hated Stamp Act was in force. In 1775 he favors the continuance of the colonial currency.

He was enjoying his accustomed life in the city—and his acquaintance with the Shippen family into which the dashing young Benedict Arnold married.

There is a strange intermingling of all the tragic figures of the play: Benedict Arnold marries the girl for whom Major André wrote a parlor play. Major André, during his period of captivity as an American prisoner of war and before his exchange, was often at the home of David Franks. And David Solesbury Franks, at his post as agent of the Franks syndicate at Montreal, is placed by a strange turn of the wheel of destiny in the military family of Benedict Arnold for a considerable period preceding and including the great treason.

So, for the moment let us leave the Jewish family of Franks—all of them still stationed as we first described them: Moses in England, Jacob at New York, David at Philadelphia, David S. at Montreal—and let us scrutinize the young American officer, Benedict Arnold.

These facts would most of them be lost, had they not been preserved in the Jewish archives, by the American Jewish Historical Society. You will read any history of Benedict Arnold without perceiving the Jews around him. The authors of the accepted histories were blind.

The principal defect in Benedict Arnold's character was his love of money. All of the trouble which led up to the situation in which he found himself with reference to the American Government and Army, was due to the suspicion which hung like a cloud over many of his business transactions. There have been attempts to paint Arnold as a dashing martyr, as one who was discouraged by the unmerited slights of the Continental Congress, as a victim of the jealousy of lesser men, as one from whom confidence was unjustly withheld. Nothing could be further from the fact. He was a man to whom men were instinctively drawn to be generous, but so general was the knowledge of his looseness in money matters that, while admiring him, his brother officers acted upon the protective instinct and held aloof from him. He was tainted by a low form of dishonesty before he was tainted with treason, and the chief explanation of his treason was in the hard bargain he drove as to the amount of money he was to receive for his guilty act.

Arnold's own record makes this clear. Let us then take up his career at a certain point and see how the Franks strand and the money strand weave themselves through it like colored threads.

Extraordinary efforts have been made in recent years to extenuate Arnold's treason by the recital of his daring services. These services need not be minimized. Indeed, it was his great achievement of the winter march to Montreal and Quebec in 1775-6 that seems to begin the chapter of his troubles. To rehearse this feat of courage and endurance would be to tell a tale that has thrilled the American schoolboy. It was at Montreal that Benedict Arnold came into contact with the young Jew, David Solesbury Franks, the Canadian agent of the Franks army-purveying syndicate. And the next thing known about young Franks is that he returns to the American Colonies in the train of Benedict Arnold as an officer of the American Army.

How this change was effected is not explained in any of the records. There is a moment of darkness, as it were, in which the "quick change" was made, which transformed the young Montreal Jew from an army-contractor for the British into an officer of Benedict Arnold's staff.

But it is impossible for every fact to be suppressed, there are here and there indications of what might have been, what indeed most probably was, the basis of the attraction and relation between the two. It was very probably—almost certainly—the opportunities for graft which could be capitalized by a combination of General Arnold's authority and young Frank's ability in the handling of goods.

From the day they met in Montreal until the hour when General Arnold fled, a traitor, from the fort on the Hudson, young David Solesbury Franks was his companion.

In one of the numerous court-martials which tried General Arnold for questionable dealings in matters pertaining to army supplies, Franks, who was aid-de-camp to Arnold, and by rank of major, testified thus:

"I had, by being in the army, injured my private affairs very considerably, and meant to leave it, if a proper opportunity of entering into business should happen. I had several conversations on the subject with General Arnold, who promised me all the assistance in his power; *he was to participate in the profits of the business I was to enter in.*"

This testimony was given by Major Franks in 1779; the two men had met in the winter of 1775-1776, but, as the records will show, Major Franks was always General Arnold's reliance on getting out of scrapes caused by questionable business methods in which Arnold's military authority was used quite freely. Major Franks admits that he was to enter business and General Arnold was to share the profits. On what basis this arrangement could exist, is another point not known. Arnold had no capital. He had no credit. He was a spendthrift, a borrower, notorious for his constant need of money. The only credible inducement for Franks to accept a partnership with him was on the understanding that Arnold should use his military authority to throw business to Franks. Or, to state it more bluntly, the "profits" which Benedict Arnold was to receive were payments for his misuse of authority for his own gain.

A complete opening of the records will show this to be the most reasonable view of the case.

It was at Montreal that Benedict Arnold's name first became attainted with rumors of shady dealing in private and public property. General George Washington had laid down the most explicit instructions on these matters, with a view to having the Canadians treated as fellow-Americans and not as enemies. General Washington had cashiered officers and whipped soldiers who had previously disobeyed the order against looting and theft.

General Arnold had seized large quantities of goods at Montreal and had hurried them away without making proper account of them. This he admits in his letter to General Schuyler: "Our hurry and confusion was so great when the goods were received, it was impossible to take a particular account of them." This means only that Arnold seized the goods without giving the Canadian citizens proper receipts for them, so that he had in his hands a large amount of wealth for which he was under no compulsion to account to anybody. This mass of goods he sent to a Colonel Hazen at Chambley, and Colonel Hazen, evidently aware of the conditions under which the goods were taken, refused to receive them. This disobedience of Colonel Hazen to his superior officer, especially in a question relating to goods, made it necessary for Arnold to take some self-protective action, which he did in his letter to General Schuyler. Meantime, a very ugly rumor ran through the American Army that General Benedict Arnold had tried to pull a scurvy trick of graft, but had been held up by the strict conduct of Colonel Hazen. Moreover, it was rumored (and the fact was admitted by Arnold in his letter) that in the transfer the goods were well sorted over so that when they finally arrived a great part of them was missing. All the principal facts were admitted by Arnold, who used them, however, to throw blame on Colonel Hazen. He even went so far as to prefer charges against Colonel Hazen, forcing the matter into a court-martial. The court was called and refused to hear the witnesses chosen by General Arnold in his behalf, on the ground that the witnesses were not entitled to credibility. Whereupon General Arnold flouted the court, who ordered him arrested. General Gates, to preserve the useful services of Arnold to the United States Army, dissolved the court-martial, to that extent condoning the conduct of Arnold. Before the court-martial dissolved, however, it informally acquitted Colonel Hazen with honor.

Here, then, almost immediately, as it would seem, upon his new connection with David Solesbury Franks, Benedict Arnold is involved in a bad tangle concerning property which had come into his possession irregularly and which disappeared soon after. His attempt to throw the blame on an officer whose disobedience was the factor that disclosed the true state of affairs, failed. It was his bold scheme to forestall an exposure which must inevitably have come.

While it is true that on this Montreal case, no verdict stands recorded against Benedict Arnold, for the theft of goods, it is also true that the American Army became suspicious of him from that day.

Had Benedict Arnold been innocent then and had he kept his hands clean thereafter, the Montreal episode would have been forgotten. But as a matter of fact such affairs came with increasing frequency thereafter, all of them, strangely enough, involving also the Jew whom he associated with himself at the time of that first exposure.

The story of this Jew's relations with Benedict Arnold all through the period ending with the great treason, may now be taken up with greater consecutiveness, for now their formerly separate courses run together. In another article this relationship and all that it meant will be illustrated from the government records.

Issue of October 8, 1921.

LXVIII.

Benedict Arnold and Jewish Aid in Shady Deal

WHILE Benedict Arnold was in Canada and David Solesbury Franks, the Jew of Montreal and a British subject, was serving as quartermaster to the American troops, David Franks, of Philadelphia, a member of the same Jewish family and of the same Jewish syndicate of army-contractors, was also engaged in an interesting business.

It has already been shown that this David Franks, the Philadelphia Jew, had gone part way with the colonists in their protests against British colonial rule. That this was not sincerity on his part, his subsequent actions proved. He first comes into the purview of this narrative in 1775, the year in which Benedict Arnold performed the remarkable feat of marching into Canada, whence he was sending back into the colonies numerous Canadian prisoners. These prisoners were kept in the New England colonies for a time, but were later collected into Pennsylvania, some of them being quartered in the city of Philadelphia.

How inspired it is impossible now to tell, but presently a committee of the Continental Congress proposes that Mr. David Franks be commissioned to feed and otherwise care for these British prisoners, and be allowed to sell his bills for as much money as may be necessary for the purpose. Of course, in accepting this proposal, Franks was only pursuing the course for which he and his numerous relatives had come to America. He was really doing business with and for Moses Franks, the head of the family syndicate in London. Shortly afterward we read of David under the mouth-filling title of

"Agent to the Contractors for Victualing the Troops of the King of Great Britain," and to check him up, a British officer was allowed to pass the lines once a month and spend a few hours with David. That this was a dangerous practice may be deduced from his further story.

In the records of the Continental Congress is a request from Franks that he be permitted to go to New York, then the British headquarters; and such was the power of the man that his request was granted on condition that he pledged his word "not to give any intelligence to the enemy" and to return to Philadelphia.

In January, 1778, six months before Benedict Arnold took command of Philadelphia, David Franks got himself into trouble. A letter of his was intercepted on its way to England. The letter was intended for Moses Franks, of London, and was concealed under cover of a letter to a captain in a regiment commanded by a British general who had married Frank's sister. It appears on the record of the American Congress "that the contents of the letter manifest a disposition and intentions inimical to the safety and liberty of the United States."

Whereupon it was "Resolved, that Major General Arnold be directed to cause the said David Franks forthwith to be arrested, and conveyed to the new gaol in this city (Philadelphia), there to be confined until the further order of Congress."

Thus Benedict Arnold comes into contact with another member of the Franks family, whose name was to be so closely associated with the great treason.

And now begins a serpentine course of twistings and turnings which are so delightfully Jewish as to be worth restating if only to show how true the race remains to its character through the centuries. It is in October, about the eleventh day of the month. Franks is imprisoned and remains a week. Then by strange reasoning it is discovered that the United States has no jurisdiction over the charge of treason against the United States (!) and that the prisoner should be handed over to the Supreme Executive Council of the state of Pennsylvania. It follows that the state of Pennsylvania has nothing to do with the crime of treason against the United States either, and in spite of the contents of the letters and the findings of the Congressional Committee thereon, David Franks smiles pleasantly and goes free! It was a time, of course, when much money was lent by Jews to public officials. The Jew, Haym Salomon, was credited with having most of the "fathers" on his books, but he did not charge them interest nor principle. He grew immensely wealthy, however, and was the recipient, in lieu of interest and repayment, of many official favors. David Franks, likewise a wealthy man, charged with treason, has his case transferred and finally dismissed. It is a trick not unknown today.

The Jewish records give much credit to Mr. Franks for not being daunted by this experience. Whether he is entitled to particular credit for his courage when he was master of so much influence, is a matter for the reader to decide, but that he was undaunted his subsequent actions show. He is very soon on the records again with an appeal for permission for his secretary to go again to New York within the British lines. He appeals to the Council of Pennsylvania. The Council refers him to Congress. Congress says it has no objection, if the secretary will be governed by General George Washington's orders in the matter. Washington's aid-de-camp gives permission, and the secretary gives sufficient bonds and sets out for New York.

Arrived in New York, the secretary discovers that Mr. Franks' presence is necessary and has made all arrangements for his master to go to New York, having even secured British permission to pass the lines. It was made very easy for Congress, it had only to say yes. But this time Congress said "no." The former escape of Franks made people aware of an un-American influence at work. After his first arrest he was regarded as dangerous to the American cause. He apparently succeeds in living well in Philadelphia in spite of his difficulties, living even gayly with the society of the city.

Up to this time, David Franks had come into contact with the two principal figures in Arnold's treason. As purveyor to the captured troops, Franks had met and entertained, in 1776, the young and engaging Major André, who in 1780 was to become the tragic victim of Arnold's perfidy. And in 1778 Franks had been the subject of an order of arrest given to General Benedict Arnold. Jacob Mordecai "mentions that it was at Mr. Franks' house that he met Major André, then a paroled prisoner, who was passing his idle hours and exercising his talents in the most agreeable ways by taking a miniature likeness of the beautiful Miss Franks." (American Jewish Historical Society, Vol. 6, page 41.)

In the meantime, Benedict Arnold was pursuing his career, a career strangely checkered with brilliant bravery and subtle knavery, a career sustained by the confidence of noble friends who believed in Arnold even against himself. Except for this strange power of holding friends in spite of what they knew of him, Arnold's career would have terminated before it did. That psychic gift of his, and the desperate need of the Continental cause for military leaders, held him on until his moral turpitude matured for the final collapse. As before stated, there is no intention to minimize Arnold's services to his country, but there is a determination to show what were his associations during the period of his moral decline, and thus fill in the gaps of history and account for the distrust with which the American Congress regarded the young general.

David Solesbury Franks, the Montreal Jew, who was an agent of the Franks army-contractor syndicate in Canada, came south to the American colonies with Arnold when the American Army retreated. In his own account of himself, written in 1789—eight years after the treason—he makes so little of his association with Arnold that were it not for the reports of certain courts-martial it would be impossible to determine how close the two men had been. In his record of himself, as preserved in the tenth volume of the American Jewish Historical Society's publications, he admits leaving

Canada with the Americans in 1776 and remaining attached to the American Army until the surrender of Burgoyne, which occurred late in 1777. He then lightly passes over an important period which saw the command of Philadelphia bestowed on General Arnold. He mentions simply that he was "in Arnold's military family at West Point until his desertion," which was in 1780. Reference to the first court-martial of Arnold, in which Colonel David Solesbury Franks was Arnold's chief witness, will show, however, that Franks and Arnold were more closely associated than the former would care to admit after Arnold's name had become anathema. Indeed, as the Jewish Historical Society's note correctly observes, the account of this court-martial "is of much interest, as it bears directly upon the relations of General Arnold and his aid, Major David S. Franks, before the traitor's final flight in September, 1780."

There were in all eight charges preferred against Arnold, the second one being—"In having shut up the shops and stores on his arrival in the city (Philadelphia), so as even to prevent officers of the army from purchasing, while he privately made considerable purchases for his own benefit, as is alleged and believed."

Follows a supporting affidavit, printed in the style of the original, with emphatic italics added:

"On the seventh day of May, A. D. 1779, before me, Plunket Fleeson, Esq., one of the justices, etc., for the city of Philadelphia, comes Colonel John Fitzgerald, late aid de camp to his excellency General Washington, and being duly sworn according to law, deposeth and saith: That on the evening of the day on which the British forces left Philadelphia, he and Major David S. Franks, aid de camp to Major Arnold, went to the house of Miss Brackenberry, and lodged there that night; *and the next morning, major Franks having gone down stairs, the deponent going into the front room of the said house,* to view Colonel Jackson's regiment then marching into the city, *saw lying in the window two open papers*; that on casting his eye on one of them, he was surprised *it contained instructions to the said major Franks to purchase European and East Indian goods in the city of Philadelphia, to any amount, for the payment of which the writer would furnish major Franks with the money, and the same paper contained also a strict charge to the said Franks not to make known to his most intimate acquaintance that the writer was concerned in the proposed purchase*; that *these instructions were not signed*, but appeared to the deponent to be in the handwriting of major general Arnold, whether or not there was a date to it the deponent doth not collect; that the other paper contained instructions signed by major general Arnold, directing major Franks to purchase for the said general Arnold some necessaries for the use of his table; *that the deponent compared the writing of the two papers and verily believes that they were both written by major general Arnold's own hand; and soon afterward major Franks came into the room and took the papers away*, as the deponent supposes. And further the deponent saith not.

"Sworn, etc. John Fitzgerald."

That such a charge involved as much the trial of Major Franks as General Arnold, will at once appear. The statements in the charge argue close association between Arnold and Franks. Yet in Franks' written record of himself in 1789 he passes over this Philadelphia period thus lightly: "In 1778, after the evacuation of Philadelphia by the British Army & on the arrival of Count d' Estaing I procured Letters of recommendation from the Board of War . . . .and joined him off Sandy Hook, I continued with that Admiral until he arrived at Rhode Island, where on the failure of the Expedition I returned to Philadelphia where my military duty called me."

No reference here, nor anywhere in his record, to a closeness of bond between the two which his testimony, now offered from the records, amply proves to have existed.

"The judge-advocate produced major Franks, aid-de-camp to Major General Arnold, who was sworn.

"Q. On General Arnold's arrival in Philadelphia, do

you know whether himself or any person on his account, made any considerable purchases of goods?

"A. I do not.

"Q. At or before general Arnold's arrival in Philadelphia did you receive orders from general Arnold to purchase goods, or do you know of general Arnold's having given orders to any other person to make purchases of goods?

"A. *I did receive from general Arnold that paper which colonel Fitzgerald has mentioned in his deposition.* There are circumstances leading to it which I must explain. I had, by being in the army, injured my private affairs very considerably, and meant to leave it, if a proper opportunity *to enter into business* should happen. *I had several conversations on the subject with General Arnold,* who promised me all the assistance in his power; *he was to participate in the profits of the business I was to enter into.* At that time, *previous to our going to Philadelphia, I had several particular conversations with him, and thought that the period in which I might leave the army with honor and enter into business (had come). I received at that time, or about that time, I think several days before the enemy evacuated the city, the paper mentioned in colonel Fitzgerald's deposition that was not signed, as well as the other.* Upon our coming into town we had a variety of military business to do. I did not purchase any goods, neither did I leave the army. That paper was entirely neglected, neither did I think anything concerning it until I heard of colonel Fitzgerald's deposition. General Arnold has told me since, which is since I came from Carolina some time in August last, that the reason for his not supporting me in business was, supposing that I had left the army, it was incompatible with his excellency's instructions and the resolution of Congress."

This testimony, seemingly straightforward in form, is rather damning to the characters of both the men involved. Arnold, upon taking command of Philadelphia, ordered the stores and shops to be closed and no goods sold. He stopped business outright. It was a most unpopular order, because it prevented the merchants profiting by the new order of things, the return of the Americans.

The very first day the closing law is in force, Arnold writes an order to Franks to make large purchases of European and East Indian goods "to any amount: and to keep the transaction secret from his most intimate acquaintance. That is, Benedict Arnold and the Jewish major on his staff, have an understanding that under cover of the military closing, they will loot the city of its most profitable goods at the enforced low selling prices—for the obvious purpose of selling at higher prices when the military order was rescinded.

These are the undisputed facts. Colonel Fitzgerald saw the papers and knew the unsigned one to be in Arnold's handwriting, even as the signed one was. They were both addressed to the Jewish Major Franks. In his testimony, Major Franks admits the existence of the unsigned order as Colonel Fitzgerald saw it, and admits also its character.

Even Benedict Arnold admitted the order, but he endeavored to show that having exhibited General Washington's orders to him (Arnold) to command Philadelphia, that fact would be a sufficient countermand to the order given to Franks to load up on valuable goods.

"General Arnold to Major Franks. Did you not suppose my showing you the instructions from general Washington to me, previous to your going into the city, a sufficient countermand of the order I had given you to purchase goods?

"Major Franks. I did not form any supposition on the subject."

This admission that he wrote the order, and the fact that no large purchases of goods could be shown, constituted

Arnold's defense. It requires no keen legal mind to show its weakness. If the order was countermanded several days before they entered the city, what was it doing in Miss Brackenberry's house in Philadelphia on the first morning of Arnold's command and the first morning of the operation of his order to close the stores? And why did Franks come in search of it? Discarded orders are not thus carried around and preserved.

Probably no purchases were made. Probably the order was not carried out. When Colonel Fitzgerald walked into the room early in the morning and saw the papers, and when soon thereafter Major Franks walked into the room and saw both Colonel Fitzgerald and the papers, there was nothing else to do than to call the plan off. It had become *known*. Colonel Fitzgerald waited in the room to see what became of the papers. He saw the Jew Franks come and get them. He saw him go out with them. He knew what those papers directed the Jew to do, and he knew that the directing hand was Benedict Arnold's. Doubtless with this clue he kept his eyes open in Philadelphia during the operation of the closing order. And doubtless Franks lost no time in transmitting to General Arnold the fact that he found Colonel Fitzgerald in the room where the papers had been left. The inadvertent visit of Colonel Fitzgerald is the key fact in that phase of the matter.

But the Jewish major becomes talkative in his effort to explain the situation. "There are circumstances which I must explain," he says. And then, in words that were frequently in the mouth of Arnold, he represents that his service in the army was injuring his private affairs very seriously, and that he was contemplating retiring from the army and going into business.

It is worth noting at this point that numerous opportunities were given Franks to retire, both before and after the Arnold treason, but he developed into a persistent clamorer after official jobs. In spite of his testimony, he could not be shaken loose from public employment.

And then Franks revealed the whole secret of his relations with Arnold. They were in close association in profiteering matters. "I had several conversations on the subject with general Arnold. . . . he was to participate in the profits of the business I was to enter into." Arnold was to remain a general in the army; his aide was to get out of the army and work with him privately, sharing the profits.

But what had all this to do with the orders to close the stores at Philadelphia? What had this to do with the papers found by Colonel Fitzgerald? For after all, this was the "circumstance" which Major Franks had set out to explain. At last he reaches it: "At that time, previous to our going into Philadelphia, I had several particular conversations with him . . . . I received at that time, or about that time, the paper mentioned in Colonel Fitzgerald's deposition which was not signed, as well as the other."

The paper authorized him to get the most merchantable goods out of the closed stores. It followed upon "several particular conversations" about the business of which Arnold was to "participate in the profits." But, apparently, the deal did not go through. Colonel Fitzgerald's untimely appearance, and the carelessness of some one in leaving the papers about, were most unfavorable to the Arnold-Franks project.

There can be no question of the intimacy of the relations between the Jew and Arnold and the use that both made of their relationship. There can be no question, either, that these relationships must have been the result of continuous acquaintance and testing.

Merely to show that a Jew once crossed the path of Benedict Arnold and was implicated with him in a discreditable scheme that probably did not fully mature, means nothing. But that this Jew was involved in Arnold's fortunes from the time the two first met in Canada until the day that Arnold betrayed his country, may mean something. And that is the case. From the time of their first meeting, their lines run along together—Frank always being relied upon by Arnold as the credible witness who extricates him from his scrapes, and Franks usually doing it with a sort of clumsy success, as in the instance just cited.

The reader may refer now to the reference made above to Franks' record of himself in which he mentions having joined Count d'Estaing, the French admiral, at Sandy Hook. This was just a month after Arnold took command at Philadelphia, just a month after the events on which the above charge was based. Evidently Franks got out of town for a little while. He would notice the coolness of his fellow officers among whom reports of Colonel Fitzgerald's discovery must have circulated. There would be no prejudice against him because he was a Jew, it would be solely due to the suspicions concerning him. Indeed, readers of the ordinary history will never learn that Arnold had Jews around him. There were David Franks, moneyed man and merchant in the city, and David Solesbury Franks on Arnold's staff—both outstanding figures, yet wholly passed over by the historians, with one or two exceptions, and even these have never caught the Jewish clue. In that day there was no prejudice against Jews as Jews, even as there is none now.

Franks, then, easily gains letters which permit him to join the French fleet of d'Estaing, within a month after the Philadelphia business. And strange to relate, at precisely the same time, Benedict Arnold conceived the notion that he too should go into the navy, and a month after his appointment to Philadelphia he writes to General Washington suggesting nothing less than that he be given command of the American Navy!—at precisely the time Major Franks takes to the water.

" . . . . being obliged entirely to neglect my private affairs since I have been in the service," Arnold writes to General Washington, "has induced me to wish to retire from public business, unless an offer, *which my friends have mentioned,* should be made to me of the command of the navy . . . .I must beg leave to request your sentiments respecting a command in the navy."

So far as the historians have been able to discover, no one ever proposed such a thing as making Arnold the admiral of the American Navy. But, then, the historians did not know David S. Franks. He, a landsman, had gone for a few weeks with the French ships. Perhaps he was the friend who "mentioned" the matter. At any rate, when Franks came off the ships again, it was to serve as witness once more for Benedict Arnold.

The charges against Arnold were such as these: Permitting an enemy ship to land, and buying a share in her cargo; imposing menial service on soldiers (a charge brought about by an action of Major Franks): issuing passes unlawfully—the case in point being that of a Jewess, named Levy; the use of army wagons for his private affairs, and so forth.

This is Major Franks' testimony concerning Arnold's permitting "The Charming Nancy" to land at a United States port, contrary to law:

"Q. (by the court) Do you know whether general Arnold purchased any part of the Charming Nancy or her cargo?

"A. I do not know of my own knowledge, but I have heard general Arnold say he did, and I have also heard Mr. Seagrove say he did.

"Q. Was it previous or subsequent to general Arnold's granting the pass?

"A. It was subsequent."

Here is a complete admission of all the facts, but the defense consisted in laboriously showing, by means of quite leading questions addressed to Franks, that the owners of "The Charming Nancy" were indeed good Americans, though residing and doing business in enemy territory. Franks was rather useful in this part of the business, and the court, overlooking the other elements, simply found that the permission which Arnold gave to "The Charming Nancy" was illegal. The fact that a major general of the United States Army speculated in the cargo of the ship which had come into port in violation of law and on his military permission, was not considered at all. Neither was the fact, stated in the charge, that he gave his permission while he was in camp with

General Washington at Valley Forge, whom he did not consult in any way.

But here again the fact is established that Major Franks was privy to the whole matter, and was the chief witness for Arnold's defense.

If it had occurred but once, as at Montreal, that Arnold had been charged with irregularities involving profitable goods; or if it had occurred but once, as at Philadelphia, that Major Franks happened to be the chief available witness, no serious notice could be taken of it.

But time and again Arnold is caught in shady acts involving profitable goods, and time and again the Jewish Major Franks is his accomplice and chief witness. And this partnership in shady transactions, extending from the time Arnold first met Franks till the time Arnold betrayed his country, is significant, at least as a contribution to history, and possibly as a side light on the gradual degeneration of Benedict Arnold.

Arnold could no longer wholly escape. But still the good fortune that seemed patiently to accompany him, as if waiting for his better nature to recover from some dark spell, remained with him; the court could not exonerate him entirely, but neither could they punish him as he deserved; and so it was given as a verdict that General Arnold should be reprimanded by General Washington, his best friend.

Washington's reprimand is one of the finest utterances in human record. It would have saved a man in whom a shred of moral determination remained:

"Our profession is the chastest of all; even the shadow of a fault tarnishes the luster of our finest achievements. The least inadvertence may rob us of the public favor, so hard to be acquired. I reprimand you for having forgotten that in proportion as you have rendered yourself formidable to our enemies, you should have been guarded and temperate in your deportment toward your fellow-citizens. Exhibit anew those noble qualities which have placed you on the list of our most valued commanders. I will myself furnish you, as far as it may be in my power, with opportunities of regaining the esteem of your country."

It was a bad day for Benedict Arnold when he got into touch with the Jewish syndicate of army-contractors. There was hope for him even yet, if he would cast off the evil spell. But time pressed; events were culminating; the alien, having gripped him, was about to make the best of the baleful opportunity. The closing chapter was about to be written in glory or in shame.

Issue of October 15, 1921.

LXIX.

Arnold and His Jewish Aids at West Point

AFTER General Washington had delivered the reprimand to Benedict Arnold, he proceeded at once to make good the intimation which he had given the unhappy officer—"I will myself furnish you, as far as may be in my power, with opportunities of regaining the esteem of your country." It was late in July, 1780, that General Washington had learned of the British plan to march to Newport and attack re-enforcements of the American cause before they could land and entrench themselves. Washington therefore decided to harry the British and perhaps prevent the attack by crossing the Hudson and marching down the east shore to menace New York, the British headquarters.

It was the last day of July, and General Washington was personally seeing the last division over at King's Ferry, when Benedict Arnold appeared. It is true that he had been wounded, it is also true that his accounts had not been allowed by Congress; but his wound was the fortune of war, and the delay in allowing his accounts was due to his already acquired reputation for shady dealing in money matters, neither of which justified him in betraying his country, but both of which might have stimulated him to recover the status he had so early lost.

It was thus that Benedict Arnold appeared before George Washington, that last day of July, 1780—a man whom Congress rightly distrusted, a man who had just been rightly reprimanded, a man whose fellow-officers looked at him askance.

Yet it was to such a man that Washington made good his

word. The army was on the way to New York to attack the British. As Arnold rode up, General Washington said to him, "You are to command the left wing, the post of honor."

Those who were present report that, at Washington's words, Arnold's countenance fell. The magnanimity of the First American meant nothing to him. The opportunity to retrieve his good name had somehow lost its value.

So patent was Arnold's disappointment, that Washington asked him to ride to headquarters and await him there. At headquarters Arnold disclosed to Washington's aid, Colonel Tilghman, that his desire was not for a command in the army, but for the command of West Point. West Point was then but a post up the Hudson River, far outside the zone of important fighting, and certainly the last place it was thought the intrepid Arnold would desire to be. The inconsistency between Arnold's desire for action and West Point's lack of action, struck General Washington very forcibly. He had offered Arnold a chance to rehabilitate his reputation; Arnold hung back, asking for a place where no distinctive service could be rendered.

Now let the reader take note of this fact: it may be important, it may be unimportant; it may have some bearing on Benedict Arnold's action, it may have none; but the fact nevertheless is this: The Forage Master, that is, the quartermaster at West Point, was Colonel Isaac Franks, a member of the same family which we have been considering in these articles. This Colonel Isaac Franks, we are informed by the Jewish records which make a great deal of the fact, was once confidential aide-de-camp to General Washington, though for what reason the relationship was dissolved we are are not informed.

The reader will recall that the narrative of Benedict Arnold has already included two members of the Franks family— David, of Philadelphia, and David Solesbury Franks, who came down from Montreal.

The third Franks is now in view—Colonel Isaac Franks. He is in charge of supplies at the post of West Point. It is to

West Point that Benedict Arnold wishes to go, even though General Washington is offering him the post of honor in the forward movement which the Continental Army is about to make. It is the last day of July, 1780.

On August 3, General Washington gave Arnold his orders and allowed him to proceed to take command of West Point. Accompanying him, of course, was Colonel David Solesbury Franks, his aide-de-camp, whose testimony had been so useful at the court-martial. There were then two Franks at West Point—Colonel D. S. Franks, aid to the commandant, and Colonel Isaac Franks, in charge of supplying the post.

It appears that Arnold had already been in communication with the enemy and had asked for the command at West Point, not for any of the reasons he alleged to General Washington, but because he had already chosen it as the gateway through which he was to let the British through into the weakened American territory. For two months Arnold had been writing to "Anderson," or John André. He had been reaching out toward the enemy for a longer time than that, and had at length requested that a man equal to himself be appointed to negotiate with him. Major John André, adjutant general of the British Army in America, was chosen as one of rank sufficiently high to deal with Arnold. They had already come into touch with each other before Arnold asked General Washington for the post at West Point. And André, as we have previously seen, knew the Franks.

Apologists for Arnold have said that the reason he showed so deep a disappointment when General Washington offered him the command of the left wing of the army, was that he had never expected such magnanimous treatment, and for the moment was conscience-stricken that he had gone so far with the enemy when his own country offered him such fine prospects. If that were the true state of Arnold's mind, he need only have taken command of the left wing, or, having been committed to take West Point, he need only have gone there and performed his soldierly duty.

The history and personality of Major John André, who completed the negotiations with Arnold, and lost his life as a spy, while Arnold lived long as a traitor, have been the object of much interest and research. His descent is obscure. His parentage was known as "Swiss-French." It is thought that the first André came into England in the train of a Jewish family. André himself had those accomplishments which were most highly prized in the society of the day. In any event, of Jewish or non-Jewish descent, he was a far finer character than Benedict Arnold.

On Arnold's staff at West Point, besides the two Jewish Franks—Isaac and David—there was Lieutenant Colonel Richard Varick. This Varick was a wise young fellow who preferred to have as little as possible to do with Arnold's affairs. He refused to take any responsibility connected with Arnold's dealings with money or goods. For some apparently good reason, which will not be difficult for the reader to surmise, Varick adopted the strict policy of keeping his hands off all supplies. Thus it was left to Major Franks to attend all such matters, to which he was apparently nothing loath. In fact, Major Franks even looked after General Arnold's private cupboard.

Not to delay longer over details, suffice it to say that on September 22, 1780, less that two months after assuming command at West Point, the treason of Benedict Arnold was accomplished. One more day, and it was discovered and foiled.

Instant inquiry was made to detect accomplices. Major Franks is placed under arrest. David Franks, of Philadelphia, is arrested. It may or may not be significant, but it is nevertheless a fact, that upon the accomplishment of Arnold's treason the authorities ordered that the two Jews, David Franks and David Solesbury Franks, be put under arrest.

The experience of David Franks adds a bit of Jewish comedy to this serious scene. It appears that he still has influence to save him from severe treatment and to gain him time. On the occasion of his previous arrest in 1778, Benedict

Arnold was commander of the city of Philadelphia and David Solesury Franks was on Arnold's staff, and if Arnold and Franks could concoct a scheme of profiteering off the closed stores of the city, it was probably not beyond them to see that the elder David Franks received favor in his case. At least, as the reader of previous articles knows, David Franks went free, although caught in the act of communicating with the enemy.

But this time there is no Benedict Arnold to help him, and his nephew, like himself, is under arrest because of Arnold's treason. Yet the Philadelphia Jew discloses a marvelous facility of playing horse with the law.

He remained in jail until October 6, and then, strange to relate, he is given two weeks to get within the enemy's lines. Investigation somehow has been stopped; prosecution has been sidetracked. But David found 14 days too brief a time to wind up his affairs, and he petitions for an extension of time. It is denied. Then when one week of the time had passed, Franks asks for a pass to New York for himself, daughter, manservant and two maid-servants; this is refused and passes are authorized for himself, daughter, and one maid-servant, "provided she be an indented servant." But David does not use these passes. He applies again for an extension of time on account of an "indisposition of body." Thus, by keeping officials busy with his evasions and his counter-suggestions the record finds him still in Philadelphia on November 18, a month after he was supposed to be out of the country.

He makes application for another pass. The Council obediently sends him one, the secretary making this observation in his note: "The Council are much surprised that you still remain in this city, and hope that you will immediately depart this state, agreeable to their late order, otherwise measures will be taken to compel you to comply with the same."

Does David go? He does not. He writes an extremely polite letter. Incidentally he gives a hint of what may be keeping him. In his letter to the Council he says:

"Being apprehensive that a report raised and circulated that

I had *depreciated the currency by purchase of specie* may have given rise to prejudice against me with the Honorable Council . . . ."

More than likely this is precisely what David was doing. It was done later by another Jew in American history, Judah P. Benjamin, and it was done everywhere by Jews during the recent war. With David's racial itch for money and his disloyalty to the American cause, there was probably sound foundation for the report.

And then, in the last line of his letter, he finds fault with his pass, and asks for another. All this time, of course, he is gaining time, and is fulfilling his purpose with regard to the specie.

This, by the way, is a common Jewish stratagem. It is very much observed in lawsuits. The non-Jew can always be depended on to desire justice and humanity, and these traits are systematically played upon. The non-Jew is also inclined to take men's word at face value, which is also a trait which can be used to his hurt. If, for example, in a business transaction which is to be consummated a week hence, the non-Jew could absolutely fortify himself if he had the slightest suspicion of sharp dealing, it is to the advantage of the Jew who tries to "do" him to give him his word as to exactly what steps will be taken a week hence at the final settlement. If the non-Jew believes that word, he is quieted for a week. He does nothing. He rests implicitly on the given word. Then the morning comes, and the dishonest Jew steps up without warning and drives through ruthlessly to a tricky gain. This is so common that thousands who have been tricked by it have told the full details. Keep the Gentiles so busy, or satisfy him so fully, that he will not bother—that's the strategy. David knew it even in his day and it was ancient then.

His request for a new pass is refused. But still he does not go. Finally, an aroused Council sends him notice to be gone by the next day. And then he goes, but not, we may well believe, until he had done all he intended to do. David is delightfully

Jewish and the Council are naively Gentile.

Up at West Point other matters are proceeding. When General Washington arrived and heard the startling news, he asked Colonel Varick to walk with him. He spoke to the young officer most considerately, told him he did not question his loyalty, but under the circumstances he would ask him to consider himself under arrest. It was very like Washington to do this, to make the arrest himself, gently. There is no record, however, that a like courtesy was shown the Jewish Major David Solesbury Franks. Washington probably remembered him as the witness for Arnold in the case which led to Arnold's court-martial and reprimand.

On that frontier post (as West Point then was) there were no witnesses. Franks and Varick were confronted with the necessity of testifying for each other. That is, the Jewish major was his own representative in court and practically his own witness. Franks put Varick on the stand to testify for him. The resulting testimony shows that Franks knew much and was eager to tell how much he knew of Arnold's traitorous intentions—but he did not tell it until Arnold's treason was exposed and he himself under arrest.

The purpose of this article being merely to fill up the gaps which are left in the Jewish propagandist boasting of the part they have played in public affairs in the United States, the reader must himself be a judge as to how far Major David Solesbury Franks was in Arnold's secret. (The "Smith" mentioned in the testimony was Joshua Hett Smith, who did secret work for Arnold and rowed André ashore for the night conference with Arnold.) Following are vital extracts from the testimony:

Major Franks—"What was my opinion of Joshua H. Smith's character and conduct, and of his visits at Arnold's headquarters . . . .?"

Colonel Varick—"When I first joined Arnold's family . . . . Arnold and yourself thought well of him as a man, but I soon prevailed on you to think him a Liar and a Rascal; and you ever after spoke of him in a manner his real character merited...."

Arnold, of course, knew what Smith was. Arnold and Smith were already partners in treason. But Varick did not know of this partnership. All that Varick knew was that both Arnold and Franks appeared to hold the same opinion, that Smith was all right. Here Arnold and Franks appear as agreed again. Varick regarded them as holding the same opinion. Varick says so to Franks' face in answer to Franks' question. He does it, however, from a friendly purpose. But the fact is significant that Franks and Arnold are found holding the same front—"Arnold and yourself thought well of him as a man."

Now, Arnold *knew* what Smith was, knew enough about Smith to hang him. Smith was one of the tools of his long extended treason. The question is, did Franks also know? Was Franks kept in ignorance of Arnold's real knowledge of Smith, or was Franks actually deceived as regards Smith? It may be, but let this be observed, that Varick, who was not at all in Arnold's confidence, nevertheless was not deceived about Smith, but saw through him at once. Did not Franks see through him, too? Until the time that Varick dared speak about the matter, Franks and Arnold were preserving the same appearance of opinion—they "thought well of him as a man."

Then Varick honestly spoke out. He got hold of the Jewish Franks and told him all that he knew and suspected about Smith. The evidence was too overwhelming for Franks to scoff at. Any man scoffing at Varick's tale would himself be under suspicion. Varick was given to understand that he had changed Franks' opinion of Smith. Thereafter Franks comported himself in a manner to convince Varick that he regarded Smith as a "Liar and a Rascal."

It is permissible to ask, was this pretense or reality? If Varick knew things, Varick was a man to handle wisely. If Varick knew things, it would be foolish to lose touch with him and thus lose the benefit of knowing how much was known or surmised outside. These, of course, are the arguments of suspicion, but they are made concerning the same Jewish officer who, on finding that Colonel Fitzgerald had discovered the profiteering venture in which Franks and Arnold were partners, was wise enough to inform Arnold and permit the plan to drop. Major Franks' previous behavior, like Benedict Arnold's, arouses the suspicion. Benedict Arnold appeared to Varick to regard Smith as a good man; Franks appeared to Varick to share Arnold's opinion; but whether Franks really *knew*, as Arnold knew, and only pretended to change his opinion that he might keep the confidence of Varick, is a point on which Franks' previous conduct compels the mind to waver.

How well Franks knew Arnold may be gathered from other points brought out in this testimony:

Major Franks—"How often did Arnold go down the river in his barge, whilst I was at Robinson's House (Arnold's headquarters)? Did I ever attend him, and what were our opinions and conduct on his going down and remaining absent the night of the twenty-first of September?" (This was the night of his meeting André.)

Colonel Varick—(answers that Franks, to his knowledge, never accompanied Arnold) "But when I was informed by you or Mrs. Arnold, on the twenty-first, that he was not to return that evening, I suggested to you that I supposed he had gone to Smith's, and that I considered Arnold's treatment of me in keeping up his connection with Smith, in opposition to the warning I had given him, as very ungenteel, and that I was resolved to quit his family" (meaning his staff). "We did thereupon concert the plan of preventing their further intimacy by alarming Mrs. Arnold's fears . . . .

"You did at the same time inform me that you could not account for his connections with Smith—that you knew him to be an avaricious man and suspected he meant to open trade with some person in New York, under sanction of his command, and by means of flags and the unprincipled rascal Smith; and that you were induced to suspect if from the letter he wrote to Anderson in a commercial style as related to you by me. We thereupon pledged to each our word of honor that if our suspicions should prove to be founded in fact, we would instantly quit him."

It is the honest Varick talking, Franks questioning him. It will be observed that it is Franks who tells Varick of Arnold's absence and that he will not return that night. Franks knew, but Varick did not. It will be observed also, that it was Varick who protested and threatened to quit Arnold. It was indeed the second time he had threatened to quit, but the Jewish major seems never to have had a similar thought. But most important to observe is Varick's statement in answer to Franks, and in Franks' presence, that it was Franks who opened up with information regarding Arnold's character—that Arnold was an avaricious man, that Franks suspected him of opening up trade with the enemy "under sanction of his command" (just as he had planned to misuse his authority at Philadelphia) and that Smith was to be the go-between. Then he mentions a letter to "Anderson in a commercial style"—this "Anderson" being none other than Major John André of the British Army.

Here we find Major Franks intimate with every element of the conspiracy—every element of it!—and giving a certain explanation of it to Varick. Did Franks know more than he told, and was he quieting Varick with an explanation which seemed to cover all the facts, and yet did not divulge the truth? It is a question that occurs, directly we recall the close collusion of Arnold and Franks at Philadelphia.

There is other testimony, that it was Varick, not Franks, who prevented Arnold selling supplies of the government for his own profit. Time and again this occurred, but never with Franks, the long-time aid and confidant of Arnold, in the rôle of actor. But every time Varick did it, Franks knew of it, as he testified.

Now we approach the "Day of his Desertion," as the records call the day of Arnold's treason.

Major Franks—"What was Arnold's, as well as my conduct and deportment on the Day of his Desertion, and had you the slightest reason to think I had been or was party or privy to any of his villainous practices and correspondence with the enemy, or to his flight? Pray relate the whole of our conduct on that day to your knowledge."

Colonel Varick—"I was sick and a greater part of the time in my bed in the morning of his flight. Before breakfast he came into my room" (and talked about certain letters) "and I never saw him after it but betook myself to my bed. I think it was about an hour thereafter when you came to me and told me Arnold was gone to West Point—also a considerable time thereafter you came to the window of my room near my bed and, shoving it up hastily told me with a degree of apparent surprise that you believed Arnold was a villain or rascal, and added you had heard a report that one Anderson was taken as a spy on the lines and that a militia officer had brought a letter to Arnold and that he was enjoined secrecy by Arnold. I made some warm reply, but instantly reflecting that I was injuring a gentleman and friend of high reputation in a tender point, I told you it was uncharitable and unwarrantable even to suppose it. You concurred in opinion with me and I lay down secure in the high idea I entertained of Arnold's integrity and patriotism . . . ."

Here is a record of Major Franks' conduct, told at his own solicitation before a court of inquiry. It reveals that Arnold told Franks, but did not tell Varick, where he was going. It reveals also that Franks knew of the message which came to Arnold, the bearer of which had been bound by Arnold to secrecy. ("For the reader's benefit it is recalled that Arnold's treason was prematurely exposed by André being lost in the woods at night after his interview with Arnold, and his consequent inability to get back to the British ship. He was sighted and halted in daylight, and discovery was made of the West Point plans in his stockings. The innocent soldiers sent word to Benedict Arnold, their commanding officer, that they had captured a spy named Anderson. This gave Arnold information that the plot had fallen through. Enjoining absolute secrecy on the messenger, Arnold made off hastily as if to investigate, but really to rush to the ship to which André had failed to return.) But, observe: the messenger arrived and immediately Franks appears to be informed what the message contains. He is informed also that Arnold is going to West Point. He is informed of "Anderson's" capture. Once again *Franks is in instant touch with all the points of the matter,* but this time he goes further and accuses Arnold. In the peculiar phraseology of Varick, which may or may not be significant, Franks "hastily told me with a degree of apparent surprise" that he believed Arnold to be a villain or rascal.

Then the difference between these two men appeared again; it shines out luminously. When it was possible to save Arnold, it was Varick who was most concerned, while Franks appeared to be hand-in-glove with the traitor. But when it was apparent that something irrevocable had happened, it was the Jew who was first and bitterest to denounce, while Varick remembered the conduct expected of gentlemen. Likewise, as at first, the Jewish major changed his opinion of Smith to agree with Varick's opinion, so now he "concurred in opinion" with Varick, although he had just violently uttered the opposite opinion concerning Arnold.

Varick was charitable because he did not have the facts. Was Franks as outspoken as he was because he had all the facts? If so, where did he get them? From Arnold?

How much did Franks know? That question will probably never be answered. There is, however, this additional testimony of his on record:

"I told you that I thought Arnold had corresponded

with Anderson or some such name before from Philadelphia, and had got intelligence of consequence from him."

David Solesbury Franks was implicated in every major crime of Benedict Arnold and in the great treason he gave evidence of knowing every movement of the game, from its far beginning in Philadelphia.

Franks was exonerated by the court.

From his safe retreat on the British man-of-war, Benedict Arnold wrote a letter in which he exculpated Smith, Franks and Varick, writing that they were "totally ignorant of any transactions of mine, that they had reason to believe were injurious to the public."

Smith was neither ignorant nor innocent. He had rowed out to the British ship and brought André ashore for his conference with Arnold. He had been a go-between on many shady missions. That fact seriously affects his exoneration of Franks. If Arnold can lie about Smith's innocence, why cannot he lie about Franks' innocence. As to Varick, he is the only one of the three who can do without Arnold's exoneration; to Varick it is an insult to have Benedict Arnold vouch for him. Franks, however, was always afterward inclined to lean upon Arnold's letter. An impartial study of the testimony, upon the background of a knowledge of Franks' history, leaves grave doubts as to the unimpeachability of his relations with Benedict Arnold. So much so, indeed, that in the study of Arnold's treason it is a grave omission to pass over Franks' name.

The reader who will make a complete study of Franks' character as revealed in the records will testify to this: the present study has been exceedingly charitable to his character; he could easily have been prejudiced in the reader's mind by the presentation of a series of facts omitted here; the object has been to judge him solely on his acts with relation to Benedict Arnold.

Rightly or wrongly, Franks was suspected ever afterward.

It was the Philadelphia incident that stamped his reputation. The suspicion of perjury on that occasion never left him. Franks insisted on having himself vindicated all round, but he was never satisfied with his vindications, he always wanted more. Jewish propagandists have misrepresented his subsequent work as a diplomatist. It was of the merest messenger-boy character, and he was intrusted with it only after the most obsequious appeals. He peddled petitions reciting his services and asking for government favor. The man who asserted in his defense at Philadelphia that he was eager to leave the army and enter business, could not be induced to leave the public service, until the allotment to him of 400 acres of land seems to have effectually weaned him from public life. What his end was, no one appears to know. His present-day use, however, is to furnish Jewish and pro-Jewish propagandists with a peg on which to hang extravagant praise of the Jew in Revolutionary times.

There can be no objection whatever to Jewish propagandists making the most of their material, but there is strong objection to the policy of concealment and misrepresentation. These impositions on public confidence will be exposed as regularly as they occur.

Issue of October 22, 1921

LXX.

The Gentle Art of Changing Jewish Names

THE Madansky brothers—Max, Solomon, Benjamin, and Jacob—have written that their names henceforth will be May. It is a good old Anglo-Saxon name, but the Madanskys are of Asiatic origin.

Elmo Lincoln, a movie actor, comes into a Los Angeles court on the motion of his wife, and it is discovered that he is only Otto Linknhelt.

A large department store owner was born with the name Levy. He is now known as Lytton. It is quite possible he did not like Levy as a name; but why did he not change it for another Jewish name? Or perhaps it was the Jewishness of "Levy" that displeased him.

A popular tenor star recently brought suit against his wife, who married him after allowing him to believe that she was of Spanish origin. "I understood from her misleading stage name that she was Spanish when I married her. Later I found that she was Jewish and that her real name was Bergenstein."

One of the biggest and best known stores in the United States goes under an honored Christian name, though every one of the owners is Jewish. The public still carries a mental picture of the good old merchant who established the store, which picture would speedily change if the public could get a glimpse of the real owners.

Take the name Belmont, for example, and trace its history. Prior to the nineteenth century the Jews resident in Germany did not use family names. It was "Joseph the son of Jacob," "Isaac ben Abraham," the son being designated as the son of this father. But the Napoleonic era, especially following upon the assembly of the Great Sanhedrin under Napoleon's command, caused a distinct change in Jewish customs in Europe.

In 1808 Napoleon sent out a decree commanding all Jews to adopt family names. In Austria a list of surnames was assigned to the Jews; and if a Jew was unable to choose, the state chose for him. The names were devised from precious stones, as Rubenstein; precious metals, such as Goldstein, Silberberg; plants, trees and animals, such as Mandelbaum, Lilienthal, Ochs, Wolf, and Loewe.

The German Jews created surnames by the simple method of affixing the syllable "son" to the father's name, thus making Jacobson, Isaacson; while others adopted the names of the localities in which they lived, the Jew resident in Berlin becoming Berliner, and the Jew resident in Oppenheim becoming Oppenheimer.

Now, in the region of Schoenberg, in the German Rhine country, a settlement of Jews had lived for several generations. When the order to adopt surnames went forth, Isaac Simon, the head of the settlement, chose the name of Schoenberg. It signifies in German, "beautiful hill." It is very easily Frenchified into Belmont, which also means beautiful hill or mountain. A Columbia University professor once tried to make it appear that the Belmonts originated in the Belmontes family of Portugal, but found it impossible to harmonize this theory with the Schoenberg facts.

It is noteworthy that a Belmont became American agent of the Rothschilds, and that the name of Rothschild is derived from the red shield on a house in the Jewish quarter of Frankfort-on-the-Main. What the original family name is has never been divulged.

The Jewish habit of changing names is responsible for the immense camouflage that has concealed the true character of Russian events. When Leon Bronstein becomes Leo Trotsky, and when the Jewish Apfelbaum becomes the "Russian" Zinoviev; and when the Jewish Cohen becomes the "Russian" Volodarsky, and so on down though the list of the controllers of

Russia—Goldman becoming Izgoev, and Feldman becoming Vladimirov—it is a little difficult for people who think that names do not lie, to see just what is transpiring.

Indeed, there is any amount of evidence that in numberless cases this change of names—or the adoption of "cover names," as the Jewish description is—is for purposes of concealment. There is an immense difference in the state of mind in which a customer enters the store of Isadore Lemy and the state of mind in which he enters the store of Alex May. And what would be his feeling to learn that Isadore Levy painted up the name of Alex May with that state of mind in view? When Rosenbluth and Schlesinger becomes "The American Mercantile Company," there is justification for the feeling that the name "American" is being used to conceal the Jewish character of the firm.

The tendency of Jews to change their names dates back very far. There was and is a superstition that to give a sick person another name is to "change his luck," and save him from the misfortune destined upon his old name. There was also the Biblical example of a change of nature being followed by a change of name, as when Abram became Abraham and Jacob became Israel.

There have been justifiable grounds, however, for Jews changing their names in Europe. The nationalism of that continent is, of course, intense, and the Jews are an international nation, scattered among all the nations, with an unenviable reputation of being ready to exploit for Jewish purposes the nationalistic intensity of the Gentiles. To mollify a suspicion held against them wherever they have lived (a suspicion so general and so persistent as to be explainable only on the assumption that it was abundantly justified) the Jews have been quick to adopt the names and colors of whatever country they may be living in. It is no trouble at all to change a flag, since none of the flags is the insignia of Judah. This was seen throughout the war zone; the Jews hoisted whatever flag was expedient at the moment, and changed it as often as the shifting tide of battle required.

A Polish Jew named Zuckermandle, emigrating to Hungary, would be anxious to show that he had shuffled off the Polish allegiance which his name proclaimed; and the only way he could do this would be to change his name, which would very likely become Zukor, a perfectly good Hungarian name. Originally the Zukors were not Jews; now the usual guess would be that they are. In the United States it would be almost a certainty. Such a change as Mr. Zuckermandle would make, however, would not be for the purpose of concealing the fact that the was a Jew, but only to conceal the fact that he was a foreign Jew.

In the United States it has been found that Jews change their names for three reasons: first, for the same reason that many other foreigners change their names, namely, to minimize as much as possible the "foreign look" and the difficulty of pronunciation which many of those names carry with them; second, for business reasons, to prevent the knowledge becoming current that So-and-So is "a Jew store"; third, for social reasons.

The desire not to appear singular among one's neighbors, when stated in just these words, very easily passes muster as being a natural desire, until you apply it to yourself. If you were going abroad to Italy, Germany, Russia, there to live and engage in business, would you cast about for a changed name immediately? Of course not. Your name is part of you, and you have your own opinion of an alias. The Jew, however, has his own name among his own people, regardless of what "cover name" the world may know him by, and, therefore, he changes his outside name quite coolly. The only likeness we have to that in America is the changing of men's pay numbers as they move their employment from place to place. John Smith may be No. 49 in Black's shop and No. 375 in White's shop, but he is always John Smith. So the Jew may be Simon son of Benjamin in the privacy of the Jewish circle, while to the world he may be Mortimer Alexander.

In the United States it is hardly to be doubted that business and social reasons are mostly responsible for the changes in Jewish names. The designation "American" is itself much coveted, as may be gathered by its frequent use in firm names, the members of which are not American in any sense that entitles them to blazon that name throughout the world.

When Moses is changed to Mortimer, and Nathan to Norton, and Isadore to Irving (as for example, Irving Berlin, whose relatives, however, still know him as "Izzy"), the concealment of Jewishness in a country where so much is done by print, must be regarded as a probable motive.

When "Mr. Lee Jackson" is proposed for the club there would seem to be no reason, as far as reading goes, why anything unusual about Mr. Jackson should be surmised, until you know that Mr. Jackson is really Mr. Jacobs. Jackson happens to be the name of a President of the United States, which names are quite in favor with the name-changers, but in this case it happens also to be one of the "derivatives" of an old Jewish name.

The Jewish Encyclopedia contains interesting information on this matter of derivatives.

Asher is shaded off into Archer, Ansell, Asherson.

Baruch is touched up into Benedict, Beniton, Berthold.

Benjamin becomes Lopez, Seef, Wolf (this is translation).

David becomes Davis, Davison, Davies, Davidson.

Issac becomes Sachs, Saxe, Sace, Seckel.

Jacob becomes Jackson, Jacobi, Jacobus, Jacof, Kaplan, Kauffmann, Marchant, Merchant.

Jonah becomes by quite simple changes, Jones and Joseph, Jonas.

Judah (the true Jewish name) becomes Jewell, Leo, Leon, Lionel, Leoni, Judith.

Levi becomes Leopold, Levine, Lewis, Loewe, Low, Lowy.

Moses becomes Moritz, Moss, Mortimer, Max, Mack, Moskin, Mosse.

Solomon becomes Salmon, Salome, Sloman, Salmuth.

And so on through the list of Jewish "changelings"—Barnett, Barnard, Beer, Hirschel, Mann, Mendel, Mandell, Mendelsohn, with various others which are not even adaptations but sheer appropriations.

The millinery business, which is one of the principle Jewish grafts off American women, shows the liking of the Jews for names which do not name, but which stand as impressive insignia—"Lucile," "Mme Grande," and the like. Reuben Abraham Cohen is a perfectly good name, and a good citizen could make it immensely respected in his neighborhood, but Reuben thinks that the first round in the battle of minds should be his, and he does not scruple at a little deceit to obtain it, so he painted on the window of his store, R. A. Le C'an, which, when set of with a borrowed coat of arms, looks sufficiently Frenchified for even observant boobs among the Gentiles. Similarly a Mr. Barondesky may blossom out as Barondes, or La Baron.

Commonly Mr. Abraham becomes Miller. Why Miller should have been picked on for Judaization is not clear, but the Millers of the white race may yet be compelled to adopt some method of indicating that their name is not Jewish. It is conceivable that a Yiddish and an American form of the same name may some time be deemed necessary. Aarons becomes Arnold—there are a number of Jewish Arnolds. Aarons became Allingham. One Cohen became Druce, another Cohen became Freeman. Still another Cohen became a Montagu; a fourth Cohen became a Rothbury and a fifth Cohen became a Cooke.

The Cohens have an excuse, however. In one ghetto there are so many Cohens that some distinction must be observed. There is Cohen the rag gatherer, and Cohen the schacet (ritual meat killer), and Cohen the rising lawyer, as well as Cohen the physician. To make the matter more difficult their first names (otherwise their "Christian" names) are Louis. It is not to be wondered at, therefore, that the young lawyer should become Attorney Cohane (which does all the better if thereby certain Irish clients are attracted), and that the young doctor should become Doctor Kahn, or Kohn. These are some of the many forms that the priestly name of Cohen takes.

The same may be said with reference to Kaplan, a very common name. Charlie Chaplin's name was, in all probability, Caplan, or Kaplan. At any rate, this is what the Jews believe about their great "star." Non-Jews have read of Charlie as a "poor English boy."

There is the Rev Stephen S. Wise, for another example. He booms his way across the country from one platform to the other, a wonder in his way, that such pomposity of sound should convey such paucity of sense. He is an actor, the less effective because he essays a part in which sincerity is requisite. This Rabbi, whose vocal exercise exhausts his other powers, was born in Hungary, his family name being Weisz. Sometimes this name is Germanized to Weiss. When S. S. Weisz became S. S. Wise, we do not know. If he had merely Americanized his Hungarian name it would have given him the name of White. Apparently "Wise" looked better. Truly it is better to be white than to be wise, but Dr. Stephen S. is a fresh point in the query of "what's in a name?"

The list of Jews in public life whose names are not Jewish would be a long one. Louis Marshall, head of the American Jewish Committee, for example—what could his old family name have been before it was changed for the name of the Chief Justice of the Supreme Court of the United States?

Mr. Selwyn's name, now so widely known in motion pictures, was originally Schlesinger. Some of the Schlesingers become Sinclairs, but Selwyn made a really good choice for a man in the show business. A rabbi whose real name was Posnansky became Posner. The name Kalen is usually an abbreviation of Kalensky. A true story is told of an East Side tinsmith whose name was very decidedly foreign-Jewish. It is withheld here, because THE DEARBORN INDEPENDENT prefers in this connection to mention only the names of those who can take care of themselves. But the tinsmith moved to a non-Jewish section and opened a new shop under the name of

Perkins, and his luck really did change! He is doing well, and, being an industrious, honest workman, deserves his prosperity.

Of course, there are lower uses of the name-changing practice, as every employer of labor knows. A man contracts a debt under one name, and to avoid a garnishee, quits his job, collects his pay, and in a day or two attempts to hire out under another name. This was once quite a successful trick, and is not wholly unknown now.

There is also much complaint among the stricter observers of the Jewish ritual requirements that the word "Kosher" is greatly misused, that indeed it covers a multitude of sins. "Kosher" has come to signify, in some places, little more than a commercial advertisement designed to attract Jewish trade. For all it means of what it says, it might just as well be "The Best Place in Town to Eat"—which it isn't, of course; and neither is it always "strictly" Kosher.

It must be conceded, however, that the tendency to mislabel men and things is deep set in Jewish character. Jews are great coiners of catchwords that are not true, inventors of slogans that do not move. There is a considerable decrease in the power they wielded by such methods; their brilliancy in this respect is running to seed. This may be explained by the fact that there are so many song titles to write for the Jewish jazz factories, and so much "snappy" matter for screen descriptions. Their comeback is painfully thin and forced. Without peers in dealing with a superficial situation like a dispute over the beauty of two rival "stars," or the amount and method of distributing confetti, they are the veriest dubs in dealing with a situation like that which has arisen in this country.

Immediately upon the appearance of the Jewish Question in the United States the Jews reverted naturally to their habit of mislabeling. They were going to fool the people once more with a pat phrase. They are still seeking for that phrase. Slowly they are recognizing that they are up against the Truth, and truth is neither a jazzy jade nor a movie motto, which can be recostumed and changed at will.

This passion for misleading people by names is deep and varied in its expression. Chiefly due to Jewish influences, we are giving the name of "liberalism" to looseness. We are dignifying with names that do not correctly name, many subversive movements. We are living in an era of false labels, whose danger is recognized by all who observe the various underground currents which move through all sections of society. Socialism itself is no longer what its name signifies; the name has been seized and used to label anarchy. Judaistic influence creeping into the Christian church has kept the apostolic labels, but thoroughly destroyed the apostolic content; the disruptive work has gone on quietly and unhindered, because often as the people looked, the same label was there—as the same old merchant's name stays on the store the Jews have bought and cheapened. Thus there are "reverends" who are both unreverend and irreverent, and there are shepherds who flock with the wolves.

Zionism is another misnomer. Modern Zionism is not what its label would indicate it to be. The managers of the new money collection—millions of it, badly used, badly accounted for—are about as much interested in Zionism as an Ohio Baptist is in Meccaism. For the leading so-called "Zionists," Mt. Zion and all that it stands for has next to no meaning; they see only the political and real estate aspects of Palestine, another people's country just at present. The present movement is not religious, although it plays upon the religious sentiments of the lower class of Jews; it is certainly not what Judaized orators among the Christians want the Christians to think it is; Zionism is at present a most mischievous thing, potentially a most dangerous thing, as several governments could confidentially tell you.

But it is all a part of the Jewish practice of setting up a label pretending one thing, while quite another thing really exists.

Take anti-Semitism. That is a label which the Jews have

industriously pasted up everywhere. If ever it was an effective label its uses are over now. It doesn't mean anything. Anti-Semitism does not exist, since the thing so named is found among the Semites, too. Semites cannot be anti-Semitic. When the world holds up a warning finger against a race that is the moving spirit of the corruptive, subversive and destructive influences abroad in the world today, that race cannot nullify the warning by sticking up a false label of "Anti-Semitism," any more than it can justify the sign of gold on a $1.50 watch or the sign of "pure wool" on a $11.50 suit of clothes.

So with the whole group of labels which the Jews have trotted out like talismen to work some magic spell upon the aroused mind of America. They are lies. And when one lie fails, how quickly they hitch their hopes to; another. If "Anti-Semitism" fails, then try "Anti-Catholic"—that might do something. If that fails, try "Anti-American"—get the biggest talent that can be hired for a night on the B'nai B'rith platform to shout it. And when that fails, as it has, —?

The American Jewish Committee is itself a misnomer. The committee is not exclusively American, and its work is not to Americanize the Jews nor even to encourage real Americanization among them. It is a committee composed of Jews representing that class which profits most by keeping the mass of the Jews segregated from Americans and in bondage to the "higher-ups" among the Jews. They are the "big Jews," as Norman Hapgood used to call them, who say to the "little Jews," "You hang together; we will be your representatives to these foreign peoples, the Americans and others." If the American Jewish Committee would change its name to this: "The Jewish Commission for America," it might be nearer the truth. It has dealt with America in the recent past very much as the Allied Commissions deal with Germany. There are certain things we may do, and certain things we may not do, and the Jewish Commission for America tells us what we may and may not do. One of the things we may not do is to declare that this is a Christian country.

There is one absolutely safe rule in dealing with anything emanating from the American Jewish Committee. Don't rely on the label, open the matter up. You will find that the Kehillah is not what it pretends to be; that the Jewish labor union is not what it pretends to be; that Zionism is a camouflage for something entirely different, which is the reason for a particular name being chosen. It runs all the way through Jewish practice, and presents another little job for the Jewish reformer.

Issue of November 12, 1921

What the American Jew needs to develop is the habit of self-criticism. If the spokesmen of the Jewish people would devote one-half the energy they now expend in answering attacks to attacking the evils that stare everyone in the face, they would make a real contribution to American life. But judged by their public utterances, they seem to be supersensitive to trivial prejudice in non-Jews. They are hypochondriac and morbidly defensive about their critics, and indulgent and complacent about what the Jewish people is and does. Races, not cursed with a sense of inferiority, do not shrink from criticism. They initiate it."—Walter Lippmann, in The American Hebrew.

LXXI.

Jewish "Kol Nidre" and "Eli, Eli" Explained

"I have looked this year and last for something in your paper about the prayer which the Jews say at their New Year. But you say nothing. Can it be you have not heard of the Kol Nidre?"

"Lately in three cities I have heard a Jewish religious hymn sung in the public theaters. This was in New York, Detroit and Chicago. Each time the program said 'by request.' Who makes the request? What is the meaning of this kind of propaganda? The name of the hymn is 'Eli.'"

THE Jewish year just passed has been described by a Jewish writer in the *Jewish Daily News* as the Year of Chaos. The writer is apparently intelligent enough to ascribe this condition to something besides "anti-Semitism." He says, "the thought that there is something wrong in Jewish life will not down," and when he describes the situation in the Near East, he says, "The Jew himself is stirring the mess." He indicts the Jewish year 5681 on 12 counts, among them being, "mismanagement in Palestine," "engaging in internal warfare," "treason to the Jewish people," "selfishness," "self-delusion." "The Jewish people is a sick people," cries the writer, and when he utters a comfortable prophecy for the year 5682, it is not in the terms of Judah but in terms of "Kol Yisroel"—All Israel—

the terms of a larger and more inclusive unity which gives Judah its own place, and its own place only, in the world. The Jewish people are sick, to be sure, and the disease is the fallacy of superiority, with its consequent "foreign policy" against the world.

When Jewish writers describe the year 5681 as the Year of Chaos, it is an unconscious admission that the Jewish people are ripening for a change of attitude. The "chaos" is among the leaders; it involves the plans which are based on the old false assumptions. The Jewish people are waiting for leaders who can emancipate them from the thralldom of their self-seeking masters in the religious and political fields. The enemies of the emancipation of Judah are those who profit by Judah's bondage, and these are the groups that follow the American Jewish Committee and the political rabbis. When a true Jewish prophet arises—and he should arise in the United States—there will be a great sweeping away of the selfish, scheming, heartless Jewish leaders, a general desertion of the Jewish idea of "getting" instead of "making," and an emergence of the true idea submerged so long.

There will also be a separation among the Jews themselves. They are not all Jews who call themselves so today. There is a Tartar strain in so-called Jewry that is absolutely incompatible with true Israelitish raciality; there are other alien strains which utterly differ from the true Jewish; but, until now these strains have been held because the Jewish leaders needed vast hordes of low-type people to carry out their world designs. But the Jew himself is recognizing the presence of an alien element; and that is the first step in a movement which will place the Jewish Question on quite another basis.

What the Jews of the United States are coming to think is indicated by this letter—one among many (the writer is a Jew) :

"Gentlemen:

" 'Because you believe in a good cause,' said Dr.

Johnson, 'is no reason why you should feel called upon to defend it, for by your manner of defense you may do your cause much harm.'

"The above applying to me I will only say that I have received the books you sent me and read both with much interest.

"You are rendering the Jews a very great service, that of saving them *from themselves.*

"It takes courage, and nerve, and intelligence to do and pursue such a work, and I admire you for it."

The letter was accompanied by a check which ordered THE DEARBORN INDEPENDENT sent to the address of another who bears a distinctively Jewish name.

It is very clear that unity is not to be won by the truth-teller soft-pedaling or suppressing his truth, nor by the truth-hearer strenuously denying that the truth is true, but by both together honoring the truth in telling and in acknowledging it. When the Jews see this, they can take over the work of truth-telling and carry it on themselves. These articles have as their only purpose: First, that the Jews may see the truth for themselves about themselves; second, that non-Jews may see the fallacy of the present Jewish idea and use enough common sense to cease falling victims to it. With both Jews and non-Jews seeing their error, the way is opened for co-operation instead of the kind of competition (not commercial, but moral) which has resulted so disastrously to Jewish false ambitions these long centuries.

Now, as to the questions at the beginning of this article: THE DEARBORN INDEPENDENT has heretofore scrupulously avoided even the appearance of criticizing the Jew for his religion. The Jew's religion, as most people think of it, is unobjectionable. But when he has carried on campaigns against the Christian religion, and when in every conceivable manner he thrusts his own religion upon the public from the stage of theaters and in other public places, he has himself to blame if the public asks questions.

It is quite impossible to select the largest theater in the United States, place the Star of David high in a beautiful stage heavens above all flags and other symbols, apostrophize it for a week, with all sorts of wild prophecy and all sorts of silly defiance of the world, sing hymns to it d otherwise adore it, with out arousing curiosity. Yet the Jewish theatrical managers, with no protest from the Anti-Defamation Committee, have done this on a greater or smaller scale in many cities. To say it is meaningless is to use the words lightly.

The "Kol Nidre" is a Jewish prayer, named from its opening words, "All vows," (kol nidre). It is based on the declaration of the Talmud:

"He who wishes that his vows and oaths shall have no value; stand up at the beginning of the year and say: 'All vows which I shall make during the year shall be of no value.' "

It would be pleasant to be able to declare that this is merely one of the curiosities of the darkness which covers the Talmud, but the fact is that "Kol Nidre" is not only an ancient curiosity; it is also a modern practice. In the volume of *revised* "Festival Prayers," published in *1919* by the Hebrew Publishing Company, New York, the prayer appears in its fullness:

"All vows, obligations, oaths or anathemas, pledges of all names, which we have vowed, sworn, devoted, or bound ourselves to, from this day of atonement, until the next day of atonement (whose arrival we hope for in happiness) we repent, aforehand, of them all, they shall all be deemed absolved, forgiven, annulled, void and made of no effect; they shall not be binding, nor have any power; the vows shall not be reckoned vows, the obligations shall not be obligatory, nor the oaths considered as oaths."

If this strange statement were something dug out of the misty past, it would scarcely merit serious attention, but as being part of a revised Jewish prayer book printed in the United States in 1919, and as being one of the high points of the Jewish religious celebration of the New Year, it cannot be lightly dismissed after attention has once been called to it

Indeed, the Jews do not deny it. Early in the year, when a famous Jewish violinist landed in New York after a triumphant tour abroad, he was besieged by thousands of his East Side admirers, and was able to quiet their cries only when he took his violin and played the "Kol Nidre." Then the people wept as exiles do at the sound of the songs of the homeland.

In that incident the reader will see that (hard as it is for the non-Jew to understand it!) there is a deep-rooted, sentimental regard for the "Kol Nidre" which makes it one of the most sacred of possessions to the Jew. Indefensibly immoral as the "Kol Nidre" is, utterly destructive of all social confidence, yet the most earnest efforts of a few really spiritual Jews have utterly failed to remove it from the prayer books, save in a few isolated instances. The music of the "Kol Nidre" is famous and ancient. One has only to refer to the article "Kol Nidre" in the Jewish Encyclopedia to see the predicament of the modern Jew: he cannot deny; he cannot defend; he cannot renounce. The "Kol Nidre" is here, and remains.

If the prayer were a request for forgiveness for the broken vows of the past, normal human beings could quite understand it. Vows, promises, obligations and pledges are broken, sometimes by weakness of will to perform them, sometimes by reason of forgetfulness, sometimes by sheer inability to do the thing we thought we could do. Human experience is neither Jew nor Gentile in that respect.

But the prayer is a holy advance notice, given in the secrecy of the synagogue, that no promise whatever shall be binding, and more than not being binding, is there and then violated before it is ever made.

The scope of the prayer is "from this day of atonement, until the next day of atonement."

The prayer looks wholly to the future, "we repent, aforehand, of them all."

The prayer breaks down the common ground of confidence

between men—"the vows shall not be reckoned vows; the obligations shall not be obligatory, nor the oaths considered as oaths."

It requires no argument to show that if this prayer be really the rule of faith and conduct for the Jews who utter it, the ordinary social and business relations are impossible to maintain with them.

It should be observed that there is no likeness here with Christian "hypocrisy," so-called. Christian "hypocrisy" arises mostly from men holding higher ideals than they are able to attain to, and verbally extolling higher principles than their conduct illustrates. That is, to use Browning's figure, the man's reach exceeds his grasp; as it always does, where the man is more than a clod.

But the "Kol Nidre" is in the opposite direction. It recognizes by inference that in the common world of men, in the common morality of the street and the mart, a promise passes current as a promise, a pledge as a pledge, an obligation as an obligation—that there is a certain social currency given to the individual's mere word on the assumption that its quality is kept good by straight moral intention. And it makes provision to drop below that level.

How did the "Kol Nidre" come into existence? Is it the cause or the effect of that untrustworthiness with which the Jew has been charged for centuries?

Its origin is not from the Bible but from Babylon, and the mark of Babylon is more strongly impressed on the Jew than is the mark of the Bible. "Kol Nidre" is Talmudic and finds its place among many other dark things in that many-volumed and burdensome invention. If the "Kol Nidre" ever was a backward look over the failures of the previous year, it very early became a forward look to the deliberate deceptions of the coming year.

Many explanations have been made in an attempt to account for this. Each explanation is denied and disproved by those who favor some other explanation. The commonest of all is this, and it rings in the overworked note of "persecution": The Jews were so hounded and harried by the bloodthirsty Christians, and so brutally and viciously treated in the name of the loving Jesus (the terms are borrowed from Jewish writers) that they were compelled by wounds and starvation and the fear of death to renounce their religion and to vow that thereafter they would take the once despised Jesus for their Messiah. Therefore, say the Jewish apologists, knowing that during the ensuing year the terrible, bloodthirsty Christians would force the poor Jews to take Christian vows, the Jews in advance announced to God that all the promises they would make on that score would be lies. They would say what the Christians forced them to say, but they would not mean or intend one word of it.

That is the best explanation of all. Its weakness is that it assumes the "Kol Nidre" to have been coincident with times of "persecution," especially in Spain. Unfortunately for this explanation, the "Kol Nidre" is found centuries before that, when the Jews were under no pressure.

In a refreshingly frank article in the Cleveland *Jewish World* for October 11, the insufficiency of the above explanations is so clearly set forth that a quotation is made:

"Many learned men want to have it understood that the Kol Nidre dates from the Spanish Inquisition, it having become necessary on account of all sorts of persecution and inflictions to adopt the Christian religion for appearances' sake. Then the Jews in Spain, gathering in cellars to celebrate the Day of Atonement and pardon, composed a prayer that declared of no value all vows and oaths that they would be forced to make during the year . . . .

"The learned men say, moreover, that in remembrance of those days when hundreds and thousands of Maranos (secret Jews) were dragged out of the cellars and were tortured with all kinds of torment, the Jews in all parts of the world have adopted the Kol Nidre as a token of faithfulness to the faith and as self-sacrifice for the faith.

"*These assertions are not correct.* The fact is that the formula of Kol Nidre was composed and said on the night of Yom Kippur quite a time earlier than the period of the Spanish Inquisition. We find, for instance, a formula to invalidate vows on Yom Kippur in the prayer book of the Rabbi Amram Goun who lived in the ninth century, about five hundred years before the Spanish Inquisition; although Rabbi Amram's formula is not 'Kol Nidre' but 'Kol Nidrim' ('All vows and oaths which we shall swear from Yom Kippurim to Yom Kippurim will return to us void.') ....."

The form of the prayer in the matter of its age may be in dispute; but back in the ancient and modern Talmud is the authorization of the practice: "He who wishes that his vows and oaths shall have no value, stand up at the beginning of the year and say: 'All vows which I shall make during the year shall be of no value.'"

That answers our reader's question. This article does not say that all Jews thus deliberately assassinate their pledged word. It does say that both the Talmud and the prayer book permit them to do so, and tell them how it may be accomplished.

Now, as to the Jewish religious hymn which is being sung "by request" throughout the country: the story of it is soon told.

The name of the hymn is "Eli, Eli"; its base is the first verse of the Twenty-second Psalm, known best in Christian countries as the cry of Christ on the Cross.

It is being used by Jewish vaudeville managers as their contribution to the pro-Jewish campaign which the Jew-controlled theater is flinging into the faces of the public, from stage and motion picture screen. It is an incantation designed to inflame the lower classes of Jews against the people, and intensify the racial consciousness of those hordes of Eastern Jews who have flocked here.

At the instigation of the New York Kehillah, "Eli, Eli" has for a long time been sung at the ordinary run of performances in vaudeville and motion picture houses, and the notice "By request" is usually a bald lie. It should be "By Order." The "request" is from Jewish headquarters which has ordered the speeding up of Jewish propaganda. The situation of the theater now is that American audiences are paying at the box office for the privilege of hearing Jews advertise the things they want non-Jews to think about them.

If even a vestige of decency, or the slightest appreciation of good taste remained, the Jews who control the theaters would see that the American public must eventually gag on such things. When two Jewish comedians who have been indulging in always vulgar and often indecent antics, appear before the drop curtain and sing the Yiddish incantation "Eli Eli," which, of course, is incomprehensible to the major part of the audience, the Jewish element always betrays a high pitch of excitement. They understand the game that is being played: the "Gentiles" are being flayed to their face, and they don't know it; as when a Yiddish comedian pours out shocking invectives on the name of Jesus Christ, and "gets away with it," the Jewish portion of his audience howling with delight, and the "boob Gentiles" looking serenely on and feeling it to be polite to laugh and applaud too!

This Yiddish chant is the rallying cry of race hatred which is being spread abroad by orders of the Jewish leaders. You, if you are a theatergoer, help to pay the expense of getting yourself roundly damned. The Kehillah and the American Jewish Committee which for more than ten years have been driving all mention of Christianity out of public life, under their slogan "This is not a Christian Country," are spreading their own type of Judaism everywhere with insolence unparalleled.

"Eli, Eli" is not a religious hymn! It is a racial war cry. In the low cafes of New York, where Bolshevik Jews hang out, "Eli, Eli" is their song. It is the Marseillaise of Jewish solidarity. It has become the fanatical chant of all Jewish Bolshevik clubs; it is constantly heard in Jewish coffee houses and cabarets where emotional Russian and Polish Jews—all enemies to all government—shout the words amid torrential excitement. When you see the hymn in point you are utterly puzzled to understand the excitement it rouses.

And this rallying cry has now been obtruded into the midst of the theatrical world.

The term "incantation" here used is used advisedly. The term is used by Kurt Schindler, who adapted the Yiddish hymn to American use. And its effect is that of an incantation.

In translation it is as follows:

"My God, my God, why hast thou forsaken me?
With fire and flame they have burnt us,
Everywhere they have shamed and derided us,
Yet none amongst us has dared depart
From our Holy Scriptures, from our Law.

My God, my God, why hast thou forsaken me?
By day and night I only yearn and pray,
Anxiously keeping our Holy Scriptures
And praying, Save us, save us once again!
For the sake of our fathers and our father's fathers!

"Listen to my prayer and to my lamenting,
For only Thou canst help, Thou, God, alone,
For it is said, 'Hear, O Israel, the Lord is Our God,
The Lord is One!' "

The words of the hymn are so much resembling a lament that they strangely contrast with the spirit which the hymn itself seems to arouse; its mournful melody inspires a very different spirit among the Jewish hearers than the same sort of melody would inspire among other people. Those who have heard its public rendition can better understand how a hymn of such utterly quiet and resigned tone could be the wild rage of the anarchists of the East Side coffee houses.

The motive, of course, for the singing of the hymn is the reference to non-Jewish people.

"With fire and flame *THEY* have burnt us, everywhere *THEY* have shamed and derided us?" Who are "they"? Who but the goyim, and the Christians who all ussuspectingly sit near by and who are so affected by Jewish applause that they applaud too! Truly, in one way of looking at it, Jews have a right to despise the "gentiles."

THEY have burnt us; *THEY* have shamed us," but we, the poor Jews, have been harmless all the while, none among us daring to depart from the Law! That is the meaning of "Eli, Eli." That is why, in spite of its words of religious resignation, it becomes a rallying cry. "They" are all wrong;; "we" are all right.

It is possible, of course, that right-minded Jews do not approve all this. They may disapprove of "Kol Nidre" and they may resent the use which the Jewish leaders are making of "Eli, Eli." Let us at least credit some Jews with both these attitudes. But they do nothing about it. These same Jewish, however, will go to the public library of their town and put the fear of political or business reprisal in the hearts of the Library Board if they do not instantly remove THE DEARBORN INDEPENDENT from the library; these same Jews will form committees to coerce mayors of cities into issuing illegal orders which cannot be enforced; these same Jews will give commands to the newspapers under their patronage or control—they are indeed mighty and active in the affairs of the non-Jews. But when it is a matter of keeping "Eli, Eli" out of the theatre, or the "Kol Nidre" out of the mouths of those who thus plan a whole year of deception "aforehand," these same Jews are very inactive and apparently very powerless.

The Anti-Defamation Committee would better shut up shop until it can show either the will or the ability to bring pressure to bear on its own people. Coercion of the rest of the people is rapidly growing less and less possible.

The "Kol Nidre" is far from being the worst counsel in the Talmud; "Eli, Eli" is far from being the worst anti-social misuse of apparently holy things. But it will remain the policy of THE DEARBORN INDEPENDENT, for the present at least, to let all such matters alone except, as in the present case, where the number of the inquiries indicates that a knowledge of the facts has been had at other sources. In many instances, what our inquirers heard was much worse than is stated here, so that this article is by way of being a service to the inquirer to prevent his being misled, and to the Jew to prevent misrepresentation.

Issue of November 5, 1921

LXXII.

Jews as New York Magistrates See Them

THE DEARBORN INDEPENDENT has been frequently importuned to make exposure of the Jewish crime record in New York and other cities, but up to this time has chosen not to do so. The material is mountainous and the facts are damaging, but THE DEARBORN INDEPENDENT will continue to assume that the majority of the Jewish people do not approve of criminal acts, even against non-Jewish life and property. This paper prefers to confine its attention to those matters which are plainly within the purpose and approval of the Jewish leaders. There is a decided criminal element in the Jewish Question, and no small part of the criminality flows directly or indirectly from the attitude of the Jewish leaders, but the Great Crime is the introduction of corruptive and anti-American ideas into American life, and Jewish leaders cannot escape responsibility for that.

The magistrates of every city with a considerable Jewish population know the facts. In practically every state in the Union there is today a celebrated case where some Jew, through money or influence, is playing horse with American law. It is locally known, but not generally, except in two or three instances. The local press—deriving 80 per cent of its support from Jewish advertising—is usually very discreet, preferring to leave the matter to the courts. Strange things occur in the courts, such as judges being taken into very lucrative partnerships after giving decisions favorable to wealthy Jewish defendants.

The following extracts of opinions given THE DEARBORN INDEPENDENT by magistrates of the City of New York are offered in the hope that the Jewish leaders will read and digest them, and see, if possible, what a hopeless game they are playing. The Jewish Question of today is turning about in the direction of the Jewish Question of tomorrow—which is, When are the Jewish Leaders going to admit that their game is a losing one? The *see* it now; but they must *admit* it and *quit* it. And it will not be surprising if a mass movement of the Jewish people compels them to do so.

"The Jewish race," said one of the magistrates, "seems deliberately blind to its own faults. Some twelve years ago General Bingham, then police commissioner, found it necessary to call attention to certain criminal tendencies of the East Side Jews. His criticisms were bitterly resented. I venture to say, however, that there are few men who preside in our inferior courts who will not readily indorse those views of General Bingham in their application to the conditions of the present day."

(It was because of General Bingham's criticisms that the New York Kehillah was increased in power—not to clean up conditions, but to shut up the critics.)

"The different groups, racial or religious, of New York City, have always each supported institutions for the care of its fallen women. We have the Magdalen Home, the Protestant Episcopal House of Mercy and the Catholic House of the Good Shepherd. The Jews alone are the exception. Yet it does not require more than a short experience in the Magistrates' Courts to convince one that more than two-thirds of the fallen women in the metropolis are of the Jewish race. This fact and the urgent necessity of caring for these unfortunates was laid before some prominent Jews. They gave the assurance that ample provision was being made by a group of wealthy Jewish families to endow an institution of the kind. However, nothing was done or even contemplated. The Jews absolutely ignored the issue. And today we magistrates are compelled, as usual, to commit such women to the Protestant Episcopal and Catholic homes.

"This is indicative of a strange refusal to look facts in the face, if the facts reflect on the Jews. A lawyer, once highly prominent in Jewish circles here, became involved in a blackmailing scandal with a notorious member of his race known as the 'Wolf of Wall Street.' The 'Wolf' was convicted and sent to a Federal prison. The lawyer was scathingly denounced by the Appellate Court and only escaped disbarment because of his age. The Jews of New York deliberately refused to condemn this man's nefarious acts. Only the other day they 'honored' him by dedicating a library to him in one of their charitable institutions, and hanging his portrait on the wall. An action such as this smacks a great deal of an absence of moral sense."

One magistrate prefaced his remarks by stating that he had no desire to dwell upon any special misdemeanors or crimes that might be considered peculiar to the Jewish race. But he pointed out that a more serious situation than one caused by sporadic criminality had been created by reason of a persistent class movement among the Jews.

"Any law," he said, "which appears to be obnoxious to the self-centered Jewish element, is deliberately ignored by them, or opposed with a stubborn resistance which neither time nor education seems to mitigate. The result is that our Magistrates' Courts and the Court of Special Sessions are crowded with cases of violations of that character. The newly arrived Jews especially are apparently determined to subordinate this country to their own desires, rather than to accommodate themselves to the conditions here as other races do.

"The most blatant example of this attitude is in connection with the law relating to Sabbath breaking. Our Penal Law is plain and specific on this matter. It states:

> The first day of the week, being by general consent set apart for rest and religious uses, the law prohibits the doing on that day of certain acts hereinafter specified, which are serious interruptions of the repose and the religious liberty of the community.

A violation of the foregoing prohibition is Sabbath

breaking.

"Sabbath breaking is a misdemeanor, punishable by a fine or by imprisonment in a county jail, and where the offense is aggravated by a previous conviction, the fine and jail sentence are doubled. Yet the various acts specified as Sabbath breaking are violated openly and with insolent impunity by thousands of Jews every Sunday in New York. Their race has much to say about its own religious liberty, but it thinks nothing of outraging the religious liberties of other races. If any serious attempt were made to enforce this statute in the Jewish districts, the police would be compelled to arrest the larger part of the population.

"These Jews are determined to trade and traffic and to keep their factories and workshops going on the American Sunday. They impose their will upon the greatest city in the United States, through silent resistance and the sheer force of numbers.

"The Jews of whom I am speaking are mostly from Eastern Europe—Russia, Galicia, and Poland. They are of the first or second generation of immigrants. They generally speak and read only the Yiddish tongue. *But is a deplorable fact that Americanized Jews of prominence, openly encourage these ignorant people in their defiance of the law.* Whenever Yiddish tradesmen and manufacturers are arrested for Sabbath breaking, hosts of Jewish lawyers spring to their defense, and powerful Jewish societies intervene to protect them. The Jewish Sabbath Alliance, with offices on Fifth Avenue, *conducts a constant propaganda among the ghetto people, urging them to insist upon their alleged legal right* to pursue their ordinary vocations on the American Sunday. And it provides them with legal counsel when they get into trouble.

"Jewish lawyers set up the specious claim that these people from Eastern Europe observe another day as 'holy time,' and therefore have a right to labor and traffic on Sunday. Some of the Jewish magistrates encourage this contention by discharging such lawbreakers. But there is no question of religion in these Sunday violations. It is merely money greed. These Jews are so hot after money that they are afraid of losing some if they close their shops on Sunday. This is easily proved by the fact that *when the Jews find it to their interest or convenience to observe Sunday closing, they do it by agreement among themselves.*

"This was demonstrated during last summer. In Rivington and Delancy streets, and in fact throughout the ghetto, there were signs posted in the shop windows of Jews, authorized by an organization calling itself 'The Independent Ladies' Garment Merchants Association, Incorporated.' The notices read:

This Store will be
closed on
SUNDAYS
from
June 26th until the end of AUGUST
The Independent Ladies' Garment
Merchants Association, Incorporated.

"In other words *these shopkeepers were spending weekends at the Yiddish summer resorts. They didn't want any of their competitors to steal the trade of customers during their absence. So they all agreed to close up. The question of religion did not enter their minds.*

"Jews of the more intelligent and well-to-do class are also constantly attempting to break the Sabbath laws in sections of the city where their race does not predominate. Non-Jewish merchants have had to organize associations to protect themselves against this unfair competition. If a non-Jew is arrested for Sabbath-breaking, he suffers. The Jewish Sabbath-breaker goes free. This gives the Jew an unfair advantage.

"Not long ago there was a large advertising sign posted conspicuously on the platforms of the elevated railroad. *A Jewish wholesale house on Fifth Avenue* notified buyers that its salesrooms would be open from 2 p. m. to 5 p.m. every Sunday afternoon. I thought this was going a little too far, and I called the attention of several of the protective associations to the methods practiced by this firm. The signs soon afterward disappeared. However, such tactics are continually being attempted by Jewish merchants and manufacturers in the Bronx and on the West Side of the city, in an effort to gain a business advantage over their non-Jewish competitors.

"But there are means of putting an immediate and effective stop to all this rascality. This would be by enforcing Section 2149 of the Penal Law, which provides for the forfeiture of commodities exposed for sale on Sunday. The section reads:

> In addition to the penalty imposed by Section 2142, all property and commodities exposed for sale on the first day of the week in violation of the provisions of this article shall be forfeited. Upon conviction of the offender by the justice of the peace of a county, or by a police justice or magistrate, such officer shall issue a warrant for the seizure of the forfeited articles, which when seized shall be sold on one day's notice, and the proceeds paid to the overseers of the poor, for the use of the poor of the town or city.

"This statute is not enforced. But I believe we shall yet be compelled to enforce it in New York. The seizure of the stocks of some of these Jewish shopkeepers would be the most effective lesson one could administer in teaching them to respect the law."

Another magistrate expresses himself still more forcibly on the Jewish question. "These people from Eastern Europe," he said, "are tending to destroy all American conceptions of right and justice. Day after day my court is crowded with Jewish people. I am compelled to fine and warn them. The attitude of the women is especially truculent. They have adopted a misconception of woman's suffrage. They say to me: "This is a woman's country. Woman can do what she likes—men can't.'

"There is no denying the fact that New York is falling more and more under the dominance of Jews. Americans are gradually being driven from public life. It will not be long before we shall have a Jewish mayor and a Jewish board of aldermen.

This in itself should be no great misfortune were it not for *the tendency of the Jew to abuse his power.* He is ambitious and restless to obtain authority. But the moment he gets it, *he becomes oppressive. This is evident already* wherever the Jews are obtaining monopolies. A friend, a young man, came to me the other day, complaining bitterly that he was deliberately being driven out of business by the Jews. He was the owner of a prosperous laundry. But the large machine laundries of the city are now mostly in the hands of Jews. They refuse to do his work for him, saying: You are not a member of our syndicate.'

(This is one of the new phases of the Jewish invasion—the almost complete absorption of the laundry business.)

"We all remember the time when the Jews began to clamor for special news stand privileges. They formed Jewish organizations of news dealers, until the business was entirely in their hands. While they still had non-Jewish competition they were obliging and attentive enough. They did everything to curry favor. But today they carry themselves like lords. *No Jewish news dealer in New York will deliver newspapers to his non-Jewish customers on Jewish holidays.*

"In the New York post office, where there are now some 11,000 employes, about one-half of whom are Jews, the same conditions exist. The Jewish postal employes complained that they were being deprived of their constitutional rights if they were compelled to work on Rosh Hashana, the Jewish New Year, and on Yom Kippur, the Jewish Day of Atonement. The postmaster was compelled to grant their demands, *at the same time pointing out that leaves of absence could not be granted to Christian employes on Christmas, New Year's and Good Friday, otherwise the postoffice would be swamped with mail.*

Another phase of this Jewish insistence upon special rights was emphasized by one of the magistrates. "I have often observed," he said, "that there is generally a good result when a Jew settles n a small New England town where there are only three or four stores. The situation develops social stimulus and competitive spirit. Too often there is a tendency toward dry-rot among the native population. They stagnate.

"But where Jews assemble in large numbers, as they do in New York City and the industrial towns of New Jersey, they immediately develop a class and racial consciousness that is unfortunate. It is not surprising that Jews should cling to their traditional customs. *But it is a peculiar fact that of the forty different nationalities in New York, it is only one race, the Jewish, which persistently tries to impose its own modes of life upon the mass of the people.*

"One dangerous feature of this tendency is a constant effort to put upon the statute books laws which favor the Jewish race, and placing weapons into the hands of the mischievous and litigious.

"In the Penal Law of the state of New York there is a statute which is outrageous in its import and should be stricken from the code. In effect it renders a man guilty of a misdemeanor if he ventures to have a process served upon a Jew on Saturday. He is equally guilty if he dares to serve a process which is made returnable on Saturday. It is a notorious fact that a large percentage of Jews deliberately alter their names in order to conceal their race. Yet if a man should induce his lawyer to procure a civil action to which such a Jew is a party to be adjourned to Saturday for trial, in ignorance of the fact that the borrowed American name conceals a Jew, that man renders himself liable to fine or imprisonment.

"This is Section 2150 of the Penal Law. Its exact wording is as follows:

> Maliciously serving process on Saturday on person who keeps Saturday as holy time—Whoever maliciously procures any process in a civil action to be served on Saturday, upon any person who keeps Saturday as holy time, and does not labor on that day, or serves upon him any process returnable on that day, or maliciously procures any civil action to which such person is a party to be adjourned to that day for trial, is guilty of a misdemeanor.

"Advantage was taken of this statute by a Jew in the city of Rochester to evade the payment of goods which had been delivered to him. The summons which had been served upon him was made returnable upon a Saturday, and upon the return day the Jewish defendant, evidently at the instigation of his Jewish lawyer, appeared in the action for the sole purpose of objecting to the jurisdiction of the court upon several grounds, but more especially for the reason that the defendant was a Jew, and that as such he uniformly observed Saturday of each week as 'holy time.'

"This case was used to tie up the business of two courts until it was finally taken to the appellate division of the Supreme Court, where Judge Adams rendered a decision in which he said:

" 'In order to give to this section the construction claimed by the defendant's counsel, we must hold that the legislature has not only utterly ignored this elementary principle (that to constitute a crime there must be not only the act itself, but a criminal intent must accompany the act), but, in violation thereof, has declared that, while in the case specified, malice of intent must exist in order to constitute the crime of procuring a process to be served on Saturday or of procuring a civil action to be adjourned to that day, the crime of serving a process which is returnable on Saturday may be committed without any intent accompanying the act.

" 'This proposition, it seems to us, has only to be stated to render its absurdity manifest; for the person who served the summons in this action, as is generally the case, was a public officer; and it is fair to assume that he performed his official duty in this instance without knowing, or having any reason to suppose, that the party served regarded one day of the week as more sacred than another.

" 'It is true that the defendant is a Jew, and certain racial characteristics may have manifested themselves to such an extent as to acquaint the officer with that fact, but there are other religions than the Jewish which require the observance of the seventh day of the week as "holy time," and, consequently, if the rule contended for is to obtain, an officer must somehow ascertain, in every instance before serving a process, that the party upon whom it is to be served does not come within the favored class; otherwise he renders himself amenable to the statute.'

" 'It is inconceivable that the legislature intended that a person thus serving a process returnable on Saturday, in ignorance of the fact that he was in any way interfering with the religious liberty of the party served, should be regarded as a criminal and it is equally certain that a conviction under such circumstances would be absurd and unjust, if not impossible. A construction of a statute, therefore, which leads to such a result should manifestly be avoided if practicable.'

"Judge Adams thereupon reversed the judgment of the county court and of the municipal court, with costs."

"Now Jewish politicians and Jewish lawyers are clever enough, as a rule," continued this magistrate. "Therefore it seems the more surprising that they should waste their time and efforts in placing such laws on the statute books, and trying to establish precedents by means of them. It is very stupid business. The ultimate effect is calculated to bring ridicule upon the Jew, and awaken suspicion, dislike and enmity against his race."

Another of the magistrates commented on the fact that in London, Jews were permitted to trade on Sunday by Act of Parliament, but only within the circumscribed limits of their ghetto. "When I was in London several years ago," he continued, "I was shown one of the Jewish Sunday markets in full swing. Opposite it was an English church. But trade was confined to the Yiddish district.

"But compared with New York, there is only a small Yiddish population in the British metropolis. Our millions of Jews are scattered throughout the city, and if we were to relax our Sunday laws in their favor, it would mean goodby to the Christian Sabbath. I cannot understand the attitude of the Jews on this question. They cheapen their own status by their conduct."

Issue of December 10, 1921

LXXIII.

Jews Are Silent, the National Voice Is Heard

BY order of Louis Marshall, the American Jewish Committee and the B'nai B'rith, American Jewry has muffled the calculated furioso of its outcry, and contents itself now with occasional yelps. No longer do the syndicated sermons of the rabbis take their course across the country, saying the same old untrue things in the same old insincere way. No longer do editorial echoes spew vilification across pages supported by advertising blackmail levied upon the community. The outcry has ceased. Suddenly, on order, orderly as a regiment on parade, American Jewry has been turned from a termagant in action to a silent mystery. A most impressive illustration of the inner control exercised by Jewish leaders.

The psychology of it all, of course, is false. Jewry decided that it was the attention which it paid to THE DEARBORN INDEPENDENT which gave these articles vogue. The leaders asserted, indeed, that had the Jews of the United States paid no attention, no one would have known that they were under scrutiny. It is a rather flattering criticism to lay upon their inability to meet the situation, but it lacks the merit of being true.

The Jews of the United States issued the order of silence, not out of wisdom but out of fear. And not out of fear of injustice, but out of fear of the truth. As soon as THE DEARBORN INDEPENDENT issued its first articles on the New York Kehillah (and only the outer edges of the fact concerning that institution have as yet been set forth) it became evident to Jewish leaders that something had to be done. They did not challenge a public investigation; rather they used discretion, refused to answer even the questions of local reporters, made absurdly untrue denials, and gave every evidence of panic. Thereafter their safest course was silence.

Not that hey were inactive. Fearing a sudden investigation by the authorities, the New York Kehillah has grown extremely busy and has doubled the guards all round. Why?

The reason is that *there is a resolution in the United States Senate which points directly at the New York Kehillah.*

Prominent Jews have invaded Washington on one pretext or another, but only to turn their influence against that resolution. Why?

The reason is that that resolution provides for an investigation by a Senate Committee into certain matters which have already been set forth in THE DEARBORN INDEPENDENT.

Senate Resolution No. 60, introduced by Senator George H. Moses, of New Hampshire, provides that the Amalgamated Clothing Workers (a Jewish Bolshevik organization that is the feeder of Red activity throughout this country) be thoroughly investigated. In the official language of the Resolution: "The purposes, objects, methods and tactics of the Amalgamated Clothing Workers of America and its relations, if any, with *other political organizations and quasi-political groups,* and to make a report to the Senate of such findings."

Why has the New York Kehillah closed the portholes and called in help—"Gentile," by the way—to face a possible storm?

Why have the most prominent Jews in the United States hurried to Washington to hold conferences with Senators, their object being to bring pressure to bear against the Resolution?

Why should the American Jewish Committee, or members of it, why should Jewish clothing manufacturers who are the principal sufferers from the Amalgamated, why should Jewish members of the Baruch "war government" go to Washington to interfere with a proposed investigation? Why?

Because such an investigation of the Amalgamated, honestly conducted, would lead straight through to the New York Kehillah and the American Jewish committee and would rip the Jewish program in the United States clean open to the public gaze—*if honestly conducted.*

Next to stopping the investigation, the Jews will try to control it. That is really the greater danger. The country does not need the investigation to get the facts. Most of the facts can be given now. The country does need an investigation that will give the facts a governmental exposure. But a pro-Jewish investigation, an investigation conducted by elective office-holders who quake under "the fear of the Jews" would simply be an additional crime.

If the Jews lose their fight to kill the resolution, they have already started on their plans to control the initiative of, divert the course of, and defeat the purpose of the investigation.

If, therefore, the Jews are silent, they are not inactive.

But, the gain has been general. For instance, the country has been given quiet and leisure to hear what the non-Jews think. During the Jewish clamor, which was nothing more nor less than an attempt to stampede the public opinion of the United States, it was impossible to hear the voice of the people. Ministers who poured adulation upon the Jews were reported in the Press; but ministers who seriously handled the Jewish Question were not reported. Publications which could be induced to act as Judah's mouthpieces, were worked to the limit; publications which desired to preserve the value of their opinions, did not join the general hue and cry. In the succeeding lull, the still, small voice of American conviction, both Jewish and non-Jewish, began to be heard.

In public propaganda, after having felt it inadvisable to print any more telegraphic news from Palestine, because even the Jews could no longer juggle the truth, the spotlight was turned on Russia, and now the newspapers are filled with headlines intended to prepare the public for a new exodus when the Russian people awake to take back their land from the Jewish usurpers.

We are told that 6,000,000 Jews in Russia are in danger of violence. It is true. Much truer than the miles of telegraphic lies which have been printed about alleged "pogroms" in Russia and adjacent countries. THE DEARBORN INDEPENDENT knows that in Eastern Europe the Jew has not been persecuted, but has consistently acted as persecutor. The proof of it is in the Jews' ability to flee; they have taken all the wealth of the people of those countries. Poles cannot flee, Rumanians cannot flee, Russians cannot flee; but after having squeezed the life out of those nations the Jews see the dark clouds of justice rolling toward them, and they are able to flee, filling the ships of the sea with their hosts. In fact, their desertion of the Jew-spoiled countries of Europe is as precipitate as was their desertion of Woodrow Wilson and the Democratic party last autumn— Barney Baruch ostentatiously staying behind to cover, if possible, the shamefulness of it. When the Jew has fried the fat and skimmed the cream, he's off. Gratitude and loyalty mean nothing to his people. They are persecutors in Poland. They are persecutors in Russia. They are persecutors in Palestine. They were the arch religious persecutors of history, as the best historians testify. They will be persecutors here as soon as they think they can start it. It is possible, however, that in the United States their anti-social career will be rolled back upon itself.

American magazines have begun to pay attention to the Jewish Question. It is a good sign. Even magazines cannot long ignore what all the people know. It is a good sign of the degree of freedom the Press still enjoys.

It is true, of course, that this freedom is not very great; indeed, not so great as it was a few years ago. But in so far as the Press is American it is impossible for Americans to think it will consent to be permanently gagged even by the Jews. There have been, it is true, some rather sad instances of editorial weakness. We know that of two oldest publishing firms, both of New York, one of them published a most scurrilous Jewish defense by a non-Jewish socialist who, if he has not deliberately lied, has shown too dark an ignorance of facts to command the confidence of a great publishing firm; and we know that that publication was made with a view to the value of the publisher's imprint and that Jews would undertake to buy tens of thousands of copies for gratuitous circulation.

Of the other old New York firm it is known that an American diplomat was advised if not compelled by it to eliminate from his forthcoming book nearly one-third of its material because it dealt in an honest, straightforward American way with what this diplomat had seen with his own eyes of the development of the Jewish subjugation of Russia. Had this diplomat been dealing with his own *opinions* about the Jews or Russia, it might have been different; but he dealt with his official *observations* on the spot—observations literally invaluable to history. But this New York firm dared not, even in the interest of history, print the truth.

The experience of G. P. Putnam's Sons, of New York, is familiar to students of the question in recent months. The name of this firm is used because it has already appeared in public print with regard to a controversy it had with the American Jewish Committee.

The Putnams, acting on the ancient and honorable principle of the freedom of the Press, nay more, the duty of the Press to inform the people, reprinted last year "The Cause of World Unrest," which had first appeared as a series of articles in the London *Morning Post* and was later put into book form by the publishing house of Grant Richards, London. Both the newspaper and the publishing house are of the highest respectability and standing, as was also the house of Eyre and Spottiswoode which brought out the Protocols. Major George Haven Putnam, head of the firm of G. P. Putnam's Sons, is an American, a fair man, a careful publisher, and one who would not stoop to propagate a lie for any wealth.

This is not a defense of "The Cause of World Unrest." In the main the book is true. But it is not the result of original research. It does not make those small but important discriminations on which the Jews always rely to lead the people astray. It too often links in the downfall of Jewry those things which shall stand independently and gloriously when freed of their present insidious Jewish connections. On the whole, however, it maintains a correct view of world affairs. But it was not a book on which the Putnams could feel obliged to make a final stand, except as regards their right to print it.

However, a proper understanding of the book called for the Protocols, to which the book made frequent reference. So, like serviceable publishers, the Putnams announced that the Protocols would follow.

Whereupon the American Jewish Committee—which means Louis Marshall—got busy, and an interesting correspondence ensued. It is included in the report of the American Jewish Committee for 1921. Throughout the correspondence Louis Marshall was the dictator, but Major Putnam's position and statement of principles were correctly maintained. However, there were personal conferences which are not reported in the American Jewish Committee's report and there were Jews crowded into those personal conferences whose names do not appear in the correspondence, and there were fists banged on the table and loud threats—"boycott," of course—and altogether a rather typical scene enacted. The upshot of that passage was that, upon Major Putnam discovering that the Boston house of Small, Maynard & Company had published the Protocols, he decided that there was no call for his firm to do so. And now, in a letter to these same people, G. P. Putnam's Sons has decided to discontinue supplying copies of "The Cause of World Unrest" to the book trade.

It is a rather interesting story.

In Britain, of course, publications of the highest standing like "Blackwood's" and the "Nineteenth Century Review" can publish articles on the Jewish Question without regard to dictatorial Jewish attempts at control of the Press. In this country, however, the spies of Jewry are on the alert for every printed letter and syllable, and attempt to make editors feel uncomfortable, as if they were the instigators of pogroms, whenever they present an intelligent view of the question. Yet editors have not been able entirely to ignore it.

The reader is rather impressed with one quality common to all the articles that have been written, namely, the facts used are always those that have been given in THE DEARBORN INDEPENDENT. Not that they necessarily have been copied from this magazine, but the facts are so well established that anyone who attempts even to "defend" the Jews must necessarily appeal to the same facts. Thus in "New York and the Real Jew," by Rollin Lynde Hartt, in the New York *Independent* for June 25, 1921, this is illustrated. It is pure Jewish publicity, but it must use the facts that have been used in this series. It must use them in order to extol the Jews. Mr. Hartt is not to be considered as a contributor to the Question; the article is mentioned merely as indicating what the American magazine editor is up against—and perhaps it is not quite fair to be hard on the editor of the New York *Independent* just at this time. The one flash of value in the entire article is this paragraph:

> "Ambassador Page, then editor of the *Atlantic*, once remarked to me, 'The most interesting fellow in America is the Jew, but don't write about Jews; without intending it, you may precipitate the calamity America should be most anxious to prevent—I mean Jew-baiting.'"

That is a strange assertion. The Jews must not be written about. To write about them, even with good intent, may bring evil upon them. Not only a strange assertion, but a strange situation. To mention the Jew has always been dangerous to the non-Jew; but why also dangerous to the Jew? The Jewish explanation of anti-Semitism, that it is in the blood of the other races, that the moment they see a Jew they hate him, cannot be defended. Most non-Jews can testify that it is untrue of them. But it is a most amazing condition if even a mention of Jews arouses this feeling. Why should it?

However, the statement is of doubtful fact-value. The Jew himself should be the first to protest against having to go concealed all his days. He should welcome the use of his definite racial name, and he should not demand that it always be used in laudatory connections. A Jew should not be a Jew when he is elected to the United States Senate, and a "Russian" or a "Pole" when he is caught bootlegging. He should take the luck of life with the other races, and this would come to him without discrimination if he did not first arouse the spirit of discrimination by insisting on discrimination in his own favor.

It is probably much nearer the truth to say that publicity is a preventive of "Jew-Baiting." People should not be confined in a condition which makes the use of the word "Jew" unusual. It should attract no more attention than does the use of any other racial name.

Mr. Page was, before his ambassadorial days, an editor of the *Atlantic Monthly* magazine which is an integral part of American life. To read the Atlantic is a certificate of character. It is one of the few publications that preserve the American spirit in literature. It is still worthy the glory of the group that first made its name known wherever sound thought expressed in good writing is appreciated. The *Atlantic* is not in need of this appraisal, it is to well established in the regard of the class of minds that give color and sinew to our intellectual life. In Mr. Page's day the *Atlantic* may never have touched the Jewish Question with even so much as the tip of a discreet pen.

Nevertheless the *Atlantic* has in more recent years done its duty toward this as toward other questions. As far back as 1917, and that is very far back in view of the crowded years between, this old Boston magazine contained an article relating to the Jewish Question. The fact that the article was written by a Jew does not militate against it, but rather adds to its value. It contained valuable suggestions which the New

York Kehillah and the American Jewish Committee might well devote the remaining years of their activity to disseminating and actualizing among the Jews of this country. Even today its counsel would save them from much of the folly which marks their attempts to combat what they call "persecution," and which is nothing but rather plain and charitable truth-telling.

This year the *Atlantic* has contained three articles of value on the Jewish Question. The first was by Professor Clay upon the situation in Palestine. Now, Professor Clay is not an anti-Semite, and certainly the *Atlantic* is not, and yet the article was received with a good deal of abuse from Jewish quarters. It told nothing but the truth, and it was rather pertinent truth too, which intelligent Jews doubtless welcomed. Professor Clay knew what he was writing about and his conclusions are not challenged by any authority on the subject.

In the May *Atlantic*, Ralph Philip Boas, who is understood to be of Jewish descent, wrote an article on "Jew-Baiting in America." He speaks rather disdainfully of publications which have endeavored to air the Jewish Question, but after having thus paid his tax to the Jews' prejudice, he proceeds in commendable fashion to contribute his thoughts to the matter. On the whole what he says is true, and the facts he uses as his foundation are of course the facts which THE DEARBORN INDEPENDENT has made its readers familiar. He sets up his straw man of "Anti-Semitism" and after having valiantly destroyed it, to the applause of all of us, he gets down to serious business, and says some things which all could hope would pierce the consciousness to its innermost stronghold and set up new vibrations there.

And in the July *Atlantic*, Paul Scott Mowrer, Paris representative of the Chicago *Daily News*, has an article on "The Assimilation of Israel." Mr. Mowrer has won the respect of students of world affairs by the conscientious ability with which he has observed and reported big events in Europe. In his news reports he has not hesitated, when the facts justified it, to cable a story of Jewish participation in this or that movement. It was reported at one time that an attempt on his job had been made by certain Jewish influences, and it is certain that sections of the Jewish press bitterly attacked him. Yet Mr. Mowrer is probably no more interested in the Jewish Question than the many other big problems which have come within his journalistic ken, and it would be extremely unfair to regard him as in any way a propagandist for anything.

Mr. Mowrer talks about Israel when, of course, he means Judah. There is a deep distinction there. And he talks also about assimilation, which the Jew will not admit as a solution. He protects himself fore and aft by attacking the "anti-Semites," whoever they are, and by expressing his confidence in the Jews, but on all the decks of his article he gives the facts—and they are the same facts. It ought to be pretty well settled by this time that there are facts, not two sets of facts, but only one set of facts, concerning Jewish influence and activity.

The *World's Work* has taken the liberty of setting before the people the only real anti-Jewish article that has appeared in the United States since the present discussion of the Question began, and that article was written by Henry Morgenthau, a Jew whom the government is accustomed to honor whenever it would pay a compliment to the Jews. It turns out that he attacks Jewry in its most tender spot—Zionism. Most people have read it, for it was immediately turned into propaganda and published in hosts of newspapers, in many of them as first-column, first-page news. Mr. Morgenthau said that Zionism was not a solution but a surrender. He attacks the whole Palestinian plan from every angle, and not only attacks but belittles it.

Of course, this is very interesting. But one doesn't understand the heat displayed. If the Jews wish to go back to Palestine, why all this objection? Mr. Morgenthau does not wish to go back, it is true; it is extremely difficult to find a Jew who does want to go back; but to desire a national land for the Jews is quite another thing, and most Jews desire that. The pity is that they carry into Palestine the same method which puts them upon question here, and they are in danger of tipping over the apple cart in their imperious disregard of the rights of men in Palestine.

Mr. Morgenthau's motive in writing the article must remain a mystery, because it would seem to leave him practically outside of American Jewry, and of course he is not outside. Not at all. Watch and see. His article was printed in a magazine read and supported by non-Jews and was intended for non-Jews; it was not a plea to his people, it was a kind of confidential explanation, whispered from behind the hand, to non-Jews.

Mr. Morgenthau knows that Zionism is the core of Jewry in this country. The Zionists rule. The Zionists, and not the Americans, dictate the policy of American Jewry. The Zionist program was the only program that went unaltered through the Peace Conference at Versailles. Zionism is the heart of Jewish aspiration. "Not of American Jews," Mr. Morgenthau may retort. But who are the American Jews? Inquire of the recent convention of Zionists at Cleveland for information.

That convention is worth a story by itself, but it explains why the *World's Work* stopped its press for the July issue and made an insertion of eight extra pages for the accommodation of Mr. Morgenthau's article. The Jews who call themselves Americans have been thrown down and out by the Cleveland convention, and Russian Jews proved themselves the stronger.

It was an event that called for quick explanation. The humiliation of the Americans was something to be covered as speedily as possible. Why the *World's Work* should have been chosen as the vehicle is not known. But the presses were stopped and the Morgenthau backfire started.

Mr. Morgenthau's article as a Jewish pronouncement is negligible, but the Editor's Note that preceded it has the value of unbiased testimony. Referring to the world organization of Zionists, whose chief officer stepped over here from Europe and simply slammed the American Jewish leaders out of office, the editor of the *World's Work* has this to say:

> "This world organization has a highly centralized form of government. This consists of an international committee, including representatives from all countries that have a local organization. But the real control is vested in what is known as the 'Inner Actions Council.' This is a compact body of only seven men and it is dominated by the Jews of Europe."

The "Jews of Europe" might be still more definitely described as the "Jews of Russia."

And "Dr. Chaim Weizmann, from London" might more accurately be described as from Pinsk, Russia.

The Russian Jews won, as they have always won, for they are the originators and corrupters of the false political Zionism which is leading so many Jews to disappointment and distress.

The point in all this is that in the silence of the Jewish regimented protest, the voice of the country has had a chance to be heard. The religious press has not been mentioned here, for it deserves a separate account, nor have the many newspapers which have reacted from the previously imposed burden of Jewish propaganda. Editorial speech is becoming freer. Jews themselves are coming to see that the call is not for abuse, but for a cleanup. The expression of the press of the country indicates that there is a Jewish Question and that the Jews used the worst possible tactics in trying to suppress the knowledge of it. They behaved in a way to show what bad masters they would be if given the chance, and what essential cowardice controls their actions. One by one the holds they gained by force of fear, are being loosened. And if the Jews would lay up capital on which to draw—the capital of public confidence in their desire to do the right thing—they would go around and loosen the holds they still have. This, however, is not expected of them. It requires too much foresight.

Issue of July 30, 1921

LXXIV.

What Jews Attempted Where They Had Power

THE time of the year has come when Christians implore the tolerance of Jews while Christmas is being celebrated. If the Jews will only permit the Christians to celebrate Christmas in their schools, their homes, their churches—in their city squares and country villages—there will be more disposition on the part of the public to believe the Jewish boasts of tolerance.

It is not yet announced whether the Jews will give their permission or not. But that there are inquiries being made into the matter is indicated by this article in the Brooklyn *Eagle*, of October 31:

"Canon William Sheafe Chase today made public a letter he has sent to the secretary of the Board of Education asking for a copy of rules and regulations which, he alleged, forbid the telling of a Christ story at Christmas time in the public schools. Canon Chase said that the attention of the Federation of Churches has been called to a statement of a kindergarten teacher who last year said she had told such a story and had been notified that 'she will be removed from her position if she repeats such an exercise this Christmas.'

"He said that the Supreme Court of the United States has said that this is a Christian country and 'the courts in the State of New York have said that Christianity is the common law of our land.' " Dr. Chase added:

" 'This government has treated the Hebrew more

generously than any other nation in the world. I believe that the people generally, Hebrew as well as Christian, are very glad to enter into the spirit of Christmas time. Any attempt, therefore, to eliminate Christ from the hymns of our Country, from the reading books, and from the religious holidays of the Christian people, I believe, is not instigated by the Hebrews as a whole, but by certain misguided leaders of Jewish religion.' "

This is a variation of the Christmas theme. Instead of looking forward to Christmas, it is a spirit of inquiry as to how far we can go at Christmas. We are asking whether we dare, as Christians in a Christian land, whisper the Name that gives Christmas its meaning. That is, the Christians are doing the Christmas asking early this year. Christian teachers want to know if they well be discharged if they give their classes a bit of Christmas flavor, as all the teachers gave us when we were young. The contrast between the schools which we of the mature generation attended when we were young, and the schools of today whose pupils are carefully screened from the fact that Christmas celebrates Christ, is such a contrast as ought to give mature Americans a pause.

But, if past experience be the standard of judgment, the appeal to Jewish tolerance in New York will be futile. If Christians do not take their rights, it is certain the Jews will never grant them. It would be un-Jewish to do so; and the ceaseless cry of the leaders is, "Be Jewish!"

Any number of instances could be cited of the whip which Jewish leaders crack across the educational and political systems of the City of New York, but one or two must serve for the present.

The first case to be considered is that of Rev. William Carter, D. D., given in "Who's Who in America" as pastor of the Throop Avenue Presbyterian Church, Brooklyn; author of "The Gate of Janus," an epic story of the War; also of "Milton and His Masterpiece" and "Studies in the Pentateuch." He is an extensive traveler and a lecturer of reputation, his specialty being history and literature. At an important Y. M. C. A. center he has lectured for thirty consecutive weeks a year on "Current Events," which course was so successful that he was asked by the New York Board of Education to start a similar one at the Erasmus High School. For ten years he has been engaged by the New York Board of Education as special lecturer in the popular evening extension courses.

The course Dr. Carter undertook was badly run down, but in six weeks he regular audience had been increased from 35 to 350. The plan of the lectures was to discuss a major topic selected by the Board, a second period was devoted to the discussion of current events, and a third period to questions from the audience.

Now it happened that for the week of November 15, 1920—just a year ago—the topic selected by the Board of Education was "The Racial Origins of the American People," a study of immigration. That is to say, Dr. Carter was asked to study that matter and discuss it publicly before his weekly lecture audience at Erasmus School. He did so, taking time to make a serious investigation of all phases of the subject.

He showed that just before the war—thirty days before the war—the highest peak of immigration was reached; the year ending June 30, 1914, having seen 1,403,000 aliens enter this country. Analyzing this great flood, he showed that whereas six per cent came from Great Britain and two per cent came from Scandinavian countries, over ten per cent were Jews. The doctor's subject was "The *Racial* Origins of the American People."

Again, on the subject, "What Has Immigration Done for America?"—this subject also scheduled by the Board of Education—Dr. Carter showed that some parts of Europe had given their worst instead of their best, and stated that the lowest percentage of immigration came from the best developed and most desirable countries, while the largest percentage came from the least desirable. For example, he differentiated between the desirable Italians and those who form the material for Black Hand activities. Speaking of Russia and Austro-Hungary, he made a reference to the Jews.

But Dr. Carter made a mistake—perhaps two. It is always difficult to tell just where the line falls between fear of giving offense and fear of being unfair. In any event, Dr. Carter gave every evidence of, let us say, fear of being unfair. But it is fear, and a Jew scents fear a long way; the man who fears even though he fear to be unfair is already marked by the Jew who may happen to be stationed to watch him.

So Dr. Carter, to avoid giving offense by this part of his lectures, did the usual thing which has always drawn sneers from the Jewish press; he began to pay compliments to the Jews on their good points. He spoke of their contributions to Art, Science, and Philosophy; to Statesmanship, Religion, and Philanthropy. He lauded their distinguished men by name, such as Disraeli, Rubenstein, Schiff, Kahn, even Rabbi Wise! He referred to his pride in counting many Jews among his personal friends. With all respect to Dr. Carter, it was the same old stuff usually handed out in such circumstances. Madison C. Peters made it unjustly famous, and American clergymen have been spouting it ever since.

If Dr. Carter will study the alleged contributions of the Jews to the Arts and Sciences, study this as carefully as he did the immigration theme, he may omit the praises from future lectures. And he may also revise his list of great Jews. But that is neither here not there.

"As we have found bad elements in these other peoples," said Dr. Carter in this portion of his lecture, "so they are to be found in the Jew, and as the majority of these 143,000 Jews who came here the year before the war were from Russia, or Russian countries, let us not forget that the Jews themselves admit the Russian Jew is the worst of his race."

Apparently the audience remained unshocked. The question period came round and two Jews, a woman and a man, asked the lecturer why he had picked out the Russian Jew in particular for criticism. Dr. Clark replied that he had only given the evidence of the Jews themselves, that he was merely quoting what the Jews themselves had alleged time and again to explain certain matters. He added that the statement was universally accepted except by some who came from Russia.

A few days afterward the Board of Education sent word to Dr. Carter that complaints had been received against him for certain statements against the Jews, and calling upon him to explain. Dr. Carter is said to have replied that as only two Jews out of 400 people had objected at the lecture, he regarded that as evidence that the proprieties had not been violated.

Within a week, however, a more insistent communication was sent out by the Board of Education, stating that more letters of complaint had been received and citing Dr. Carter to meet his accusers at a special meeting of investigation.

Now begins as strange a proceeding as American people may hope to see in this land of the free. It is really not as rare as some might think. It can be duplicated in a number of known and proved cases. The way the Carter case worked out was this:

Dr. Carter arrived, as summoned. There were seven Jews there before him. Four of these Jews admitted they had not attended the lecture, and one had never even heard of Dr. Carter before. The minister was alone. Not knowing what was afoot, and not having been told to bring witnesses who had heard his lecture, he was there—a lone Gentile before a Jewish tribunal.

The Jewish delegation was headed by a certain Rabbi C. H. Levy, who was referred to as secretary of the Board of Jewish Ministers, a union of rabbis in connection with the New York Kehillah, which is part of the general spy system of American Jewry. Rabbi Levy admitted that the had not attended the specific lecture complained of, or any other lecture in the course, but declared he was there to "represent my people."

Well, Rabbi Levy's "people" were pretty well represented. There was hardly any other kind of people there except the

Christian clergyman who was on trial for telling the truth as to public opinion, and Jewish opinion particularly, about the Russian Jew.

So the Inquisition upon the Gentile began. Six letters were read, most of them having been addressed to Dr. W. L. Ettinger, Superintendent of New York Schools. One of these letters asked Dr. Ettinger as a Jew not to allow his people to be maligned and misrepresented, but to see that this Gentile was stopped!

After the reading of the letters, Dr. Carter was permitted to speak. He called attention to the similarity of the style in all the letters, a similarity which suggested to him the possibility of their having been dictated by one person. At which Rabbi Levy flew into a passion—though no one had mentioned his name. Dr. Carter also observed that as Dr. Ettinger had been appealed to on racial, religious and prejudiced grounds, it would be right to permit Dr. Carter time to get witnesses on his side. This was not permitted. He was on trial!

Even the Jews admitted, under straight questioning, that what Dr. Carter had said was not uttered invidiously. They admitted that he had referred to the undesirable elements of other races as well as of the Jews. It was admitted that the subject was not of his own choosing, but was assigned to him by the Board of Education. There was very little left at the end of the examination except to assume that the Jews were a sacrosanct race, with special privileges, a race whom no non-Jew should presume even to mention in anything but awe-filled tones.

That was the issue as it appeared that day. With half the Jewish population of the United States centered in the city of New York, they had assumed control of American education at its source. The group of Jews sitting in judgment on Dr. Carter were as serene in their control of the education of the Christians, as if they had been a Soviet court sitting in Moscow. They had succeeded in driving everything Christian out of the schools; they had succeeded in introducing the most sickening praise of their own race; they looked forward to the teaching of Judaism as the universal morality!

It was further brought out that this Christian minister had been one of the men who had preached in favor of the Jews. He had been one of those public men on whom Jewish leaders could depend to respond with typical Christian generosity. He had delivered blows at race prejudice. He had lauded the Jewish race and its leading figures. He had interpreted its commanding influence as the reward of diligence and ability. He had thundered against what Jewish reports had led him to believe was "the Crime at Kishineff." And for this he had been duly complimented by the Jewish Publication Society, and others. *BUT* he had now spoken a word of truth which the Jews disliked, and he was before them for trial and condemnation.

In the course of the examination it developed that he had been a citizen of the United States for thirty years, having come to this country from England at the age of 15. Rabbi Levy apparently missed the full fact, getting only the fact that Dr. Carter was born in England.

"May I inquire as to whether the gentleman is or is not a citizen of the United States?" said the rabbi in the air of one who was innocently uncovering a great exposure.

I became a citizen over thirty years ago, as soon as the law allowed—as I trust you did," was Dr. Carter's straight thrust.

The rabbi dropped the subject. He did not take up the challenge as to his own citizenship. But that the matter burned in him is evidenced by his later remark:

"I'll see to it, notwithstanding all this, that you shall never speak again from any platform in New York, you dirty Englishman!"

Dr. Carter called the attention of the committee to the hatred and malignity expressed in the face, attitude and words of the enraged rabbi, and said he did not know whether it was a threat against his life, his pastorate, or his position as lecturer for the New York Board of Education.

The term "dirty" is rather an unusual one to apply to a race that has so long astonished Semitic countries by its insistence on its "bawth." That is to say, the accuracy of Rabbi Levy's description would draw about the same degree as would an appraisal of his gentlemanliness.

There was, fortunately, one other non-Jew present, namely, Ernest L. Crandall, supervisor of lectures, who was American enough to enter the fray. He addressed the hysterical little rabbi:

"I never have seen nor heard such bitterness and hatred expressed by any human being toward another as you have manifested here. You ought to be ashamed of yourself, and if I hear another word from you along such lines, I will have you thrown out!"

The future of Mr. Crandall should be worth watching. If he is apologetic for his principles, they will "get" him. If not, he may be the instrument of "getting" some things that are wrong with New York.

At any rate, Mr. Crandall acquitted Dr. Carter, and the Jews went out muttering.

It is rather an unusual and noteworthy fact, the acquittal of a man against whom the Jews had moved the charge and against whom the secretary of the Board of Jewish Ministers had uttered the aforesaid threat.

Dr. Carter went back to Erasmus school. He received from the Board of Education his appointments for the ensuing months. Affairs seemed to be going along as before.

Then one day all the lecturers on "Current Events" in New York public schools received simultaneous notice that they must refrain from discussing the *Jewish* and *Irish* questions. With Zionism crowding the newspapers, and breeding a war in Mesopotamia, and dictating the policy of the diplomatic departments of Great Britain and the United States; with the Irish Question uppermost in the minds of millions and coloring the politics of the United States as well as challenging the full ability of the British Government—that is, with the two foremost "Current Events" seething throughout the world, orders were given through the New York Board of Education that lecturers must remain mum.

It was plain to be seen what had happened. Rabbi Levy, and those who worked with him, having failed in their personal attack, had achieved what they wanted another way—by an order given to lecturers not to speak about the Jewish or Irish question.

Why lug in the Irish? The Irish were not protesting against discussion of the Irish Question. The Irish wanted the Irish Question discussed; they believed that the successful issue of the matter depended on wide and free discussion. It is beyond the realm of imagination that the Irish should ever ask, desire or sanction a gag on popular discussion of Irish affairs.

As to Dr. Carter, his audiences had been asking him questions about the Irish Question for three years. In Y. M. C. A., in public school, in people's forum, everywhere he had been asked for information about one or another phase of the Irish Question; and being a well informed man he was able to give answers. And no one had ever complained before. Indeed, it is said that at the next lecture he gave at Erasmus School, following the encounter with Rabbi Levy, the audience had asked questions touching the Irish Question, and Mr. Crandall was present, and found no ground for criticism.

Yet soon thereafter came the order to observe complete silence on the Irish Question. Why?

Even the tyro in Jewish policy knows the answer. The Irish Question was lugged in to camouflage the order regarding the Jewish Question. That is a very common Jewish practice: any Gentile name will serve for concealment!

Imagine an Irishman and his family attending an evening lecture on "Current Events" and asking a question about the Irish situation. Imagine the lecturer saying, "I am forbidden to mention Ireland, or the Irish, or the Irish Question on these premises." The Irishman, being a white man, would not be slow to see that somehow he was being discriminated against.

He would demand to be told *why* the lecturer dared not mention the matter. And, being forbidden to mention the Jews either, the lecturer would not be able to say, "Those Jews down at the Board of Education have put their taboo on both the Jews and the Irish!" He would be breaking the rules even in giving the explanation.

But imagine the Irishman being classed with the Jew—the Irishman who wants publicity, with the Jew who fears it! How long would it take an Irishman to see what was intended to be discrimination *in favor of* the Jews was discrimination against the Irish.

Yet that was precisely what the Jews of New York brought about in the public lecture system to make their point against a Christian clergyman who had told a very well-known truth about the Jews.

Of course, there is nothing in such an order that would appear to the Jew as being subversive. Suppression is his first thought. Suppress the paper! Suppress the investigation! Suppress the out-and-out speaker! Suppress the immigration discussion! Suppress the facts about the theater, about the money system, about the baseball scandal, about the bootlegging business! Suppress the lecturers of the City of New York! Fire them from their jobs unless they stand up like phonographs and recite what men like the sentinel rabbis of New York dictate!

The order was Jewish in every element of it. And as an American citizen who did not believe that American free speech should be the plaything of a crowd of aliens, Dr. Carter resigned his lectureship. It meant serious inconvenience and financial loss to him to do so at the end of December, when it was late to make further plans for the winter, but a principle was at stake, and he resigned.

Immediately the matter came into the newspapers and there was the usual ado—the Jewish writers throwing threats about recklessly; a few timid Americans asking what New York was coming to! One newspaper came out with an

American editorial defending the right of free speech, but changed its tone somewhat upon receiving a deluge of Jewish protests threatening the paper with the displeasure of the Jews.

A man of less ability and of lower standing than Dr. Carter might have been overwhelmed by the storm. But he had at last struck rock and there he stood. At that time he was not known to have said anything detrimental to the Jews, and he is not known to have made subsequent remarks upon his experience. That is, being attacked by the Jews, he is not known to have attacked them in return. It is quite possible that he might be induced to do the Madison C. Peters stunt again and speak in praise of them, giving them the usual laudation which they themselves first prepared for our consumption. But nevertheless he has been, through no fault of his own, the focus of the vindictive policy which pursues the truth-teller. It may be distasteful to Dr. Carter to have his story thus told, but if he will begin anew his studies in the history and character of the International Jew, he will find his own experience a valuable commentary thereon.

Dr. Carter is only one of many. There are teachers in New York who could a tale unfold that would stir indignation to its depths—but there has never been any one to tell their story or take their side. Many of these stories are in the possession of THE DEARBORN INDEPENDENT.

Issue of November 19, 1921

LXXV.

The Jewish Question in Current Testimony

THE Jewish Question continues to attract more and more attention. In many quarters a new tendency toward freedom of the press is observed, and the long-concealed truth is getting itself spoken bit by bit. It has been thought worth while, before going on to other phases of the study of the Jewish Question, to present in this article a few of the informative or confirmatory articles that have appeared in the public press. It need not be said that, with a single possible exception, none of the writers or publications here quoted could be called "anti-Semitic." Not even the most unreasonable Jew could append that term to any writer or publication here cited.

The Associated Press sent out a dispatch which was printed in American papers of August 24, as follows:

"Thousands of Russian Jews are crossing the Estonian, Lithuanian and Polish borders every month, many sent from Soviet territory under protection of high Bolsheviki officials, according to travelers in the border states who recently have returned here. The opinion in neighboring states is that the exodus is prompted by fear of an approaching crisis. "The fact that no appreciable organized Russian anti-Bolshevik movement has appeared since Baron Wrangel's forces were dissipated, leads observers of the situation here to believe that, should the overthrow of the Soviets occur this winter, it will take the nature of a popular uprising, supported by such troops as are not at the front. Many fear it will result in a widespread anti-Jewish program.

For these reasons every Jewish family of means, and many that are destitute, are attempting to get out of Russia. They have no desire to tarry in Lithuania or Estonia, but are seeking to enter Germany, with the idea of eventually reaching America."

To give the reader the background of this fear, we offer part of a letter from Kishinev which was received by a North Dakotan:

"My Dear Friend Gutsche:

"For one month no fugitives arrived, but now again many of them are coming from the Ukraine to Bessarabia, most of whom are Jews. They are a different lot than the former fugitives were; for they are wearing costly clothes, furs, precious stones, jewels, and so on, such as was seen before the war only by very well-to-do people, landowners and the like; they have money and money's worth. There is no doubt that these fugitives had leading positions in the Bolshevik regime, perhaps they were commissars, or even 'judges' on the "Blood and Inquisition courts' of the so-called 'Tschreswytschaika' or short 'Tscheka'—their purses and pockets are filled, not with worthless paper money—for they themselves have manufactured that, millions and billions of it, which they have thrown before the Christian brood, the 'goies'—no, filled with money and precious jewels which no more show traces of blood and tears, but shine and glitter the same as in those happy hours of their rightful owners.

"But the people over there (in Russia.—Ed.) are awakening; they wonder about the source of all this terror. The children of Judah know the answer thereto, but they prefer to leave the ground which is becoming unsafe to stand upon; it is getting too hot for them. The Nemesis is raising her head from out the blood of innocence which calls to heaven for revenge. Yes, they fear the result of their actions and wish to save their skins before it is too late. In this they succeed, but not always are they allowed to keep their furs, their stones and precious metals; they overlooked the Rumanians. These people are very vain and greedy for costly things! The newcomers are on their way to America and the doors on all borders are willingly opened them, even to the soldier in the army. Only on again! The faster the better! I think that some day America will have so many Semites that they (the Semites) will be looked upon the same as the colored, the black, yellow and brown races.

"Imagine for a moment that there were no Semites in Europe. Would the tragedy be so terrible now? Hardly! They have stirred up the people in all countries, have incited them to war, revolution and communism. They believe in the saying that 'there is good fishing in troubled waters.'

"But enough of 'the chosen people.' Some day they will reap what they have sown. . . .

" . . . . .Another picture—Every three or four days a 'razzia' (domiciliary search, graze) is being conducted in the city. Terror, fear and oppression drive the people from the streets, looking for hiding places. The people do not work, eat or sleep. Only stamping, cursing patrouilles are seen on the streets with their victims. In this manner 200 or 300 persons are often driven together: former civil and military officials, teachers, landlords, business men, and so on (only Christians, seldom Jews): among them also women. This group is led to the 'Tschreswytschaika.' In front of the group are 40 to 50 armed red guards, infantry and on horses, right and left about the same number of guards, in the rear several carriages or an automobile with machine gun, and behind that again infantry and horseback riders. When this group is seen on the streets, everyone flees terrified; occupants of houses peep through cracks and press their hands to their hearts to see—what?— Father, brother, son or other relatives led away from their once happy homes, perhaps never to return again. This they know, whose behind doors and windows, where occur hysterical spells, heart failures and deaths. Words cannot express the terror of it all.

"And then at the 'Tschreswytschaika'? There are youths, mostly circumcised, often half or wholly drunk! Should there be personal enemies among the 'judges' the unfortunate ones are executed either or on the same day or the next one, but are sometimes also 'tried' like they 'tried' the heretics in the Inquisition chambers. Several of these creatures of the 'Tschreswytschaika' and especially a certain Wichmann—a Jew, of course—carry on terribly; he is the terror of the city and the flat land; he even kills Bolshevist Commissars and their wives should they now and then reveal a more humane feeling.

"They fear the reprisal and hasten across the borders, laden down with valuables.

"More suffering is caused in the cities by hunger and cold. The dead bodies are buried without coffins and often without clothes. How the people dwell in houses I shall, perhaps, relate next week. Enough for today.

F. Horch."

The freedom of the Balkan Jew from the hunger and suffering which afflict the native peoples is vividly set forth in the words of an American:

"Our ship is the first to enter Libau on a peaceful mission since the war, they say. At any rate, our arrival has caused a great excitement, on account of the food cargo we have for these people. At present we are tied up to a quay, in a narrow stream that seems to be also a sewer. Unloading our flour is a ticklish piece of work, due to the terrible hunger of the crowd that watches us. Whenever a bag breaks, people fight to scrape up the loose flour, which they put into cans along with a good portion of dirt that is mixed into it . . . .Everyone has a tin can and at noon there was almost a riot over a bucket of potato peelings that were tossed into the water. The people tied strings to their cans and went fishing for the peelings. They stand all day and beg us for food. . . . It is not a very pleasant sight—this crowd of emaciated, white-faced men and women, and big-eyed children.

"The most damnable thing about it all is the dozen Jews who flit like magpies through the crowd. They are young, soft, well-groomed and prosperous. They carry canes, wear new straw hats, and resemble the kind you see in the States. They have nothing in common with the other people. They have money, plenty of it, and they seem to think this ship is a floating pedlar's cart and tobacco store. They come up to the gangway and wave British five-pound notes in the air, offering them for a carton of cigarets. Or, they have gold watches that they will trade for a few pounds of soap. From the looks that other people favor them with, I do not wonder that we hear about periodic slaughters of the Jews in Russia. These fellows look too prosperous in comparison with the rest of the population to suit me."

The peculiar character of Jewish cruelty in Russia is so little in accord with the character of the Jew as we propagandized Americans have been taught to conceive it, that even THE DEARBORN INDEPENDENT, in its desire to present a consistent account of Jewish activities as they relate to the United States, has not opened this special phase of the study of Jewish psychology. The Sadism displayed throughout the Russian Terror has been discussed briefly in "The World Significance of the Russian Revolution," by George Pitt-Rivers.

There is, however American Jewish testimony on the same point. It is found in the April, 1921, number of *the Hebrew Christian Alliance Quarterly*. In an article entitled "Persecution Is Not the Monopoly of Christianity and Is Contrary to Its Principles," the Rev. M. Malbert, B. A., of Ottawa, Ontario, says:

"We must now proceed to deal with our last point. The Jews blame Christianity for its persecuting spirit. They consider it a monstrous thing to persecute another person for his convictions. Now, the question is, are they themselves free from the persecuting zeal? I am going to show that real religious persecution is uniquely Jewish, and that they themselves have been the relentless persecutors. In the year 120 B.C., John Hyrcanus, son of Simon, the last of the Maccabean brothers, who fought against the Syrian hosts in defense of their religion, persecuted other religions. He destroyed the Samaritan Temple on Mount Gerizin. Next, he conquered the Idumeans and bade them choose between exile or Judaism. They chose the latter. That he made a mistake in forcing his religion on an unwilling people, may be seen in the treacherous Herodian dynasty, Idumean converts, who were a curse to the Jewish nation.

"The intolerant religious spirit among the Jews themselves is unique in history. In the Maccabean princes the royalty and the high priesthood were united in one person, King Alexander, third son of John Hyrcanus, who was a Sadducee. The Pharisees therefore hated him. In the year 95 B.C., on the Feast of Tabernacles, as he was officiating in his high priestly capacity in the Temple, instead of pouring the water on the altar, he spilled it at his feet. The congregation worshiping with the palm branches and citrons in their hands, noticing the water spilled at the high priest's feet, started to pelt him with them. The King's life was in danger and he was constrained to summon to his aid the Pisidean and Cilician mercenaries. Those fell on the people and slew 6,000 within the precincts of the Temple. The hostility of the Pharisees was more bitter against the king, and their hatred knew no bounds. But the king endeavored to make peace with them. He therefore summoned their chief men and told them that he was tired of the feuds and that he desired peace. What were their conditions? They replied, the death of the king. *Then they actually set out to betray their country.* They invited the Syrian king, Eucaerus, to invade Palestine and treacherously offered him their aid. Eucaerus advanced upon Judea with 43,000 men. The Pharisees kept their promise and fought in the camp of their country's enemy against their king, who was eventually defeated. The poor king, the descendant of the heroic Maccabees, wandered about in the mountains of Ephraim. At last, 6,000 Pharisees, conscience-stricken, returned to him from the Syrian camp. With these 6,000 penitents, he was able to force the Syrians from Judea. But the majority still remained hostile and made war against him, but they were finally defeated and reaped the fruits of punishment

that they deserved.

"The Jewish king himself was intolerant and he forced many heathen cities to embrace Judaism; those who refused were destroyed. Simon ben Shetach, president of the Synhedrion, *condemned 80 women to be crucified for witchcraft.* The son of Simon ben Shetach was accused by his enemies of some breach of a religious precept and although the father himself knew him to be innocent, he nevertheless sentenced him to death and allowed him to be executed.

"Between the school of Hillel and Shammai there was constantly bloodshed. The trial and execution of Jesus were the natural outcome of religious intolerance. The greatest service to God a Jew thought possible was to persecute the Christians. Rabbi Tarphon said that the Gilion, that is, the Gospels and all the writings of the Minim, that is, the Apostolic Epistles, should be burned even with the holy name of God in them. He maintained that Christianity was more dangerous than paganism and he would rather fly to a heathen Temple than to a meeting house of the Minim. A curse against the Minim was inserted into the Jewish daily prayers at that time, which is still used by the congregations. Bar-Kosibah, the false Messiah, persecuted the Christians without mercy. Even in the time of Justinian, in the sixth century, the Jews massacred Christians in Caesarea and destroyed their churches. When Staphanus, the governor, attempted to defend the Christians, the Jews fell on him and slew him. In 608, the Jews of Antioch fell upon their Christian neighbors and killed them with fire and sword. The Patriarch Anastasius, surnamed the Sinaite, was disgracefully ill-treated by them and his body dragged through the streets, before he was finally put to death. About 614, the Persians advanced upon Palestine and the Jews, after joining their standard, massacred the Christians and destroyed their churches. Ninety thousand Christians perished in Jerusalem alone. The Jews expected fair play from the Persians as a reward, but were treated worse by them than by the Christians. In 628, the Emperor Heraclitus had retaken

Palestine from the Persians and when marching through Tiberius, he was entertained by a wealthy Jew named Benjamin, the same man who invited the Jews to join the Persians against the Byzantines; the emperor asked him what had induced him to betray so great an animosity against the Christians, to which he replied that they were the enemies of his religion. *Yet they claim the prophecy of Isaiah in the fifty-third chapter, to have been fulfilled in them. 'He was oppressed, and he was afflicted yet he opened not his mouth.'* They even persecuted Mohammed in the incipient stages of his career. They prejudiced the chief Arabs against him, helped his enemies to discredit him and endeavored to alienate his followers."

The article continues to give in detail the persecution to which the Jews subjected their own people who were progressive. It reminds one of the warning given to Rabbi Isaac M. Wise by Rabbi Lilienthal, when the former was urging the reform of Judaism: "If you want to be Christ you must expect to be crucified." ("Isaac Meyer Wise," p. 92)

Readers of Gibbons' "Rise and Fall of the Roman Empire" will recall that in Volume 1, Chapter 16, he wrote severe words about the cruelty of the Jews. It will be agreed that only records of the most staggering cruelty could have driven the calm historian to the use of such terms. Readers will also observe, in the passage herewith quoted, that the desire for "the empire of the earth" which actuated the Jews of that period is the same as that discovered in the Protocols:

"From the reign of Nero to that of Antonius Pius, the Jew discovered a fierce impatience of the dominion of Rome, which repeatedly broke out in the most furious massacres and insurrections. Humanity is shocked at the recital of the horrid cruelties which they committed in the cities of Egypt, of Cyprus and of Cyrene, where they dwelt in the treacherous friendship with the unsuspecting natives; and we are tempted to applaud the severe retaliation which was exercised by the arm of the legions against a race of fanatics, whose dire and credulous superstitions seemed to render them the implacable enemies not only of the Roman Government, but of human kind. The enthusiasm of the Jews was supported . . . .by the flattering promise which they derived from their ancient oracles, that a conquering Messiah would soon arise, destined to break their fetters and to invest the favorites of heaven with the empire of the earth."

In footnotes to this passage, Gibbons gives revolting details of the methods used by the Jews of that period.

In all this work the Jewish Idea has the assistance of certain Christian sects who gloss over the inhumanity and immorality of certain courses of actions by saying that "these are doubtless the means by which God is giving the Jew his promised control of the world." This is one form of the un-Biblical conception, the un-Scriptural teaching, that the Jews are God's Chosen People.

Of all the sects following this error, none is more active than the so-called "Russellites," the followers of Pastor Russell, and officially known as the International Bible Students' Association.

It has been reported to THE DEARBORN INDEPENDENT by numerous witnesses that Jewish interpreters at points of debarkation in Canada and the United States have circulated Russellite literature. The fact that a Jew would circulate any kind of Christian literature is sufficiently astonishing to cause inquiry. It is explained by the elaborate pro-Jewish propaganda which Russellism is conducting

Not to go into this extensively at this time, suffice it to refer to handbill advertising in the Russian quarters of American cities. The fact that the literature is circulated among Russians and that meetings are held in Russian sections of our cities would seem to indicate a desire to explain to credulous Russians that Bolshevism, too, should be received as part of the circumstance by which the Jews are to obtain world rule. The handbills are headed "The Fifth Universal Kingdom," and in every meeting reported the speakers have declared that in

1914 the rule of the world was taken away from "us"—that is, the non-Jews who are the so-called "Gentiles"—and was given to God's Chosen People, who, according to this sect, are the Jews. Thus, acquiescence in Bolshevism and every other form of revolutionary overturning is acquiescence in the will of God.

The teaching that world rule is already in the hand of the Jew is so novel, so unrelated to Biblical sources, as to warrant careful scrutiny for possible pro-Jewish connections.

But Palestine is not yet a fact, and other Bible students see in the present political movement a daring and God-defiant scheme destined to failure. Certainly there are great obstacles in the way—moral obstacles, matters of honor and humanity—which do not promise easily to disappear. The Jews of the world are discovering that they read too much into the Balfour Declaration and that Great Britain is not ready to violate her obligations to the Arabs. Jewish leaders are beginning to feel the weight of realities in the settlement of the land itself. The Jews are not going back. Those who have gone back are, a considerable and influential number of them, tainted with Russian Bolshevism.

The English people themselves are becoming dubious about the situation as is shown by the dispatch of the London correspondent of the Detroit *News* printed in the August 14 issue of that paper:

"Then there is the scarcity of accurate information from Palestine. The high commissioner, Sir Herbert Samuel, transmits reports to the British Government, but they are not published. Even the report which he made on going to Palestine two years ago to inquire into the exact status of affairs never has been made public. Lord Sydenham asked for it in the House of Lords, and, though Lord Curzon replied that the report contained nothing unsuitable for publication, it has never been given out. It is also charged that the Zionist Commission maintains a strict censorship; that even a petition to the king disappeared in transit; that letters have to be written guardedly. A series of articles by the special correspondent of the *Times* suddenly ceased, though the last, May 17, bore the line, 'To Be Continued.'

"News from Palestine is exceedingly scanty, and no one knows whether what does come through is trustworthy. It has been printed that Sir Herbert Samuel does not dare ride through the streets of Jerusalem without an armored car in attendance. For these reasons there is a great deal of suspicion in England that all is not well in Palestine."

The most outspoken word that has yet been uttered on the political dilemma in which Zionism places the Jew, appeared in an editorial entitled, "Political Judaism" in the *Christian Century*, of Chicago, a publication of weight and character:

"Political loyalty is one. Under the present world order it does not admit of division. The citizens of any nation may maintain a Platonic admiration for the political systems of neighboring nations, but their ultimate loyalty cannot be 'Platonized.' Spiritual Judaism is one thing. A Palestinian state, or a Jewish political organization anywhere else, is a very difficult thing—at least in Gentile estimation. . . . .

"Once a Jewish state is set up in Palestine, in so far as it is accepted as the proper expression of Judaism, the Jew of the diaspora must surrender his religion. Is there any escape from this issue? The Jew can be a Jew anywhere, so long as his religious adherence carries with it no political implications. At least he can be an acknowledged Jew in every land where religious freedom is guaranteed or practiced. And even in states where an established religion other than Jewish debars him from the fullest and highest participation in the affairs of state, he can still hold to his religion without too serious embarrassment.

"But what would be the status of the Jew in any land of the present world when the profession of his religion would inevitably identify him with the fortunes and aspirations and diplomacy, even with the military policies, of a political state alien to the society of his residence and citizenship? The status seems, at least to the Gentile mind, altogether impossible. A revival of anti-Semitism, and its spread to lands where heretofore it has not prevailed, is not the least embarrassing of the inevitable results of such a move. How can the Jewish outlander maintain his own spiritual and mental integrity? It is not even necessary to imagine a possible precipitation of war between the new Jewish state and the land of his citizenship. War is not, let us hope, the necessary condition or even potentiality among separate political states. But it remains true, by the very nature of the present system of political organization, that political loyalty is one, and cannot be divided. Hyphenation, discriminating Americans are by this time well aware, must remain spiritual, or racial, or sentimental; it dare not become political under any circumstances.

"If the proposed new Jewish state in Palestine is to be and remain a province or dominion of the British Empire the way is smoothed for any Jew residing and claiming citizenship in any portion of the British Empire. But the way is decidedly roughened for the Jew elsewhere. The Briton is honored, especially in times of peace, in most regions of the world for his connection with so magnificent a political structure, but for that very reason his political loyalty is the more emphasized in his own mind and scrutinized by citizens of other political units. A Jew identified with so insignificant a power as an independent Palestinian state must forever be, would, in many lands and on many occasions, be in a far more advantageous position when a resident of an outlying nation, than if he were recognized as a Briton. The anticipated dependence of a new Palestine upon British sovereignty thus fails to relieve the embarrassment of Zionism; it would seem rather to compound it."

Issue of August 27, 1921

LXXVI.

America's Jewish Enigma—Louis Marshall

SOMETHING of an enigma is Louis Marshall, whose name heads the list of organized Jewry in America, and who is known as the arch-protester against most things non-Jewish. He is head of nearly every Jewish movement that amounts to anything, and he is chief opponent of practically every non-Jewish movement that promises to amount to something. Yet he is known mostly as a name—and not a very Jewish name at that.

It would be interesting to know how the name of "Marshall" found its way to this Jewish gentleman. It is not a common name, even among Jews who change their names. Louis Marshall is the only "Marshall" listed in the Jewish Encyclopedia, and the only Jewish "Marshall" in the index of the publications of the American Jewish Historical Society. In the list of the annual contributors to the American Jewish Committee are to be found such names as Marshutz, Mayer, Massal, Maremort, Mannheimer, Marx, Morse, Mackler, Marcus, Morris, Moskowitz, Marks, Margolis, Mareck—but only one "Marshall," and that is Louis. Of any other prominent Jew it may be asked, "Which Straus?" "Which Untermeyer?" "Which Kahn?" "Which Schiff?"—but never, "Which Marshall?" for there is only one.

This in itself would indicate that Marshall is not a Jewish name. It is an American, or an Anglo-Saxon name transplanted into a Jewish family. But how and why are questions to which the public as yet have no answer.

Louis Marshall is head of the American Jewish Committee, and the American Jewish Committee is head of all official

Jewish activity in the United States.

As head of the committee, he is also head of the executive committee of the New York Kehillah, an organization which is the active front of organized Jewry in New York, and the center of Jewish propaganda for the United States. The nominal head of the Kehillah is Rabbi Judah L. Magnes, a brother-in-law of Louis Marshall. Not only are the American Jewish Committee and the Kehillah linked officially (see chapter 33, Volume II, reprint of this series), but they are linked domestically as well.

Louis Marshall was president of all the Jewish Committees of the world at the Versailles Peace Conference, and it is charged now, as it has been charged before, that the Jewish Program is the only program that went through the Versailles conference as it was drawn, and the so-called League of Nations is busily carrying out its terms today. A determined effort is being made by Jews to have the Washington Conference take up the same matter. Colonel House was Louis Marshall's chief aid at Paris in forcing the Jewish program on an unwilling world.

Louis Marshall has appeared in all the great Jewish cases. The impeachment of Governor Sulzer was a piece of Jewish revenge, but Louis Marshall was Sulzer's attorney. Sulzer was removed from the office of governor. The case of Leo Frank, a Jew, charged with the peculiarly vicious murder of a Georgia factory girl, was defended by Mr. Marshall. It was one of those cases where the whole world is whipped into excitement because a Jew is in trouble. It is almost an indication of the racial character of a culprit these days to note how much money is spent for him and how much fuss is raised concerning him. It seems to be a part of Jewish loyalty to prevent if possible the Gentile law being enforced against Jews. The Dreyfus case and the Frank case are examples of the endless publicity the Jews secure in behalf of their own people. Frank was reprieved from the death sentence, and sent to prison, after which he was killed. That horrible act can be traced directly to the state of public opinion which was caused by raucous Jewish publicity which stopped at nothing to attain its ends. To this day the state of Georgia is, in the average mind, part of an association of ideas directly traceable to this Jewish propaganda. Jewish publicity did to Georgia what it did to Russia—grossly misrepresented it, and so ceaselessly as to create a false impression generally. It is not without reason that the Ku Klux Klan was revived in Georgia and that Jews were excluded from membership.

Louis Marshall is chairman of the board and of the executive committee of the Jewish Theological Seminary of America, whose principal theologian, Mordecai M. Kaplan, is the leading exponent of an educational plan by which Judaism can be made to supersede Christianity in the United States. Under cover of synagogal activities, which he knows that the well known tolerance of the American people will never suspect, Rabbi Kaplan has thought out and systematized and launched a program to that end, certainly not without the approval of Mr. Marshall.

Louis Marshall is not the world leader of Jewry, but he is well advanced in Jewry's world counsel, as is seen by the fact that international Jewry reports to him, and also by the fact that he headed the Jews at the "kosher conference'—as the Versailles assemblage was known among those on the inside. Strange things happened in Paris. Mr. Marshall and "Colonel" House had affairs very well in hand between them. President Wilson sent a delegation to Syria to find out just what the contention of the Syrians was against the Jews, but that report has never seen the light of day. But it was the easiest thing imaginable to keep the President informed as to what the Jews of New York thought (that is, the few who had not taken up their residence in Paris). For example, this prominent dispatch in the New York *Times* of May 27, 1919:

"Wilson Gets Full Report of Jewish Protest
Here.
"Copyright, 1919, by the New York Times Co.
"By Wireless to *The New York Times.*

"Paris, May 26.—Louis Marshall, who has succeeded Judge Mack as head of the Jewish Committee in Paris, was received by President Wilson this afternoon and gave him a long cabled account of the Jewish mass meeting recently held in Madison Square Garden, including the full text of the resolutions adopted at the meeting . . .and editorial comment in *The Times* and other papers . . . ."

When Russia fell, Louis Marshall hailed it with delight. The New York *Times* begins its story on March 19, 1917:

"Hailing the Russian upheaval as the greatest world event since the French Revolution, Louis Marshall in an interview for the New York *Times* last night said"—a number of things, among which was the statement that the events in Russia were no surprise. Of course they were not, the events being of Jewish origin, and Mr. Marshall being the recipient of the most intimate international news.

Even the new Russian revolutionary government made reports to Louis Marshall, as is shown by the dispatch printed in the New York *Times* of April 3, 1917, in which Baron Gunzburg reports what had been done to assure to the Jews the full advantage of the Russian upheaval.

This glorification of the Jewish overthrow of Russia, it must be remembered, occurred before the world knew what Bolshevism was, and before it realized that the revolution meant the withdrawal of the whole eastern front from the war. Russia was simply taken out of the war and the Central Powers left free to devote their whole attention to the western front. One of the resulting necessities was the immediate entrance of America into the conflict, and the prolongation of the hostilities for nearly two more years.

As the truth became known, Louis Marshall first defended, then explained, then denied—his latest position being that the Jews are against Bolshevism. He was brought to this position by the necessity of meeting the testimony of eye-witnesses as given to congressional investigation committees. This testimony came from responsible men whom even Mr. Marshall could not dispose of with a wave of his hand, and as time has gone on the testimony has increased to mountainous proportions that *Bolshevism is Jewish in its origin, its method, its personnel and its purpose.* Herman Bernstein, a member of Mr. Marshall's American Jewish Committee, has lately been preparing American public opinion of a great anti-Semitic movement in Russia. Certainly, it will be an anti-Semitic movement, because it will be anti-Bolshevist, and the Russian people, having lived with the hybrid for five years, are not mistaken as to its identity.

During the war, Mr. Marshall was the arch-protester. While Mr. Baruch was running the war from the business end ("I probably had more power than perhaps any other man did in the war; doubtless that is true"), Mr. Marshall was running another side. We find him protesting because an army officer gave him instructions as to his duties as a registration official. It was Mr. Marshall who complained to the Secretary of War that a certain camp contractor, after trying out carpenters, had advertised for Christian carpenters only. It was to the discrimination in print that Mr. Marshall chiefly objected, it may be surmised, since it is the policy of his committee to make it impossible, or at least unhealthy, to use print to call attention to the Jew.

It was Mr. Marshall who compelled a change in the instructions sent out by the Provost Marshal General of the United States Army to the effect that "the foreign-born, especially Jews, are more apt to malinger than the native-born." It is said that a Jewish medical officer afterward confirmed this part of the instruction, saying that experience proved it. Nevertheless, President Wilson ordered that the paragraph be cut out.

It was Mr. Marshall who compelled the revision of the Plattsburg Officers' Training Manual. That valuable book rightly said that "the ideal officer is a Christian gentleman." Mr. Marshall wrote, wired, demanded, and the edition was changed. It now reads that "the ideal officer is a courteous gentleman," a big drop in idealism.

There was nothing too unimportant to draw forth Mr. Marshall's protest. To take care of protests alone, he must have a large organization.

And yet with all this high-tension pro-Jewish activity, Mr. Marshall is not a self-advertising man, as is his law partner, Samuel Untermeyer, who has been referred to as the arch-inquisitor against the Gentiles. Marshall is a name, a power, not so much a public figure.

As an informed Jew said about the two men:

"No, Marshall doesn't advertise himself like Sam, and he has never tried to feature himself in the newspapers for personal reasons. Outside his professional life he devotes himself exclusively to religious affairs." That is the way the American Jew likes to describe the activities referred to above—"religious affairs." We shall soon see that they are political affairs.

Mr. Marshall is short, stocky, and aggressive. Like his brother-in-law, Rabbi Magnes, he works on the principle that "the Jew can do no wrong." For many years Mr. Marshall has lived in a four-story brownstone house, of the old-fashioned type, with a grilled door, in East Seventy-second street. This is an old-time "swell" neighborhood, once almost wholly occupied by wealthy Jews. It was as close as they could crowd to the choice Fifth Avenue corners, which had been pre-empted by the Vanderbilts, the Astors, and other rich families.

That Mr. Marshall regards the whole Jewish program in which he is engaged, not in its religious aspect alone, but in its world-wide political aspect, may be judged from his attitude on Zionism. Mr. Marshall wrote in 1918 as follows:

"I have never been identified and am not now in any way connected with the Zionist organization. I have never favored the creation of a sovereign Jewish state."

BUT—

Mr. Marshall says, "Let the Zionists go on. Don't interfere with them." Why? He writes:

"Zionism is but an incident of a far-reaching plan. It is

merely a convenient peg on which to hang a powerful weapon. All the protests that non-Zionists may make would be futile to affect that policy."

He says that opposition to Zionism at that time would be dangerous. "I could give concrete examples of a most impressive nature in support of what I have said. I am not an alarmist, and even my enemies will give me credit for not being a coward, but my love for our people is such that even if I were disposed to combat Zionism, I would shrink from the responsibilities that might be entailed were I to do so."

And in concluding this strange pronouncement, he says:

"Give me the credit of believing that I am speaking advisedly."

Of course, there is more to Zionism than appears on the surface, but this is as close as anyone can come to finding a Jewish admission on the subject.

If in this country there is apprehension over the Jewish Problem, the activities of Louis Marshall have been the most powerful agents to evoke it. His propagandas have occasioned great resentment in many sections of the United States. His opposition to salutary immigration laws, his dictation to book and periodical publishers, as in the recent case of G. P. Putnam's Sons, who modified their publishing program on his order; his campaign against the use of "Christological expressions" by Federal, State and municipal officers; all have resulted in alarming the native population and harming the very cause he so indiscreetly advocates.

That this defender of "Jewish rights," and restless advocate of the Jewish religious propaganda, should make himself the leader in attacking the religion of the dominant race in this country, in ridiculing Sunday laws and heading an anti-Christianity campaign, seems, to say the least, inconsistent.

Mr. Marshall, who is regarded by the Jews as their greatest "constitutional" lawyer, since the decline of Edward Lauterbach (and that is a tale!) originated, in a series of legal arguments, the contention that "this is not a Christian country nor a Christian government." This argument he has expounded in many writings. He has built up a large host of followers among contentious Jews, who have elaborated on this theme in a variety of ways. It is one of the main arguments of those who are endeavoring to build up a "United Israel" in the United States.

Mr. Marshall maintains that the opening of deliberative assemblies and conventions with prayer is a "hollow mockery"; he ridicules "the absurd phrase 'In the name of God, Amen,' " as used in the beginning of wills. He opposes Sunday observance legislation as being "the cloak of hypocrisy." He advocates "crushing out every agitation which tends to introduce into the body politic the virus of religious controversy."

But Mr. Marshall himself has spent the last twenty years of his life in the "virus of religious controversy." A few of his more impertinent interferences have been noted above. These are, in the Jewish phrase, "religious activities" with a decidedly political tinge.

The following extracts are quoted from the contentions of Mr. Marshall, published in the *Menorah Journal*, the official organ of the Jewish Chautauqua, that the United States is not a Christian country:

IS OURS A CHRISTIAN GOVERNMENT?
BY LOUIS MARSHALL

When, in 1892, Mr. Justice Brewer, in rendering the decision of the Supreme Court of the United States in the case of the Church of the Holy Trinity against the United States (144 U. S. 457), which involved an interpretation of the Alien Labor Law, indulged in the *obiter* remark that "this is a Christian nation," a subject was presented for the consideration of thoughtful minds which is of no ordinary importance.

The dictum of Mr. Justice Story in Vidal against Girard's Executors (2 How. U. S., 198), to the effect that

Christianity was a part of the common law of Pennsylvania, is also relied upon, but is not an authoritative judicial determination of that proposition. The remark was not necessary to the decision.

The remarks of Mr. Justice Brewer, to which reference has already been made, were also unnecessary to the decision rendered by the court.

The fact that oaths are administered to witnesses, that the hollow mockery is pursued of opening deliberative assemblies and conventions with prayer, that wills begin with the absurd phrase, "In the name of God, Amen," that gigantic missionary associations are in operation to establish Christian missions in every quarter of the globe, were also instanced. But none of these illustrations affords any valid proof in support of the assertion that "this is a Christian nation."

Our legislation relative to the observance of Sunday is such a mass of absurdities and inconsistencies that almost anything can be predicated thereon except the idea that our legislators are impressed with the notion that there is anything sacred in the day. According to the views of any section of the Christian church, the acts which I have enumerated as permitted would be regarded as sinful. Their legality in the eye of the law is a demonstration that the prohibitory enactments relating to Sunday are simply police regulations, and it should be the effort of every good American citizen to liberalize our Sunday legislation still more, so that it shall cease to be the cloak of hypocrisy.

As a final resort, we are told by our opponents that this is a Christian government because the majority of our citizens are adherents of the Christian faith; that this is a government of majorities, because government means force and majorities represent the preponderance of strength. This is a most dangerous doctrine ...

If the Christianity of the United States is to be questioned, the last person to initiate the inquiry should be a member of that race which had no hand in creating the Constitution or in the upbuilding of the country. If Christian prayers in public are a hollow mockery, and Sunday laws unreasonable, the last person in the world to oppose them should be a Jew.

Mr. Marshall has the advantage of being an American by birth. He was both in Syracuse, New York, in 1856, the son of Jacob and Zilli Marshall. After practicing law in Syracuse, he established himself in New York, became a Wall Street corporation lawyer, and his native country has afforded him generous means to win a large fortune.

The question arises whether it is patriotic for Mr. Marshall to implant into the minds of his foreign-born co-religionists the idea that this is not a Christian country, that Sunday laws should be opposed, and that the manners and customs of the native-born should be scorned and ridiculed. The effect has been that thousands of immigrant Jews from Eastern Europe are persistently violating Sunday laws in the large industrial centers of the country, that they are haled to court, lectured by judges, and fined. American Jews who are carrying into practice the teachings of Mr. Marshall and his followers are reaping the whirlwind of a natural resentment.

Mr. Marshall was the leader of the movement which led to the abrogation of the treaty between the United States and Russia. Whenever government boards or committees are appointed to investigate the actions, conduct or conditions of foreign-born Jews, great influences are immediately exerted to have Mr. Marshall made a member of such bodies to "protect" the Jewish interests.

As head of millions of organized Jews in the United States, Mr. Marshall has invariably wielded this influence by means of a campaign of "protests," to silence criticisms of Jewish wrong-doing. He thus protested when testimony was made before the Senate Sub-Committee in Washington, in 1919, that the Jewish East Side of New York was the hotbed of Bolshevism.

Again he protested to Norman Hapgood against the editorial in *Harper's Weekly,* criticizing the activities of Jewish lobbyists in Washington.

Mr. Marshall describes himself in "Who's Who" as a leader in the fight for the abrogation of the treaty with Russia. That was a distinct interference in America's political affairs and was not a "religious activity" connected with the preservation of "Jewish rights" in the United States. The limiting expression "in the United States" is, of course, our own assumption. It is doubtful if Mr. Marshall limits anything to the United States. He is a Jew and therefore an internationalist. He is ambassador of the "international nation of Jewry" to the Gentile world.

The pro-Jewish fights in which Mr. Marshall has been engaged in this country make a considerable list:

He fought the proposal of the Census Bureau to enumerate Jews as a race. As a result, there are no official figures, except those prepared by the American Jewish Committee, as to the Jewish population of the United States. The Census has them listed under a score of different nationalities, which is not only a nondescriptive method, but a deceptive one as well. At a pinch the Jewish authorities will admit of 3,500,000 Jews in the United States. The increase in the amount of Passover Bread required would indicate that there are 6,000,000 in the United States now! But the Government of the United States is entirely at sea, officially, as to the Jewish population of this country, except as the Jewish government in this country, as an act of courtesy, passes over certain figures to the government. The Jews have a "foreign office" through which they deal with the Government of the United States.

Mr. Marshall also fought the proposed naturalization laws that would deprive "Asiatics" of the privilege of becoming naturalized citizens. This was something of a confession!

Whenever there were extradition cases to be fought, preventing Jewish offenders from being extradited, Mr.

Marshall was frequently one who assisted. This also was part of his "religious activities," perhaps.

He fought the right of the United States Government to restrict immigration. He has appeared oftener in Washington than any other Jew on this question.

In connection with this, it may be suggested to Mr. Marshall that if he is really interested in upholding the law of the land and restraining his own people from lawless acts, he could busy himself with profitable results if he would look into the smuggling of Jews across the Mexican and Canadian borders. And when that service is finished, he might look into the national Jewish system of bootlegging which, as a Jew of "religious activities," he should be concerned to break up.

Louis Marshall is leader of that movement which will force the Jew by law into places where he is not wanted. The law compelling hotel keepers to permit Jwis to make their hotels a place of resort if they want to, has been steadily pushed. Such a law is practically a Bolshevik order to destroy property, for it is commonly known what Jewish patronage does for public places. Where a few respectable Jews are permitted, the others flock. And when one day they discover that the place they "patronize" is becoming known as "a Jew hotel" or "a Jew club," then all the Jews abandon it— but they cannot take the stigma with them. The place is known as "a Jew place," but lacks both Jew ad Gentile patronage as a result.

When Louis Marshall succeeded in compelling by Jewish pressure and Jewish threats the Congress of the United States to break the treaty with Russia, he was laying a train of causes which resulted in a prolongation of the war and the utter subjugation of Russia. Russia serves the world today as a living illustration of the ruthlessness, the stupidity and the reality of Jewish power—endless power, fanatically mobilized for a vengeful end, but most stupidly administered. Does Mr. Marshall ever reflect on the grotesque stupidity of Jewish leadership?

It is regretted that space does not permit the publication here of the correspondence between Mr. Marshall and Major G. H. Putnam, the publisher, as set forth in the annual report of the American Jewish Committee. It illustrates quite vividly the methods by which Mr.. Marshall secures the suppression of books and other publications which he does not like. Mr. Marshall, assisted by factors which are not mentioned in his letter, procured the suppression of the Protocols, after the house of Putnam had them ready to publish, and procured later the withdrawal of a book on the Jewish Question which had attracted wide attention both here and in England.

Mr. Marshall apparently has no confidence is "absurdities" appearing absurd to the reader, nor of "lies" appearing false; but he would constitute himself a censor and a guide of public reading, as well as of international legislation. If one might hazard a guess—Mr. Marshall's kind of leadership is on the wane.

Issue of November 26, 1921

James Russell Lowell always declared "that he was of Jewish extraction and proud of his ancestry."

If anybody has achieved an exceptionally high grade in a difficult course, he or she was probably Jewish.

—Syracuse Jewish Monthly

LXXVII.

The Economic Plans of International Jews

THE strength of Jewish money is in its internationalism. It stretches a chain of banks and centers of financial control across the world, and plays on them on the side of the game that favors Judah. This center was, and for the moment is, in Germany, at Frankfort-on-the-Main, but feverish anxiety now accompanies the fear that it may have to be moved. Destiny is overtaking the Jewish World Power. The gold which is their god—"the God of the living" is what they call their gold—is being brought overseas on every available ship and locked up in the vaults of Jewish bankers in North and South America, not to enrich this hemisphere but to mobilize Jewish financial power for any desperate stroke. Financial Jewry is afraid. It has a right to be afraid. Its conscience, still bloody from the war whose gains have not stopped, is in a troubled state.

Single Jewish banking houses in any country, however great such banks should grow, would be no menace. In spite of the fact that the richest bankers in the world are Jews, as mere bankers in their several countries they would not occasion alarm. In straight out-and-out banking, the Jew is not a success. The Rothschilds were never bankers in a proper sense; they were money-lenders to nations whose representatives they had corrupted to seek the loans. They did business precisely on the plane of the money-lender in the side street who induces the rich man's son to borrow a large sum, knowing that the father will pay. That is scarcely banking. Brains of that sort may "get" money, but will not "make" money. The deposit banking of the world is not done in Jewish banks anyway, even Jewish depositors preferring banks which are managed by non-Jews.

It is not, therefore, the success of the individual Jewish banking house that concerns us. Flabby-minded non-Jews who have been blinded by pro-Jewish propaganda find difficulty in seeing that point. They say that the individual Jewish business man has as much right to his business success as has anyone else. Which is a perfect Jewish platitude! Certainly he has. Who ever stated that he had not? But when you are dealing with a world chain of financial consulates, all of them lining up in a world system, none of them to be regarded as American banks, or British banks, or French banks, or Italian banks, or German banks, but all of them members of the Jewish World Banking System, you are obviously not dealing with individuals who are trying to make a living. You are then dealing with a mighty force for good or ill, and thus far, sad truth to know, the ill is mountainous in comparison.

Nor does this Jewish banking system require that in each country a Jewish house be the most important. It is not the wealth and importance of single houses, but the wealth and importance of the world chain, that gives the strength. Kuhn, Loeb & Company is far from being the most important financial house in the United States, but with its foreign connections, all Jewish, it takes on a new aspect. Kuhn, Loeb & Company is far from being the most important banking house in the United States, and yet it was an idea that came out of Kuhn, Loeb & Company's office that now dominates the monetary system of the United States. Paul Warburg, a German Jew, scion of the Jewish world banking group, is boosted into undue prominence and power through the pressure of banker-bought prestige in government circles. It is his connections—Jewish ones—that count.

The Warburg idea in the United States, dovetailing with the Sterns, the Furstenbergs, the Sonenschiens and the Sassoons and Samuels and Bleichroeders overseas, was something to wonder at. Jewish bankers ran this war as they have run every great war. No informed Jew will deny that. Most informed Jews have boasted of it as indicating the importance of their people. Above the nations at war was an international financial committee, all Jewish, looking down upon all the ruction and blood as serenely as American baseball league directors look down upon a pennant series. Separated, each man tied to his country by ties of undivided nationalistic loyalty, none of these would have amounted to much. United, as a super-national financial board, knowing the secrets of all the nations, conferring one with another in all sorts of ways, even during the hardest days when all communication between countries was supposed to be locked by war, deciding the duration of the war and the hour of so-called peace, these groups constitute a danger which no one doubts after once having clearly seen it.

Men who can thus manipulate money in time of war can do so in time of peace. The United States is living under some of that peace manipulation now.

The reader of the Protocols is much impressed by the financial notes that are sounded throughout their proposals. The Jewish defense against the Protocols, that they were written by a criminal or madman, is intended only for those who have not read the Protocols, or who have overlooked the financial plans they offer. Madmen and criminals do not coolly dissect one money system and invent another, as do the Protocolists.

It will be worth while, in view of the sidelights that these articles have thrown on the money question, to recall some of the forecasts and plans made in these most remarkable documents which have been attributed to the Wise Men of Zion, the world leaders of the inner council.

"When we sink, we become a revolutionary proletariat, the subordinate officers of the revolutionary party; when we rise, *there rises also our terrible power of the purse.*" So wrote the great Jewish Zionist leader, Theodore Herzl, in his work, "A Jewish State," (p. 23). It is precisely that union of revolutionary tendencies and financial power that the world is facing now. Look at Russia, and look at the people who swarmed at Versailles and made the Peace Treaty. The Peace Treaty was written by financiers; it is the bill presented, not to a beaten foe, but to the world. Very few people have ever read it; but its operation is evident everywhere. The Jewish bankers the world over are shoveling in the gold.

Protocol VI is interesting in this connection:

"We shall soon begin to establish huge monopolies, colossal reservoirs of wealth, upon which even the big Gentile properties will be dependent to such an extent that they will all fall, together with the government credit, on the day following the political catastrophe."

Although these words were written with Europe in view (the United States not yet having been Judaized) their import is clear. At the present moment the number of business concerns in the hands of Jewish creditors, through "loans," is very large. The Jewish idea in business is to "borrow," instead of making the business stand on its own feet. The trail of that idea is seen all over our land today.

"At the same time it is necessary to encourage trade and industry vigorously, *and especially speculation*, the function of which is to act as a counterpoise of industry. *Without speculation, industry will cause private wealth to increase and tend to improve the position of agriculture by freeing the land* from indebtedness for loans by the land banks. *It is necessary for industry to deplete the land* both of laborers and capital, and, through speculation, transfer all the money in the world into our hands....

"To destroy Gentile industry, we shall, as an incentive to this speculation, encourage among the Gentiles a strong demand for luxuries, all-enticing luxuries."

There is the Idea—Extravagance and Debt support the Jewish money-lender's power. He does not lend to build

The Economic Plans of International Jews

industry, but to drain it. Independent industrial or agricultural wealth menaces his rule. Industry must be curbed by speculation; speculation must be encouraged by extravagance; an industrious people soon works itself free of its debt slavery; therefore invent new excitements to keep it in debt. Entice people from the farms, and so forth, and so forth, all which devices are now well known to the world.

"*We will force up wages*, which, however, will be of no benefit to workers, for *we will at the same time cause a rise in the price of prime necessities, pretending* that this is due to the decline of agriculture and cattle raising. *We will also artfully and deeply undermine the sources of production* by instilling in the workmen ideas of anarchy and encourage them in the use of alcohol...."

That wages were forced up, that they were of little profit to the workers, that prices did rise, that the above excuses were given, that anarchistic ideas now being circulated among the workers are Jewish and are circulated by Jews, that the illicit liquor business (as once was the legal liquor business) is entirely in the hands of Jews—these things everyone knows to be true.

The Protocols have been in non-Jewish knowledge since 1896. The British Museum has possessed a copy since 1906. Were they written by *a prophet who foresaw*, or by a *power that foreordained*?

The Jewish World Program is shown in these Protocols to be largely dependent on the *false economic ideas* it can induce the governments and peoples to accept. The false economic ideas—not only false, but cruelly deceptive and impossible—which are being sown among the masses of the people are the counterpart being sown in the upper circles of banking and government.

Jewish economic ideas are quite different from the ones which Jewish thinkers put out for others to follow.

Jewish bankers know better than anyone else the utter falsity of the present system, but they profit by that falsity, and they are ruining non-Jewish rule by that falsity, and they are establishing Judah by that falsity, and they will try to maintain that falsity until it brings the inevitable collapse, after which they hope to reorganize the world on Jewish monetary principles. So, at least, the Protocols indicate. This bad regime is for the so-called Gentile period only.

The temporary nature of the present Jewish system, and the destruction it is meant to work in the world, is shown in the Third Protocol, where, after discussing ways and means to make the lower classes hate the well-to-do, it says:

"This hostility will be still more accentuated as the result of crises which will close stock exchange operations and stop the wheels of industry. Having organized such a general economic crisis by all the underground means available to us, and thanks to the assistance of gold, all of which is in our hands, we will throw whole crowds of workingmen into the streets simultaneously in all the countries of Europe. These crowds will gladly shed the blood of those whom they, in the simplicity of their ignorance, have envied since childhood and whose property they will then be able to loot."

All this, as the world knows, has occurred in Europe. The weapons first used were economic. The subjection of the people, the revolution, was first economic. The Jewish program profited by the split which Jewish ideas had been able to make between the upper and lower classes of "Gentile" society. "Divide and Rule," is the Jewish motto, as quoted in the Protocols. "Divide the working class from the directing class. Divide the Catholic and Protestant churches." In brief, divide Christendom on economic, creedal, social and racial lines, while the Jew remains a solid body, able because of his solidarity to handle a divided world. And this plan has succeeded. Out of the disorder of the World War look how high the government of Judah has ben placed in Russia, Austria, Germany, France, Italy, England and in the United States.

The Economic Plans of International Jews

All the Jewish bankers are still in Russia. It was only the non-Jewish bankers who were shot and their property confiscated. Bolshevism has not abolished Capital, it has only stolen the Capital of the "Gentiles." And that is all the Jewish socialism or anarchism or Bolshevism is designed to do. Every banker who is caricatured with dollar marks on his clothes is a "Gentile" banker. Every capitalist publicly denounced in Red parades is a "Gentile" capitalist. Every big strike—railroad, steel, coal—is against "Gentile" industry. That is the purpose of the Red movement. It is alien, Jewish and anti-Christian.

Now, one of the interesting points about the Jewish financial scheme for the future as shown in the Protocols is the way in which it contrasts with the financial scheme which the Jewish groups now favor. As before stated, what the Protocolists now advise is not what they will adopt when their present advice has worked its hoped-for results.

The Protocols which detail the future financial plan of Jewish control are numbered XX and XXI. Protocol XX opens thus:

"Today we will speak of the financial program, the discussion of which I have postponed to the close of my report as it is the most difficult, decisive and concrete of our plans."

Throughout the recital the Protocolist harks back to the old (our present) financial system, and some of his remarks are worth transcribing here:

"You know that *the gold standard destroyed the governments that accepted it, for it could not satisfy the demand for currency, especially as we removed as much gold as possible from circulation.*"

Whether the first statement is true remains to be seen; the others are demonstrably true. The gold in the ground and the gold that is money is under Jewish control, and they withdraw it when they will.

The stupid so-called "Gentile" says, "Why should they withdraw it? They cannot make any money that way!" Once again remember the distinction: it is not a matter of "making" money but of "getting" it; panics are more quickly profitable than is a long period of prosperity for men whose commodity is money. Indeed, men who deal in money as a commodity and on the Jewish plan, lose their prestige if prosperity continues too long. The banker who is a banker, who lives to serve industry, and the community—*he* profits by prosperity, but not so the money sharks.

"We created economic crises for the *Gentiles by the withdrawal of money from circulation.* Mass capital stagnated, money was withdrawn from use by the various governments, and they in turn were obliged to turn back to the capitalists for loans. Such loans naturally embarrassed the governments, owing to the payment of interest charges, and made them subservient to the capitalists . . . ."

The withdrawal of money from circulation will create panics; every one knows that. Such withdrawal of money is within the decision of a very small group of men. Here in the United States we have been for a long fifteen months witnessing such a withdrawal and its effects. The word went by wire across the land, setting a date. On that date values began to crash all over the country, and honest bankers tried to help, while others who knew the game profited hugely. As shown in the last article, money was withdrawn from legitimate use, that it might be lent to money speculators at six per cent, who in turn lent it to desperate people at rates as high as 30 per cent.

No intelligent person will attempt to explain such events on the ground of natural law or of honest practice. These things occurred in this country within recent days. It is the "elastic" system, you know, with the public as a monkey on one end of the "elastic." A splendid idea, no doubt, if administered by the non-Jewish method of doing the greatest possible good to the greatest number, but a deliberate assassination of life and property as it has been administered.

The Protocolists then pay their respects to governmental finance with the keeness that is well justified:

"Owing to methods allowed by irresponsible Gentile governments, their treasuries became empty. Then came the period of contracting loans and using up the assets that remained. This brought all the Gentile governments to bankruptcy."

As operating groups, the governments are bankrupt now. Only their power of confiscation keeps them up. The United States, commonly referred to as the richest country in the world, is just as poor as a government as is any other. It has nothing: it is in debt and borrowing. And its creditors are constantly discounting their obligations and are putting it into worse hands than ever. Even the Liberty Bonds are almost passed out of the hands of the people into the hands of Jewish fiscal agents who "get" money out of the necessities of the people who sell and out of the necessities of the government which borrowed. And if all signs do not fail, we shall one day be hearing in Congress pleas for special legislation in behalf of "the poor bondholders." It is to be hoped when that day comes, some one will have mettle enough to stand up and declare who the "poor bondholders" are. A list should be made now, for future reference.

"Every loan proves government inefficiency and ignorance of governmental rights. Loans, like the sword of Damocles, hangs above the heads of the rulers, who, instead of placing temporary taxes on their subjects, stretch forth their hands and beg for charity at the hands of our bankers. Essentially, foreign loans are leeches, which in no instance can be removed from the government body until they fall off of their own accord or the government itself removes them. But Gentile governments, instead of removing them, continue to place more. They must perish inevitably through exhaustion by voluntary bloodletting."

This is the plainly expressed criticism of the Jewish World

Government upon the governments of the nations, and the truth of it cannot be gainsaid. It represents a statement of common wisdom upon which the Jewish World Program hopes to commend itself to the common people.

"Then why do not the Jewish world financiers help the nations out of this false financial policy?" Why, indeed? Jewish financiers are the inventors of such loans as they here describe, the barriers to such direct taxes as they here recommend. Listen—in the same page as the above:

"You may well understand that such a policy, although inspired by us, cannot be followed by us."

That is historically true, whether it will prove prophetically true or not. Compromising loans and interest are Jewish devices, historically Jewish. Practically and at present the Jew prefers not to borrow except in such a way as to place all business risks on other people's money while he keeps his own safely, and the payment of interest is an abomination to him. These statements of the Protocols have at least these historical and racial confirmations.

The whole stupidity of the "Gentile" system by which Jewish International Financiers are enriched, is clearly set forth in the same XXth Protocol:

"What is the effect of a loan, especially of a foreign loan, other than this? A loan is the issuance of government notes, pledging interest in proportion to the sum of borrowed capital. If the loan pays five per cent when in twenty years the government has paid the interest in vain, for it is equal to the sum of the loan; in forty years it has paid out an amount equal to the loan twice over; and in sixty years, three times, *while the original debt remains unpaid.*"

Extremely simple, and yet it is the most generally ignored fact of all.

We live in a democracy, yet loans are contracted that always cost more than the amount of the loan, and no one has a word to say about it. We Americans do not know how much interest we pay every year, and we don't know to whom we pay it. We are still living under the lie that "A National Debt Is a National Blessing," the most delusive doctrine ever promulgated.

The amount of our National Debt is the measure of our enslavement to Jewish World Finance.

The reader may observe in passing that Jewish apologists, John Spargo, Herman Bernstein, and others, say that the Protocols were put out by the secret police of the Russian Czarist regime. It is very unusual, is it not, to find the Czar's police interested in plans to remove graft from high finance, and preaching doctrines exactly contrary to the established system? The reader will find some amusement in searching for Russian police spies in the further development of the Jewish financial philosophy.

The purpose of Protocols XX and XXI is not to describe the present financial chaos in which the Gentiles are encouraged to continue; that system was described in previous Protocols; their purpose is rather to describe how the Jewish World Power plans to run thing when the time comes.

This is well worth considering, for there are portions of the plan which would be worth adopting. The Jewish expectation of World Rule is, of course, absurd, although the mass of Jews sincerely hold it. Their condemnation is that they regard every degeneracy in society as bringing them a step nearer their goal, which explains the great assistance they give to all degenerative processes.

"When we ascend the thrones of the world, such financial expediencies, not being in accord with our interest, will be definitely eliminated."

That is the opening note. It is another version of the statement—"You may well understand that such a policy, although inspired by us, cannot be followed by us."

What, then, did the Protocolists, looking for world power, propose to eliminate?

(1) *"The stock exchanges will be permanently suppressed,* for

we will not allow the prestige of our authority to be shaken by price fluctuations on our stocks. We will fix the full value legally without permitting any power to raise or lower it. Raising prices givens the pretext for lowering them—which was *what we started with the stocks and bonds of the Gentiles."*

(2) "The lawful *confiscation of money* in order to regulate its circulation."

(3) "We must introduce *a unit of exchange based on the value of labor units* regardless of whether paper or wood are used as the medium. We will issue money to meet the normal demands of every subject (citizen), adding a total sum for every birth and decreasing the total amount for every death."

(4) "Commercial paper will be bought by the government, which, instead of paying tribute on loans as at present, will *grant loans on a business basis.* A measure of this character will prevent *the stagnation of money, parasitism and laziness, qualities which were useful to us as long as the Gentiles maintained their independence,* but which are not desirable to us when our kingdom comes."

(5) "We will replace stock exchanges by great *government credit institutions,* whose functions will be to tax trade paper according to government regulations. These institutions will be in such a position that they may market or buy as many as half a billion industrial shares a day." (The reader will bear in mind that "police spies" of agricultural Russia "forged this document" in 1896. As a gentleman remarked: If this is the forgery, what must the original have been!—Ed.) "Thus all industrial undertakings will become dependent on us. You may well imagine what power that will give us."

The Protocolist now being quoted also gives his attention to taxation (observe again the "Russian police spy" doing some "forging"). The builders of this plan for World Rule recognize that when the overturn comes they will have to be in a position to offer the people something extremely good in order to win their favor. This, of course, was the plan in Russia, although Russia presents no parallel to what the Protocolists hope to do

The Economic Plans of International Jews

for what they call their "kingdom." Russia was simply tortured in punishment. Russia was a passover offering. Russia is an example of Jewish vengeance, destruction, rage, not of the rule which International Jewry hopes to put over a world economically conquered through its own weakness and lust. Hear then the taxation plan:

(1) "When we become rulers, our autocratic government, as a first principle of self-protection, will *avoid burdening the people with heavy taxes.* It must not forget to play the part of father and protector. But, as government organizations are costly, it is necessary to raise money for maintenance. Consequently, it is necessary to study carefully in this particular the problem of checks and balances."

(2) Kinds of taxes to be raised: (a) "The best method of taxation is to establish *a progressive tax on property.*" (b) The receipt of *purchase money* or an *inheritance* will be subjected to a progressive stamp tax." (c) "Any transfer of personal property, whether in money or other form of value . . . ." (d) A luxury tax—"the latter will be taxed through the medium of a stamp impost."

The rich are to be taxed in proportion to their wealth: "A tax on a poor man is the seed of revolution and it is detrimental to the government which loses the big things in its pursuit of the small." But there are other shrewd reasons for thus taxing the rich (a) "Aside from this, the tax on capitalists will *lessen the growth of wealth in private hands, where we have concentrated it at present as a counterweight to the governmental power of the Gentiles.* . . . (b) "Such a measure *will destroy the hatred of the poor toward the rich,* who will be regarded as the financial support of the government and the exponents of peace and prosperity. The poor will realize that the rich are paying the money necessary to attain these things."

This was written at least as early as 1896. How many forms of taxation have come precisely as here outlined!

How illuminating also the following remark: "Money

should circulate; and to hinder free circulation has a fatal effect upon the government mechanism, which it lubricates. The thickening of the lubricator may stop the correct functioning of the whole machine. *The substitution of a part of money exchange by discount paper has created just such an impediment."*

Remember that when next you hear the Jewish plan that "Gentiles" shall do business with their own bits of paper, while Jews keep the gold reserve safely in their own hands. If the crash comes, "Gentiles" have the paper and Jews the gold. If bits of paper serve ordinarily, the world may some time decide to do away with the gold. Certainly a system which rests on Cash yet works with Not-Cash, has disadvantages which depression and panic reveal. Says Protocol XXII—"We hold in our hands the greatest modern power—gold; in two days we could free it from our treasuries in any desired quantities."

The Jews are economists, esoteric and exoteric; they have one system to tangle up the "'Gentiles," another which they hope to install when "Gentile" stupidity has bankrupted the world. The Jews are economists. Note the number of them who teach economics in the state universities. Says Protocol VIII:

> "We will surround our government with a whole world of economists. *It is for this reason that the science of economics is the chief subject of instruction taught by the Jews.*

Issue of July 23, 1921

LXXVIII.

A Jew Sees His People As Others See Them

THIS week we present another Jew's comment on his race and for the good of the race. Bert Levy has said these things before Jewish Women's Councils, and B'nai B'rith lodges, and they will assist readers of this series to an understanding of some of the truer, though minority, influences which are at work in American Jewry. He sincerely exposes every obvious defect, and it is to be hoped that one day, with as sincere a pen, he will go deeper. Mr. Levy's chosen title is:

FOR THE GOOD OF THE RACE

From a far-off land I came, a sad-eyed, pale-faced, poetic young Jew, with an unspeakable love of my people burning in my heart. Of Polish-Russian parentage, there was implanted in my nature an indefinable sorrow (born perhaps of my father's and mother's persecution), which left me highstrung and sensitive to the anti-Semitic taunts of my schoolmates.

Given to idle dreaming by some old abandoned shaft or roaming the deserted alluvial diggings of the little mining town of my youth, I would conjure up visions of that new world I had so often read about—that great country where there was no prejudice against my race—the New Jerusalem.

Shyly hugging to my breast some borrowed American book or magazine I would seek the shadows of the huge decaying poppet legs and dream over the pages containing many Jewish faces, and I read with pride and gratitude of the high places occupied by my people in music, art, literature and the drama. Filled with Jewish names and good Jewish deeds was the story of this new Zion, and a longing to be among the great ones of my people took possession of me. Between my dear father and myself here was a bond of love too sacred for words, and when I looked upon his dear face for the last time in this world and bade him a sorrowful goodby before my departure for the New Jerusalem, he held me close to his breast and whispered"

"Don't forget that you are a Jew, and if you need sympathy, love or help, go to your own race and show your Arba Kanfoth." (According to Deuteronomy XXII., 12, the Jews are commanded to wear fringe upon four corners of their vestures and this command is observed to the present day by wearing a special garment with these fringes, generally hidden by the ordinary clothes.)

I carried my father's words across the ocean in my heart and the memory of his tear-dimmed eyes and the pressure of his big loving arms has never left me; in fact, it is so strong at times that I find it hard to believe that he is not by my side telling me, in spite of many disappointments, that after all, the Jews are still my brethren and sisters.

Words fail to describe my feelings as the beauties of the New World unfolded to me. In wonderful contrast to the melancholy aspect of my own country was the joyous color of Samoa, with its hallowed memories of Robert Louis Stevenson, lifted like some fairy veil out of the midst of the Pacific to give me a glimpse, as it were, of my dream of America—the New Jerusalem.

Oh, the wonderful days and wonderful nights out on that vast blue expanse, where God and His stars seemed so near that one formed a good resolution with every throb of the great engine far down below. On one of those nights I sat listening to some one playing in the music salon and I was inwardly thanking the Creator that there was a Puccini in the world and that he had given us "La Boheme." There we were, thousands of miles from anywhere, languidly rolling under a perfect moonlit sky, listening to the plaintive airs that Puccini had coined for Mimi. There was hardly a sound but the gentle lapping of the waves breaking against the vessel's side till a slight commotion on deck up ahead caused some of the listeners to investigate. One of the passengers, an ex-Harvard man, returned with the remark:

"Oh, it's only some damned Jew. He's fallen and hurt himself pretty badly."

Like a smudge on some beautiful picture was this anti-Semitic sentiment on such a night, and considering its source I felt deeply grieved. As I was the only other Jew in the first cabin I made my way to the stateroom where they had carried the victim of the accident and found him to be a tenderhearted old man who I subsequently learned had spent a long life in acts of charity toward his fellow men and women, regardless of creed. He was returning to end his days in Jerusalem (his Jerusalem, not the one of my dream), where he could touch again the beloved stones of the wailing wall.

Something in the old man's face, that "something" which was in the face of my father, my brother, drew me to him, as it has drawn me to all Jews always, and I spent many intellectual hours by his bedside, picking up grains of wisdom which he had translated from the Talmud. I wished that the ex-Harvard man could have known that the old man's wrinkles were but the pathetic records of the massacres of his kith and kin which he had witnessed in his homeland and that he daily prayed for death to efface the awful memories.

Later on the ex-Harvard man asked me to join in a deck game. I reminded him that I also was a "damned Jew."

"I'm sorry," he said. "I know what you refer to—that was an unfortunate slip I made the other night—merely a figure of speech, I assure you."

I found him a charming companion and soon in a cozy corner of the smoking room we became fast friends and I tried to win him over to think better of our people.

"I would like to hear your opinion of your fellow Jew after

you have spent, say, twelve months in America," he said.

Since then I have walked the length and breadth of the great cities of America, and my very soul has cried out to my fellow Jew: "Suppress Thyself!" The day I arrived in New York I learned that my dearest friend, my father, had passed away, and naturally my first thought was to say the kaddish, a prayer of the Jewish liturgy recited by orphans for the welfare of the souls of their deceased parents, somewhat after the fashion of the Catholic mass. Every male of Jewish blood at some time of his life recites this beautiful prayer. It does not matter how far one strays from the fold or how much one has denied the faith, there comes a time when the Jew in him asserts itself and he says the kaddish.

Public prayer among Jews can be recited only in the presence of ten males above the age of religious maturity, and this assembly is called minyan. Surely in this great city I would easily find a minyan, I thought; so I followed the line of least resistance, like any stranger in a strange land, and sought out the Jewish names best known to the public. I called at a business house uptown with the name of a great Hebrew over the door. He was the great man of whom I read with such pride in the little mining town at the other end of the world. Yes! The same Jewish face depicted in the huge photograph in the lobby I had seen in the magazine I had hugged so lovingly at home.

I made my way, full of hope, to his office and was asked by a doorkeeper of my mission. I explained—the doorkeeper was a Hebrew—that I desired to say kaddish for my father and that I wanted to form a minyan. With a sly wink he passed me on to several Hebrew clerks and office boys, each of whom smiled, sneered, and make his little joke about "greenhorns." Then I was ushered with many grimaces into the presence of the big man.

Just a minute's conversation convinced me that he was a Jew in appearance only, and that he had never known anything of the traditions, the romance, the art or the literature of our race. He didn't exactly know what minyan was, or pretended he didn't, but recommended me to "one of our people," as he put it, who ran a very popular chophouse close by. I began to realize that I was a stranger among my own people and that night I walked the streets of great New York with an aching heart. Everywhere in the hurrying crowds I saw the faces of my brethren and sisters, thousands, hundreds of thousands of them, hurrying, pushing, shoving brethren they were, with all the tenderness, the friendship and the Semitic look gone from their eyes.

"Oh, God!" I thought, "are these the children of Israel? Is this the persecuted race—that people who had been scattered to the four corners of the earth?"

Hungry and weary, I made my way as if in a dream to the café of a great hotel. Everything in the huge room was glaringly false—marble pillars, oak beams. flowers, were all imitation: a big orchestra sat in a balcony with an artificial moon and a painted sky as a background; everywhere were lights, lights, and more lights.

From table to table I went but I was roughly reminded that "this" was reserved and "that" was reserved. Presently glaringly gowned, bediamonded Jewish women, accompanied by equally vulgar Jewish men, filed in and occupied every seat, and between mouthfuls of food and drink their bodies would sway to the voices of other Jews who sang only of "Mississippi" and "Georgia." How these people did laugh when they caught sight of my foreign clothes and my pale, poetic face, and how they would have screamed with laughter had I shown them my Arba Kanfoth, that beautiful little token which my poor father fondly imagined would have made me understood in the New World.

Out into the night I went and found myself struggling in a torrent of humanity. Every time I received an extra bump or hard push I looked only to see that my antagonist was a Hebrew. On the street, in the cars, in the subway, or at the soda fountain, wherever I saw my fellow Jews blatantly shouting and rudely pushing, I, in spite of my indignation, felt the love of my race uppermost in my heart, and I wanted to cry out:

"Oh, Jew; dear brothers and sisters, suppress yourselves for the good of the race! Stand back! For the good of the race!"

Never in the world have our people known such a free country as this, and it is a privilege to be here, but at times a great fear comes over me that we are abusing that privilege. Amid the din of Jewish music and laughter, the newsboys are shouting the names of Jewish murderers (the Rosenthal case), the gunmen of the city. The bribe givers and the bribe takers depicted in the news sheets have Jewish countenances. The gambling house keepers—yes! yes! I know that there are Christians who are murderers, gamblers and informers, but the Jew is a marked man. He is distinct, apart, so distinct that in a crowd he is the first noticed.

It is for this reason that I would have my brethren and sisters suppress themselves, stand back! I would have real Jews take the worst of a bargain once in a while for the sake of the race. I would have them once in a while give up their seats in public conveyances, behave modestly in cafes, dress quietly, and give up the use of assumed Christian names.

There is nothing so pathetic as the man who, with a Hebrew face, assumes a Christian name. I never go to a public place without wishing that my fellow Jew would talk less and appear less ostentatious. When one Hebrew comes in late to a show, marches down the aisle and on the front row deliberately obstructs the view of people in the audience as he stands slowly removing and folding his coat and gloves, he seems to cause more annoyance than if half a dozen Gentiles did the same thing. When a Jew stands aside and waits patiently at a ticket window, gives his seat to a lady on a street car or behaves in a refined manner in any walk of life, he immediately makes friends for our people.

Most of our people, I have found, have aggressive personalities; it is this aggressiveness which has enabled many immigrants to pass through Ellis Island to the ownership of fine apartment houses all within a couple of years—but sometimes this aggressiveness becomes absolutely cruel, crushing from the very soul all the tender elements which go to make up a happy life.

Recently I thought with much bitterness of my father's last words to me; "If you need sympathy, love or help, go to your own race." Ill-health overcame me and I became involved in debt for a trifling amount. Each stage of my embarrassment and consequent suffering was contributed to by a brother Jew. First, the shyster lawyer, without principle or mercy, then his brutal clerks, sly and grafting. Next, a collector, absolutely callous, then the process server, and, at last, the "bouncer," sans heart, sans soul, sans everything.

If all these agents of misfortune were Gentiles I could have borne it, but the greatest heartbreak of all was the fact that one and all of them were brother Jews. Why must a Jew always be in at the death, as it were?

There came a time soon after this when I walked the streets almost penniless. Seeking work, I applied at the store of a wealthy Hebrew. I explained to the well-groomed proprietor that I was an orthodox member of his race and appealed on that ground for a chance. He pooh-poohed the idea.

"My dear fellow," said he, "These are the enlightened days, when Judaism is not taken seriously, in fact, it doesn't pay. I am a Christian Cultist, I meet nice people and it helps my business."

Here was a poor fool with his head like the ostrich's—in the sand. I explained to him that being a Jew was not a question of religion but a question of blood. I told him that if a Jewish leopard ceased visiting the synagogue to go to a Christian Cultist chapel it did not necessarily get rid of its spots. I left him scratching his head, and I also lost the chance of a job in his store.

In and out of offices presided over by men with Jewish

faces I trudged all day. Most of these men, I subsequently learned, belonged to New Thought, Christian Cultist and other up-to-date churches and societies—it was good for their business. They called themselves Christians, but nature's marks cannot be changed like one's clothes.

In the great theatrical districts I found thousands of my fellow Jews who had grown rich over night by coining perhaps a popular song that had pleased the cabaret-mad crowd or by ridiculous impersonations of their race upon the music hall stages. A good many of these were young men, sons of fathers and mothers who had been driven from their own country with fire and sword.

The mothers and fathers stay at home blessing God every hour of the day and night for guiding them to such a country as this, while the sons and daughters are out at the theatres, in the halls and cabarets singing songs of Dixie. Passing by in this great throng are prominent actors, critics and playwrights, many under assumed names, simply because their own names are Jewish.

Flashing across the horizon as I write is a notorious Jewish doctor with a consumption cure. He could have been famous and honored had he but suppressed himself, instead of which he, with his commercial instinct and his press agent methods, made more enemies for the race. Many Gentiles, I will admit, have had consumption cures, but it remained to one of our people to float companies and open institutions before the "cure" was even reported upon by the government.

Trampling the city tired and weary of looking for friendly Jewish faces I found myself near the City Hall. I approached a milk station and bought a cent's worth of the most delicious milk I have ever tasted. A rough-looking fellow next to me said, as he smacked his lips:

"Pretty good stuff, that," and perhaps noting that I was a stranger, he added; "The guy who is doing this milk thing is saving the babies all right—he's some rich Jew—God bless him—I've got three babies of my own."

Hungering to hear a Jew praised I talked with this man for an hour, listening with keen enjoyment to the story of one of my race who had caused his millions to do good for the people irrespective of creed, and had kept himself suppressed. I learned of this Jew's efforts for the dying babies at home and for his starving co-religionists in Palestine and felt proud. Proud and happy for the first time, I sat in the little park watching the passing procession till I dozed off into a sound sleep. My happiness continued in my sleep, for I had a most beautiful dream.

Before me in my dream passed a grand parade; it was a series of "For the good of the race" tableaux. All the prominent professional Jews headed the procession with their real names and the name of their race emblazoned upon silk banners in letters of gold. Then came all the Hebrew gambling house keepers bearing aloft broken roulette wheels and other emblems of a discarded and disgraced "business."

Next in order was a large army of Hebrews who were professional bondsmen for arrested street walkers headed by two crooked ward politicians carrying a huge streamer with the words: "Henceforth we will go to work." These men looked a little sad as they marched along thinking of the easy money they were leaving behind, but the cheers of the multitude exulting over their great sacrifice somewhat atoned for their agony of mind. Next followed the amalgamated Jewish usurers, real estate and company promoter's union. This part of the parade took four hours and a half to pass a given point.

All the marchers had discarded their expensive clothing and their diamonds and were modestly attired. They had also discarded their automobiles—many of the prominent men in this section carried flags and banners upon which were inscribed the legends: "We will not lie about values." "We will not charge exorbitant interest" and "We will not water our stock." These inscriptions were received with incredulous looks of astonishment, and many of the crowd called out: "We're from

Missouri," whatever that meant.

Then came a beautiful torchlight brigade called "The Hebrew Firebugs' Union." Nearly all these men had their hair close-cropped and wore prison clothes, a fact which filled the crowd with relief. Next came that part of the procession which showed the greatest following among its marchers. It was the large army of Hebrew "aggressives." Hundreds and thousands of them passed by with reformed looks upon their faces. Oh, I felt so happy as I read the buttons they wore and saw the flags they carried. Most of the streamers read: "We will suppress ourselves." "We will stand back and keep quiet." "We will be unostentatious." There they were, hundreds of well-known faces and types—end-seat hogs, front-seat hogs, loud talkers, inconsiderates, bargainers and the terrible army of people that go to make up the crowd which is directly responsible for the anti-Semitic feeling. The line of them was miles long.

I was awakened from my happy dream by a rude thump from a Jewish policeman who hurried me to a police station, where I was surrounded by shyster lawyers, my brethren, who wanted money with which they could square other brethren. I could not gain the services of a Hebrew bondsman because I had no pull. A Hebrew magistrate called me a "bum" and a loafer for going to sleep in a public park.

"Keep awake in the future," he said as I was roughly bundled out of the court.

Keep awake! This is the worst advice he could have given me, for I was so happy asleep and dreaming that my brethren and sisters had reformed and had become real Jews for the sake of the race.

I now look upon my police court humiliation as the best thing that could have happened to me, for a kindly old Jewish scholar, who acted as court interpreter, was attracted by my appearance. His long contact with human misery and his great experience with foreigners stranded in a strange country enabled him to understand me.

That night he took me to his poverty-stricken little room behind a delicatessen shop in the Ghetto. After supper he went to the street door and called the neighbors from their stoops. He called them by their first names and I said kaddish for my father as they stood around among the pickle barrels.

Since then I have lived among Jews, real Jews. I have learned that beneath the ragged coat of a push-cart vender there may beat a heart of gold, and that a poor seller of collar buttons or suspenders may be a student of the Talmud with a mind that is a gift of the gods.

Leaving the seething, modern, fashionable life of upper Broadway to enter the religious atmosphere of the numerous schools of Jewish literature on the East Side entails a violent contrast in conditions

To see the deeply furrowed, time-scarred faces of the grand old men pouring over their beloved Talmud is to get a glimpse of another world—a world of resignation, peace and love.

Within earshot of the thundering traffic of Broadway I stood gazing at the bowed figures engaged in study and prayer. As I gazed the sordid walls of the poverty-stricken room faded from my sight, and in their stead I was (in my mind's eye) the wailing wall of Jerusalem or some ruin of the Holy City—a more fitting background to the rabbinical figures so strangely out of place in hustling America.

The great passion for the dead and gone past reflected in the Rembrandtesque faces of the aged students lends to their lives a religious grandeur which the uptown tourist (hastily passing on a rubberneck wagon) would never suspect. Behind many a shabby-looking little store, or maybe above some corner saloon, are the societies for the study of Hebrew literature, where congregate the types of Jewish scholars and philosophers that make the heart of the writer and artist glad.

Gray-haired, bewhiskered, sad old men, many of whom have tasted only the bitterness of life—yet such is their faith in the Almighty that they cling to the praying shawl and Bible to blot out the memory of a Kishineff—their lives of study and prayer amid abject poverty giving the lie to the fallacy that the Jew lives but for money.

I have often wandered among these scholars picking up the crumbs of wisdom which fall from the lips of the old men, grateful that my Jewish face and blood gave me the privilege to sit and sketch among them. Somehow or other my ramblings on the East side are like the calm after the storm of the uptown struggle.

Many times I have felt the heart tug—the longing to be among my people—the real Jews—and leaving theatrical uptown, the land of make-believe and unrest, I have sought the little schools of study where the wonderful real old men who live by optimism and nourish their souls by faith teach me the lesson of patience and the love of humanity.

There is something restful and inspiring when an old man—long, long past the Biblical three score and ten—places his hand on your shoulder and murmurs in Yiddish, "It is God's will." I have envied the profound peace of many of these aged students living in the past and undisturbed by thoughts of the future. Their Jewish view of life is as beautiful as it is simple. It disregards neither earth nor heaven. It looks to earth and observes the evil prevailing among men; it thinks of heaven and ponders on the bliss of "the future state," and it urges man to strive to bring heaven on earth, to establish by justice and equity those blessed conditions on earth which so many associate with heaven.

Their Jewish view of death is equally beautiful. For those who die they feel no sorrow. Having once torn aside the veil which parts the known and the unknown, having once entered into the shadow, or rather the sunshine, of the beyond, they are better off in the other life. Whether death means eternal sleep or eternal life, those who have left our side, having passed into the arms of pitiless death, repose in a condition which should give survivors no cause for anxiety on account of their beloved dead.

In the pathetic chapter of "The Old Curiosity Shop," in which Dickens tells of the death of Little Nell, he makes the Schoolmaster utter these words of wisdom, on which all who mourn for their dead may well ponder. "If," said he, "one deliberate wish expressed in solemn terms above the bed could call her back to life, which of us would utter it?"

Dickens took this view of death from the Talmud.

The interpretation of a difficult passage from the Talmud, or the coining of an epigram, is as food and wine to the wise old students, and there is not an ill in their lives that cannot be soothed or a blessing that cannot be acknowledged in a quotation from their beloved book. To watch them at their study and devotions undisturbed by the turmoil about them is to marvel at the faith which has enabled some of them to live more than one hundred years with no other interest in life than their God and their books.

From the dingy windows of the schools the mass of sordid buildings looks to their eyes like the hills of Palestine, and the shriek of the passing elevated trains and the clanging of the car bells and the din of passing traffic disturb them not, for they live in the past.

The alleged Jew of the fashionable uptown lobster palaces—the blatant, pushing type, who is the direct cause of much anti-Semitic feeling—knows and cares nothing for the submerged student of his race. The latter is equally oblivious of the alleged Jew who is contemptuously referred to as a meshumad (apostate). But while the former stands out in the world of money and worldly success as a target for much abuse and hatred, the latter lives with books, unknown and unheeded, drawing from the Talmud a joy that riches cannot buy and solacing himself with the love of humanity.

In strong contrast to their fathers and grandfathers are the children of these old men. Modern America, with its opportunities for all, has torn them from the religious atmosphere and sent them uptown to become the lawyers, the artists and the actors.

The Jewish comedian of the vaudeville theater who nightly sets the audience shrieking at his Yiddish idioms is in nine cases out of ten the son of a scholar, and though the glamour of Broadway success claims him and he no longer lives home, in his heart of hearts he is a Jew and never forgets the old people. He will tell many stories of his parents to his Gentile friends, imitating and exaggerating their many characteristics, but he is mighty sore when he hears a Gentile do the same thing. But, after all, the comic Jew of the modern stage is but an imaginary sketch.

There is absolutely nothing humorous in these old men of Judea. Even in the sordid surroundings where you find them engaged in prayer or study, their attitude is one of quiet dignity—a dignity enhanced by their extreme old age.

In a little dark den behind a poultry store I was sketching some of the old men at study. One old fellow one hundred and four years old was explaining to a young fellow of sixty a passage in the Talmud about which the latter was in doubt. Both men were without coats. The younger man had left his push-cart at the door, entirely forgetting the perishable goods thereon and quite oblivious to the fact that hundreds of dirty children were surrounding his cart and fooling with his wares.

Other old men were in the school, and the background to their somber faces was the shop with its ghastly poultry suspended by the necks. One of the old Talmudic students would now and again leave his ponderous Bible to serve in the shop, returning, after wrapping a fowl in a newspaper, to the verse he had been propounding. There was absolutely nothing humorous in all this, but I would love to have had some of my non-Jewish friends see how little thought of money and business the real Jew has.

Sometimes when I have felt full of shame at the behavior in public places of men and women with Jewish faces but with no Judaism in their hearts, I have wished that the simple, studious lives of the old men of the East Side could be the standard by which our race is judged, and that the Talmudic saying so aptly put into verse by Rabbi Myers was better known:

> "Which is the path, both right and wise,
>   That for himself a man should find?
> That which himself much dignifies,
>   And brings him honor from mankind."

Issue of May 7, 1921

"It can hardly be an accident that antagonism directed against the Jews is to be found pretty much everywhere in the world where Jews and non-Jews are associated. And as the Jews are the common element of the situation it would seem probable, on the face of it, that the cause will be found in them rather than in the widely varying groups which feel this antagonism."
—Jesse H. Holmes, in *The American Hebrew*

LXXIX.

Candid Address to Jews on the Jewish Problem

THIS is a candid address to the Jews of the United States. Without subterfuge, without flattery, wholly without fear of all that they may threaten or can do, this attempt is made to set before them the Jewish Question as *their* question, theirs to acknowledge, theirs to consider, theirs to solve.

It is not a question of THE DEARBORN INDEPENDENT at all. This paper has merely become the vehicle of unwelcome facts which have finally thrust themselves up for final disposal in this country.

Damning this paper, compelling cheap city politicians to interfere with its sale, indulging a ribald humor concerning it, will not affect the facts at all. What THE DEARBORN INDEPENDENT says is true or it is untrue. If true, it ought to be considered. If untrue, it ought to be disproved. The present policy of Jewish leaders is to do neither, but to indulge in antics which go a long way toward illustrating what this paper has said.

What THE DEARBORN INDEPENDENT says is true, and tens of thousands of Jews know it is true.

No representative Jew has ever approached us with a denial of the truth of what has been stated in this paper. Neither has any unrepresentative Jew.

The chief objection made against the publication of the fact is always stated in this form: "What you say is true. Certain Jews are guilty of the things you charge. But why do you say 'Jew'? Why do you not say Al Wood, Morris Gest, Louis Marshall, Samuel Untermeyer, 'Wolf' Lamar, Edward Lauterbach, Felix

Warberg—why not let it go with these men's names, why say 'Jew'? When you say 'Jew," it sounds as if you blamed all the Jews."

This objection has been seriously and courteously made by a number of Jews who have conferred with THE DEARBORN INDEPENDENT on this series of articles, and has been as seriously and courteously considered.

What is the answer? First, that these men are Jews. Second, that being Jews these men constitute a problem for the Jews themselves. Third, it is time for some one to call attention to the necessity of cleaning up on that problem. There has been too much mincing of words. There has been too much concealment of names and relationship. The method which Jews were taking in this country with regard to concealment was heading them swiftly toward the same conditions which have menaced their race in Europe, and THE DEARBORN INDEPENDENT would count no labor lost that would rouse the Jews to a sense of the responsibility which rests on them to solve the Jewish Question in this country, possibly the only country where it can be solved.

Let us be frank: if this paper had mentioned only the names of individual Jews, never mentioning their race, and had exposed them as isolated persons, it would have made no difference in the general Jewish reaction, the cry would still have been that "the Jews were being attacked"; whereas the other people of the country would have been just as much in the dark regarding the close bonds which unite all the groups of evil influences in this country. The purpose of this series of articles is to let in the light—to show the Jews generally that the stench had become too great, and to show the rest of the people where the stench arose.

The list of charges for the Jews of the United States to consider as affecting the distinguished members of their race is very serious. And the charges are true.

It is true that there is a distinct "Jewish idea" in business and professional life which has eaten away the traditional principles of honor on which Anglo-Saxon life was erected. Every Jew knows that, every non-Jew knows it. Here and there a Jew in business or professional life makes a breakaway from trickery, deception, dishonesty, and exploitation of the gullible public, and achieves success with honor, but that Jew also knows that the majority of his brethren in the same line practice different methods.

It is true that behind the amazing degeneracy of the modern stage and motion picture is a solid wall of Jewish ownership and control. This ownership and control must bear the responsibility for the rapid and dangerous deterioration which has come since such ownership and control was achieved.

It is true that behind all the shoddy and make-believe and adulteration in the staples of life is the Jewish idea of profits, "making the ephah small and the shekel great," and that the initiators of American business into these shady practices were Jewish. It is idle to retort that apt pupils have been found among non-Jews; the point is that before Jewish influence began to be felt in America business, sound quality and a fair price were the rule. It is the Jew's ceaseless boast that wherever they go they change business, but not for the better.

It is true that beneath all the network of trivializing influences in literature, art, politics, economics, fashion and sport, is Jewish influence controlled by Jewish groups. Their Orientalism has served as a subtle poison to dry up the sound serum of Anglo-Saxon morality on which this country thrived in its formative years. Is it necessary to specify? In every movement toward a lower standard, a looser relationship, especially toward the overthrow of the old Christian safeguards, do not Jewish names predominate?

These charges and many more have all been made in detail with evidence submitted, and need not be repeated here. The present purpose is simply to get the problem squarely before the Jews of the United States.

These charges are true, they cannot be disproved, Jewish

leaders have not attempted to disprove them. Thousands of Jews have said that they are true.

Then where is the obstacle to a settlement?

This question is best answered by three typical replies made by Jews during the course of the present series.

1. *"What you say is true, but you should not say it."*

There is a principle, seldom expressed among the Jews, but always acted on, that Jews should not have public attention called to them except by themselves or their chosen spokesmen. This is unfortunate, because any establishment of the Jews as an accepted and trusted part of the general citizenry must include their being known as such. In this country the Jew should not only welcome the widest knowledge (unless he has something he fears to have known) but should himself undertake the exposure of those things which will eventually bring a shadow on the name of his race. The Jew has never done this. When exposure could no longer be suppressed, that Jewish attitude has always been one of defense, regardless of the merits of the case. "The Jew can do no wrong" is the principle acted upon. Never must a "Gentile" charge be admitted, however true it may be. Never must a "Gentile" reform be assisted, no matter how much needed.

Now, that principle may do for other countries, but not for the United States. If the Jew is wise, he ought speedily to take warning that in this country the old line of action will not succeed. If Jews continue to show a disposition to defend the malefactors of their race against the just expostulations of the rest of the people, they must not be surprised if the public begins to view them as all one crowd—an inner nation set against the outer nation.

2. *"What you say is true but your conclusion is wrong: it is not for the Jew to change to your standards, it is for you to change to the Jew's standards."*

This is the fighting view. It admits that there are two ideas in conflict in the United States, what it unfairly terms the "Puritanic" idea, opposed by what it calls the Jewish Universal idea.

This view would command respect if it represented a superior morality in conflict with a lesser morality, if it represented a higher civilization against a lower civilization. Will any Jew contend that it does? Will any Jew deny that the influence of the Jewish idea in this generation is to break down such morality as we had? Will any Jew deny that the civilization of the United States before the advent of the Jews thither was superior to the highest civilization ever achieved by the Jews anywhere at any period of their history?

There are *two* ideas in conflict—that is certain. The Jewish idea has a tremendous degenerative power. It is a powerfully disintegrating influence. It eats the substance out of the civilization which it attacks, destroys its moral virility, throws down its reverence, saps its respect for authority, casts a shadow on every basic principle.

That is the way the Jewish idea works in American civilization. Moral gravitation being, like physical gravitation, downward, it is not difficult to seduce human nature to lower levels, but it is a massive task to lift it to higher levels of morality and reverence and sober justice. And this latter task, organized Jewish effort has never attempted. The campaign in the United States is a campaign for the breakdown of the ideas that now obtain, not a lifting of them to a higher degree of nobility.

If it were an attempt to substitute the austerity of the Mosaic law—the law given *to* Moses, not the ordinances decreed *by* Moses—for the halfhearted Christian idealism of the day, even that would be a task in which all right-hearted men could join. But *Moses condemns the modern Jews* more severely than anyone else could. They have rejected the Mosaic law. They have built their international power upon the exact opposite of the Mosaic law. Moses was given a law of human society which would have saved civilization its greatest tragedies. Moses has a social program, obedience to which for one day would completely wreck the Jewish international power. Moses is their judge, and when the Law is established Moses will be their destroyer.

Let the Jews think seriously what is this idea which they set up to follow. Let them penetrate the mists and seek out where this idea originated. Let them think forward and visualize the effect if this idea should become regnant. It will not become regnant here; there are safeguards here which the true Israelite will understand; but it is as certain as day that the idea will in the end destroy, utterly destroy, all who trust in it.

This much is gained, however, from the attitude we are now discussing: we have gained clarity of understanding as to just what it is that is in collision; it is *two ideas*, and one of them is the idea of disruption, fostered by the false and delusive hope that disruption will spare the disruptor.

3. *"What you say is true, and we Jews could change it if we only would. The trouble is, we don't want to seem to be driven to it. But I don't see how otherwise we are to do it.*

Many Jews will recognize this sentiment as their own, but they will be readier to express it to a non-Jew than a Jew. Why? Because prophets must be prepared to suffer in Judah. "Well, if you insist on playing Christ, you must expect to be crucified," said Lilienthal to Isaac Wise. "O Jerusalem, that stonest them that are sent to thee!"

Yet there is need of prophets in Judah today, men who will rise among the people and tell them plainly. The rabbinate is utterly bankrupt of the prophetic spirit. It has fallen into the blindness of the old priesthood. Here and there a literary man attempts to speak, but Jewish "art" has so accustomed the Jews to make-believe that the writing is looked upon as a performance, nothing more.

No one with a sense for such things—and there are believers still left in Judah—will doubt that the times are ripe for a great change respecting the Jews. So strong is the feeling among the remnant of believing Jews that it is interpreted as forewarnings of the Messianic period. Among the Judaized Christian sects, other interpretations are given to the times, most of which are used to support political Zionism which represents the materialism and unbelief of present-day Judaism and which will undoubtedly fail as a national restorative and as a political program. But however misintrepretive these sectarian and Jewish conclusions may be, they indicate a sense of imminent change. A greater change is indicated than migration to Palestine would be—for that would not mean any change at all in the world, and certainly no change for the better in the fortunes of the Jews. Christians—misguided Christians, one must say—who see God's alleged will of universal Jewish dominion fulfilled by means of the Jews defiance and despite of the Law given to Moses, ought to reexamine their ground for so strange and immoral a conclusion. The breakup of this civilization, this age of civilization, will occur because of the collapse of this system by which the Jew has obtained his hold on the nations. The system that gives him his hold is doomed, is passing, and the fallacy of Jewish tribal destiny to rule the world will pass with it.

With this change already on the threshold, prophets should be expected to arise in Judah to recall their people to the Law whose previous denial meant their overthrow. These prophets will not be of the "Reform school" which denies the God of Israel as a divine Person, nor will they be of the ultra-orthodox school which makes much of fringes and cookery—they will be of the race of the ancient prophets who spake boldly against Judah's violation of the fundamental law.

Our confidence is that a sufficient number of Jews will see the truth, and act upon it.

What would be the greatest overturn the present Jewish idea, the disruptive Jewish idea, could possibly have? This: *a knowledge that the way they are going is the way their own Law fordooms to failure, and that the people they hope to triumph over are the people their own Scriptures say they are not to triumph over.*

The first is beyond dispute: there is no success for the Jew, no establishment of him in the world except upon the basic law given to Moses. In any other attempt he must fall when the structure collapses.

The second is in dispute, but is by no means beyond consideration, especially by Jews. In these matters the Jews are much wiser than the so-called Christians. There is among the Jews "the law of the brother" and "the law of the stranger." The "law of the stranger" permits several important things which the "law of the brother" prohibits. The Jews have been treating the rest of the world, often intentionally, sometimes as a matter of course, according to the "law of the stranger." This is one of the influences which has helped to solidify Jewry against the rest of the world.

Suppose it should be shown that the people in whose lands the Jews have never been persecuted, the people of those lands to which the Jews have never been "driven" but to which they have hopefully and joyfully come, are not "strangers" and are not to be treated as "strangers" and, so far from being "strangers," are really the leaders and rulers of that ethical stream of influence of which the Jews, but for their disloyalty to their destiny, might have been an important part!

Suppose it should be shown that Judah, the "driven" part of Israel, has been blindly attacking the "led" part of Israel. Suppose it should be shown that Judah is not the Israel upon whom great destiny is to come, but a small part of that Israel and not even a participating part, until it "returns, returns, returns."

If these things should once take hold of the intensified consciousness of Judah, as facts, there would be such a change in human society in general, such a change in the Jewish situation in particular, as would make a return to Palestine a mere summer excursion in comparison.

Jews are thinking about these very matters now. They are thinking from within. They are seeking a reason (the thoughtful among them) for the sense of unfitness which they feel when they adopt the traditional attitude of enmity toward the "others," the "others" in this case being the Anglo-Saxon peoples. The reason for this sense of impropriety is that here, in this land, the Jew will have to change his attitude of antagonism and dwell in peace as in a land prepared for him. Not as lord of it, by any means, but as a grateful wanderer at last come home. Not as ruler, but as adding his bit to the righteousness, prosperity and peace of the people.

It is not a question of religion. Let the Jew get back his Mosaic religion—it is the most perfect social system ever devised and directly contrary to the practical modern Jew's idea of things.

It is not a question of intermarriage. Let the Jew keep as long as he pleases his idea that he is racially different. The suggestion of intermarriage is a crude one and always indicates a lack of grasp of the Jewish Question.

Let the Jew keep all his traditions. They are not objectionable in any way; the slightest regard for them can only hold them as romantic.

But let him shed his false notion of "the Jew against the world!"

Let him shed his false program of breaking down Christendom by the infiltration of Orientalism into business, art, entertainment and the professions.

Let him abolish the false ideal that it is an honor to Jewry to save a guilty Jew from the common law, and a disgrace to Jewry to see a guilty Jew punished by the common law.

Let him draw up notice on all the Jews of the United States who by hook or crook are sowing vile seed in society that the Jewish community charges itself with their misbehavior and will use methods well known to Jews to bring that misbehavior to an end.

Let the Jew end forever the disgrace of an anti-defamation committee which grows frantic over innocent remarks on the part of "Gentiles," and is absolutely indifferent to the misdeeds of thousands of Jews who do more damage to the Jewish name than all the "Gentile" critics and newspapers could do in twenty years. No one can give the Jews a bad reputation but the Jews themselves.

Most Jews who have given this matter a thought will agree. A good deal of bad temper exists among them, no doubt, and it will be hard for them to admit that anything THE DEARBORN INDEPENDENT may contend for is right, but the idea here expressed, when divorced from this paper, does command respect from many Jews.

The question remains: When will they start on the program here suggested?

Human nature being what it is, they will hate to start at all if it will seem that the present agitation has compelled them. But would they have started without the agitation?

It is possible for an additional number of Jews to catch the thought that this series of articles cannot be so easily explained away—we are not referring to the contents now, but to the fact that these articles exist at all—as being the creation of prejudice, or hatred or vindictiveness or ignorance?

Suppose these articles should be truly a sign of the times for American Jewry! Suppose they offer a warning word, however unwelcome, and a light, however undesired, which it would be most unwise for Jews to ignore.

Suppose these articles were conceived in a spirit far different than the average pro-Jewish spouter is competent to understand. Suppose the set time has now come for the Jews to quit their attitude of attacking every one who shows them the truth, and to profit by this report of the poor figure they cut in American life today. Suppose these people who are moved to search and report the truth about Judah are truly the shophar calling the people to a new day—is it wise to let stubbornness counsel? Is it wise to let pride close the ear?

The enemies of the Jews are those who defend them for the pay of hire or praise or votes. The enemies of the Jews are those who bespeak them fair to their faces, and express quite different thoughts behind their backs. The writer of this personally knows that two of the principal "Gentile" defenders of the Jews, men who have shouted and ranted through the Press on the Jews' behalf, are men who privately hold and express thoughts about the Jews which are sheer hatred and enmity and—fear. Mostly fear! The enemies of the Jews are those who encourage them to take an attitude that they cannot hold in America—not as affecting their personal liberty at all, but their social attitude and the Public Right. These are the enemies of the Jews, and yet these are the ones whom Judah counts his friends. They are hired friends, false friends, incapable of realizing for a moment what this whole Question means. Judah's friends today are those who will speak the surgical truth to him, braving his fury in the knowledge that the future will justify the word.

Judah's leaders have betrayed him in this country —they do not know they have crossed the Jordan. The Jews are as sheep without shepherds in this land. And the chief objection which the Jewish leaders have to THE DEARBORN INDEPENDENT is *that the Jews may read it and learn how shepherdless they are,* the Jewish leaders' opposition to THE DEARBORN INDEPENDENT rises mostly from *the fear that the Jews may read it!* The Jews have read it, and they have not found hatred, they have not found abuse and calumny, they have not found ignorance and malice; they have found statements of fact calmly set forth, not to arouse hatred among the non-Jews, but to arouse a sense of social responsibility among the Jews.

These are significant times. The emergence of the Jewish Question is a part of the culmination of destiny that has come upon us, not for harm but for good. The Jews must uncover their eyes and unstop their ears, and they will see the beginning of the end of their travail, and they will hear that to which they have been too long heedless.

The justification of a discussion of the Jewish Question is the good of the Jews, and the greatest present obstacle to that good is the Jews themselves. The time is here when they shall see it.

Issue of January 7, 1922

"Everywhere they wanted to remain Jews, and everywhere they were granted the privilege of establishing a State within a State. By virtue of these privileges and exemptions, and immunity from taxes, they would soon rise above the general condition of the citizens of the municipalities where they resided; they had better opportunities for trade and accumulation of wealth, whereby they excited jealousy and hatred."
——Lazare

LXXX.

An Address to "Gentiles" on the Jewish Problem

THE heading of this article presents difficulties. The correct use of the term "Gentiles" is in question. It is a name that has been given us, not by ourselves, but by Jews, and it is by no means certain that it is accurately given. A very great chance exists that it is not. That, however, is a matter which "gentiles" do not bother to understand; they think, of course that if one is not a Jew one must be a gentile. This is only another instance of the Jewish view being "put over" without the "gentile" understanding or even questioning it.

There is another difficulty: how shall one address "gentiles" collectively? When one addresses Jews he knows that the Jew is always a Jew; that every Jew acknowledges every other Jew; that Jews understand each other and are loyal to each other as against "outsiders"; that they think together and act together; that they stand together for Jewish defense, no matter how just the charge brought against them. When you address Jews you address a unit, and when you discuss Jews you get a united reaction from them.

This cannot be said of gentiles. They are of many races, many nationalities, many religions, many tongues. They never think of themselves as being united under the name "gentiles." They are not race or class conscious; certainly they do not think of themselves as a unit with reference to the Jews as an opposite unit. "Gentiles" cannot be organized into one group nationally, let alone internationally, as Jews can. Jews of every shade of opinion, of every degree of religion and of unreligion, can unite all round the world, and do unite, having their own news service, their own telegraph service, their own "foreign department" (as they themselves describe it), by which they keep themselves united and informed for mass action. There is nothing even remotely approaching that among "gentiles."

Not that this fact can be urged against the "gentiles" as a fault. There are reasons why the "gentiles" never can be united. And one reason is that among the so-called "gentiles" there is a regnant superior strain that is not "gentile" at all; no more is it Jewish. There are racial and moral strains among the non-Jewish section of the world which never can be brought into agreement. And, outside this superior strain, among the gentiles proper, the very basis for enduring union is lacking.

So that the only union that can be expected is a union of the superior strain, which physically and morally is unconquerable, and whose task it is to liberate the lesser peoples who easily fall victims to subversion and have no reactive power to rescue themselves.

It is to this human Gulf Stream that flows through the ocean of humanity, blessing it, that this address is offered. As to the identity of this section of humanity—"He that hath ears to hear, let him hear." The others will not, because they cannot. There are many genuine gentiles mixed up in our common population, but it is not to them that these words are offered.

The Jewish Question has existed for a long time, as the Jew knows and admits, and is a consequence of certain un-Jewish, or rather un-Israelitish ideas held by Jewish persons of power. The disability under which the Jew labors is that he is not a Jew, properly speaking, and does not desire to be. Just at that point is the soil and the root of the Jewish Question.

Tackling the Jewish Question is not congenial work. The Race which this article now addresses has always shrunk from tackling it. Our Race has little disposition to chastise any portion of humanity, to arouse feeling or resist it. We have little taste for this surgical work which becomes absolutely necessary when certain corrupt influences deeply dislocate and seriously injure the common life. Nothing but a clear vision of the danger, nothing but an imperative sense of duty would impel any one of us to embark on a course which is subject to misunderstanding and which must, in the nature of things, wait long for its complete justification. Our Race is too fair, and has always been too fair, to enter hastily into judgment—and upon this fairness and longsuffering the offending groups have often seriously trespassed.

Regarded by itself, as a separate entity, the Jewish Power is most impressive. International Jews today occupy literally every controlling lever of power. Building up for centuries, perfecting their teamwork from generation to generation, from country to country, they have practically reached the summit. Nothing but the Christian religion remains unvanquished by them, though through false "liberalism" even that has felt the Jewish assault. So great is this power that the very knowledge of it kills hope that any movement can ever dislodge it. Earnest, honest men have walked round it, surveyed it, measured its strength, and have given up the dream of changing it. In Russia they tried to segregate it, but while segregation went on from one side, infiltration proceeded from the other, and even the "anti-Semitic" Russian Government was honey-combed with Jews, as the end showed. In Germany they endeavored to vote the Jewish power out of politics, only to find the root deep-set in finance—and no country has yet attacked the sacred image of gold. In England the policy of absorption was adopted, and the result is that wherever a Jew was put in power the British Empire has reaped trouble, in Ireland, in India, in Palestine, the present vice-regents of all these possessions being Jews. Other little countries, exasperated beyond endurance, tried violence, and failed just as miserably as the others.

Why? Because every one of these methods is precisely the method that the Jew prefers to have people try. He knows their futility first; they find it out later. He knows how these methods positively help him; they discover that later. The knowledge thus won would be pure gain, were it not that it also seems to discourage the hope of men who know how seriously wrong the situation is.

Besides this massive array of power, immovable as it appears, there is the veil cast over the Christian mind as to the supposedly peculiar destiny of "God's chosen people." The Christian cannot read his Bible except through Jewish spectacles, and, therefore, reads it wrong. The idea of "the chosen people" is one of the two great Biblical ideas, but that the Jews constitute this Chosen People is entirely opposed to the statement of the Bible—even of the Bible which the Jews acknowledge, the Old Testament of the Christians. The blessings of world possession, world rule, superior population, commercial greatness, military power, constituted governments, "a great nation and a company of nations"—all of these as means by which to spread light and healing among the nations—were truly promised to one people, to Israel, not to Judah. Judah's destiny was to be quite different. Very few Bible readers ever note the distinction between the House of Israel and the House of Judah, yet this distinction was marked from the time of Jacob; the prophets absolutely insist upon it. Israel seceded from Judah, being unable to live with that people any longer. Israel's destiny took them out into the world, and if the Bible be true, then Israel's destiny of greatness is being fulfilled in Israel and not in Judah. The two Houses are distinct to this day, although a future reunion, a spiritual reunion, is prophesied to come.

Yet the false idea that the Jews constitute All Israel has penetrated the Christian consciousness to an alarming extent, so that when the Jewish press insists, as it does every week, "We gave you your God, we gave you your Bible, we gave you your Christ," even Christian ministers cannot find an answer. The answer is that the Old Testament is nine-tenths an Israelitish book, and not a Jewish book. Abraham was not a Jew; Isaac was not a Jew; Jacob was not a Jew; Moses was not a Jew: Joshua was not a Jew; Gideon was not a Jew; Samuel was not a Jew; even Esther and Mordecai were not Jews, but

Benjamites; the majority of the prophets were not Jews, but Israelites. Upon the coming of Judah into power, in the persons of David and Solomon, the misrule was so great that Israel seceded, and the secession was sanctioned by the prophets. In the New Testament, Jesus Christ found his disciples in Galilee, far out of Judea, and of them there was but one, Judas, whose name indicates that he was a Jew. St. Paul was one of the tribe of Benjamin, "the light tribe," which was left with Judah "for a light."

But there is a constant patter of preaching (the Russellites make it the great theme) that "the Jews are to rule the world because it is so prophesied." The amazing blindness with which Christians have regarded the open pages of their Bible is the only explanation of this one-sided teaching which is confusing to the Christians and exceedingly dangerous to the Jews. In the Bible, Israel is the Chosen People of Blessing, and the time is announced when Judah shall walk to Israel and recognize them and become one with them. There is a chosen racial breed, a select seed, a superior strain of blood and soul in the world, but it is not Judah. One thing, therefore, that Christians can do, as a contribution to the solution of the Jewish Question, is to read their Bibles carefully.

The Jewish Question will be solved, and its solution will begin in the United States. But that does not mean that it will come as the result of a popular movement. Great changes do not occur that way. It makes little difference whether the mass of the people see this Question or not; the mass of the people are not always called into such matters. Their work is to hold the world steady while the change takes place. But a sufficient number of qualified persons have seen the Question to insure that now the era of solution has set in. The timid, the soft literary men in pulpits (with whose ilk Jeremiah had a keen acquaintance), the false preachers of "Peace, peace," the hush brothers and sisters of every name, the shallow shouters for "fairness," and all who are afraid of the truth in its surgical forms—these have no place in the healing of the hurt of these times; they are wedded to their softness. Nothing has been more shameful in the last two years than the spectacle of men bidding for the applause of bootleggers, and gamblers, and the lecherous masters of the modern stage, and the sinister Kehillah, and the anti-Christian American Jewish Committee, because, forsooth, some one has fulfilled the duty to tell the truth. However, these things must always be, and the evil influences among the Jews have learned just what kind of help they may expect and from what kind of men.

THE DEARBORN INDEPENDENT has not been making a fight but fulfilling a duty to shed light on a matter crying for light. THE DEARBORN INDEPENDENT, therefore, has never urged any individual or organization to join it in this work. Nor has it charged with cowardice those who for prudential or other reasons have kept silent. Editors especially have been absolved; not one of them was asked to lend his aid, although the files of this office hold thousands of written assurances from newspaper men all over the land, and from all parts of the world, testifying to the truth of our statements. Organizations have been proposed, for various purposes; strong organizations have offered themselves as vehicles for the carrying out of any plan THE DEARBORN INDEPENDENT might propose. But all such undertakings have been avoided, our belief being that simply to state the truth, and let it work its own right will, was sufficient at this time. And to that belief and policy we have adhered.

"But what shall we do?" is the constant question; "How shall we balk this system which surrounds us and infects so much of our common life?"

Observe it, identify it, eschew it— that is more powerful than active opposition. The clear eye of the man who sees and understands is something that even the evil powers of Jewry cannot endure.

But the most potent action any awakened person can take is this: to erect again our own moral landmarks, which the Oriental Jewish invasion has broken down. This would spell sheer doom to the whole evil system sponsored by Jews. And this is the course which has never been tried. To go back to the principles which have made our race great, the principles to which we have been recreant and therefore have fallen easy prey—this is the only invincible course. It is an opposition which evil Jews cannot understand and cannot defeat.

In place of the way of doing business which Jewish dealers have introduced, let the business man of the country adopt the old way of the white man, when a man's word was as good as his bond, and when business was service and not exploitation.

Let the men and women of the country learn how to buy, let them learn how to test quality in fabric and food, instead of being dependent on price tags. The merchandising practices of this country, in the hands of ruthless exploiters, have all but ruined honest merchants. Let any dweller in a great city recall the last twenty years, how the Christian merchants have been growing fewer and fewer. Why? Is it because the owners of Jewish department stores are better business men? No! The Jewish merchants began the practice of filling their store windows with goods that looked like the goods in reputable merchants' windows, and sold them for a much lower price. The helpless public, no longer able to determine the quality of goods, and guided solely by price tags, flocked to the Jews' store. The result is that one hears everywhere in ordinary conversation the complaint that "everything is shoddy." Of course it is, and it will remain so, until we educate people in the art of buying. That of itself will break down three-fourths of the abuses practiced in the commercial world today.

Another contribution that can be made to the defeat of Jewish subversive influence is the examination of so-called "liberal" ideas, their source, their effect, their whole tendency. Men are thinking ideas today that poison them morally, socially and economically. These ideas are as deliberately shot into society as poison gas was shot into ranks of soldiers in France. Our mental hospitality has been grossly abused, the public mind has been made a sewer. The time has come for a custom barrier to be raised for the examination of imported ideas. Unrestricted immigration of ideas has been as bad for the American mentality as unrestricted immigration of people has been for American society.

We have taken our amusements without thought of what was behind them in the way of deliberate intent to make us common and careless and coarse. We have read our newspapers, wholly innocent of the propaganda mixed with the news. We have even taken our religion in a Judaized form, without troubling to inquire whether it squared with the Bible, the textbook of religion. We have read our novels and have failed to see what serum the author was injecting along with his story. And all this has been possible because we have been asleep, enjoying, as we thought, a life which was swiftly being taken from us, and dreaming that the old principles still held sway.

It is perfectly obvious that the cure for all this is to become awake, alert, to challenge the foreign influence, and to seek out again the principles which gave us our greatness.

We have been weaned away from our natural leaders. We have been taught to look to those who cannot even speak our language and who do not hold our institutions dear. A people that turns from its own leaders, or a people whose leaders have been turned from the sacred responsibilities of the high office of leading, is in a precarious position, and becomes an easy victim to confusion of soul. There is a dearth of voices in the land today, the prophets are dumb, or are reading beautiful essays to the people. Suspicion has been sowed like darnel seed between classes of the same race, the people have been broken up, and the subversive Jewish influence supports the oligarchy of unserviceable wealth at one end of the social scale, while it stimulates the baser elements of industrial unrest at the other end. And the race thus rent asunder to its own undoing, does not see this—capital does not see, and labor does not see—that the leaders of chaos are alien in blood and soul.

To keep American and Christian the school, the church, the legislature, the jury room and the Government, is the most potent resistance that can be made to the evil influences which have been upon us and which this series of articles has partly uncovered. The strength of all subversive influence is in proportion as we cease to be what we ought to be. The evil influences surrounding this people can succeed only as they change this people into something less than it ought to be. Therefore, to go back to the old landmarks, whereby we made all the progress we ever made, is not only the part of wisdom, but the need of the hour. The school must be cleansed. The jury box must be kept inviolate—trial by jury has almost disappeared in Jewish New York. The church must be un-Judaized and Christianized. The Government must be Americanized. Let there be the utmost freedom of thought and speech, but let there be also with it a discrimination which will prevent the people being victimized by every spurious idea, every "gold brick" economic proposal which comes along. It needs only that men be awake to their better interests and to leave no place in their scheme of life for the practices which destroy the very foundations of confidence.

Surely it must be understood by this time that the Jews rule, not by reason of their brilliance or their money, but by ideas which are not even properly Jewish, but Babylonian. They have captured the castle from within. They have been able to do so only because of our ignorance of the lineage and dignity of the stock of ideas upon which our civilization has been founded. Our people needs to engraft itself again on the parent tree and draw again the sustenance which made it great and fruitful.

Many so-called "gentiles" are somewhat affected by the Jews' wails of "persecution." This has been sufficiently discussed in previous articles, but "gentiles" can further contribute to the solution of the Jewish Question by looking about them to see if they can discover any evidence of "persecution" here—unless it be persecution of the Christians by the organized agencies of the Jews! In this month's *Atlantic Monthly* a Jewish rabbi, who undoubtedly knows better assumes that his race is a hated race. He rather enjoys the thought and accepts it as a distinctive honor. Our "gentile" might also observe how untrue this is—how, indeed, in this mixture of nations, the Jew gets off with less even of the harmless kind of racial animosity than any other foreign admixture.

Above all, the "gentile," so-called, who in ninety cases out of every one hundred is no gentile at all (as the Jews may well admit) will do well to avoid fear. Nothing is more abject than "the fear of the Jew," and nothing more disastrous to the Jew than the tactics he employs to sustain that fear. The Jewish subversive power had been powerful only for evil and only where there was a disposition to evil. It has never yet succeeded in bringing shame or confusion to the right.

Indeed, there is one sure way of gaining the respect of the Jew, and that is, *Tell The Truth.* No one knows better than the Jew whether statements made about Jews are true or not. "Gentiles" may never be certain whether a statement made about the Jews may be relied upon, but Jews always know. That is why prejudice, abuse, hatred, scorn, ridicule, false charges roll off them as water off a duck. The Jews have never in all their history feared the lies of their enemies; but they have feared the truth. And if they only fear the truth in the ancient sense, not to be afraid of it but to fear to violate it, and to fear to have the truth testify against them, then the day of Judah's return to standing has come. The truth is Judah's friend, and Israel's friend, and the world's friend. It makes hard demands; it is sometimes not easy to speak and harder still to hear; but the truth heals, as Judah is due to discover.

There is this to say, that among the many thousands of persons who have written to THE DEARBORN INDEPENDENT confirming out of their own observation and experience the statements made in this series of articles, there has been a most gratifying absence of the spirit of violence. At the beginning a few rabid Jew-baiters made themselves known and expressed their hope that at last a regular program of pogroms was to be instituted. We never knew how far these advances were made with knowledge of the Jewish leaders, but we do know that for a year and a half in this United States the Jewish press, and Jewish thugs, and Jewish politicians, and even some of the most respectable of the Jewish organizations did their utmost, and in some of the strangest ways, to compel this Study of the Jewish Question to lead into violence and disorder. There was nothing that the Jewish leaders more desperately desired or more tirelessly worked for.

That was their first setback. Everywhere else in the world they had always been able to foment this sort of thing and label it "anti-Semitism." The label "anti-Semitism" is one of the choicest weapons in the Jewish armory. But in the United States their plan failed. It is their first notification that in this country the Question is going to be solved; it is not to be given a new lease of life by following the old mistakes.

THE DEARBORN INDEPENDENT knows the temper of the American people on this question, that it is cool, fair, and somewhat more determined than it formerly was. But the Jews know this temper better than anyone else. Hence the magnitude and superb rashness of the propaganda with which they are literally flooding the country. THE DEARBORN INDEPENDENT is grateful for the flood of Jewish propaganda. It has served in hundreds of important cases to give the confirmation to our statements which was wanted. Jewish literature has been a powerful informer of the gravity of the Jewish Question in the United States. The result was not what the Jewish leaders wished, of course, but it was serviceable to the truth just the same.

Now that the Question is open, now that the press is able to print "Jew" when necessary, now that a bunch of keys has been provided by which the people may unlock doors and make further inquiries, THE DEARBORN INDEPENDENT will follow other aspects of the Question, discussing them from time to time as circumstances may warrant.

Issue of January 14, 1922.

www.ingramcontent.com/pod-product-compliance
Lightning Source LLC
LaVergne TN
LVHW091250080426
835510LV00007B/191